THE
CRIME
BUSTERS

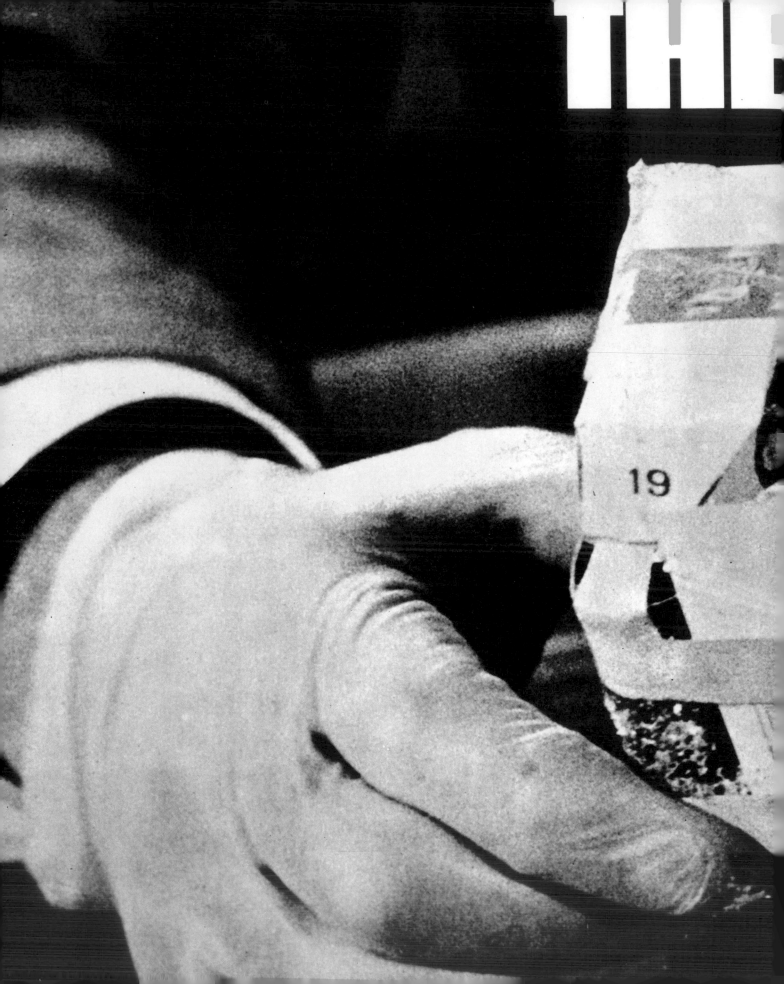

19

CRIME BUSTERS

The FBI, Scotland Yard, Interpol –
the Story of Criminal Detection

Edited by ANGUS HALL

TREASURE PRESS

First published in Great Britain
in 1976 by Verdict Press

This edition published in 1984 by
Treasure Press
59 Grosvenor Street
London W1

© 1973/1974/1976 Phoebus Publishing Company/
BPC Publishing Ltd (A division of Macdonald & Co (Publishers) Ltd)

ISBN 0 907812 89 9

Printed in Portugal, by Gris Impressores, S.A.R.L.

D.L. 3825/84

Jacket front: All illustrations Popperfoto;
Jacket back: left BPC, centre Popperfoto,
top right Pinkerton's Detective Agency,
bottom right Scotland Yard; Back flap:
Scotland Yard; Titlespread: Syndication
International; This page: below F. Wilkinson,
bottom right Popperfoto.

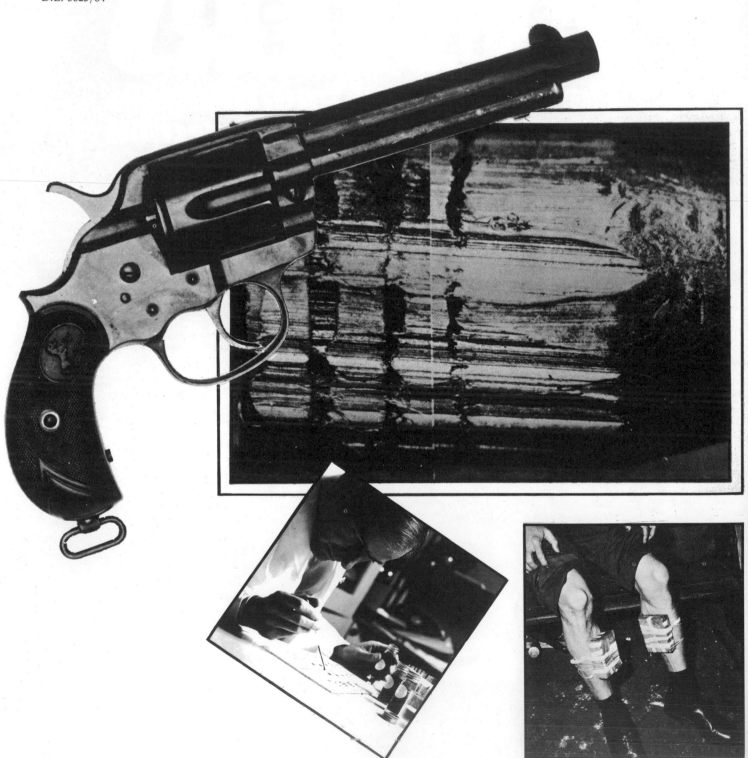

CONTENTS

FOREWORD

Ever since criminals first turned their hands against Society, Society has been forced to protect itself; and as criminals have become increasingly violent, skilful and cunning, so the police have become increasingly skilful at thwarting them before they commit their crimes and at detecting them afterwards.

Police detection does not often bear much resemblance to the feats of Sherlock Holmes, who would sometimes solve a case without even leaving his study. Real police investigation is a matter of laborious checking and counter-checking; interviewing hundreds, perhaps thousands, of possible witnesses; or combing every yard of long grass on a desolate heath or dredging miles of muddy canal for a discarded weapon. The Holmesian principles of observation and deduction are still essential, but to these are now added the sophisticated skills of the scientist. In a modern police laboratory the most delicate analyses are carried out, and conviction of guilt may depend upon the matching of a single faint fingerprint, on the microscopic examination of a single hair, or on the markings on an ejected cartridge case.

In this book some of the most modern methods used in the detection of crime are described. We are told, too, of the élite police forces in the United States and in Britain—the F.B.I. with its special agents, and Scotland Yard's Special Branch. Crime in the mid-twentieth century is big business, with fortunes being made in drug traffic and Mafia activities. The enforcers of the law need all the resources that Society can give them to bring these criminals to book.

Crime is now international, with its tentacles stretching round the world, and international cooperation between national police forces is needed to counter it. It is for this reason that Interpol has been set up, and we may read here of some of the many cases where the information provided by Interpol has enabled an arrest to be made.

We may read, too, of real-life cases of deduction, based upon forensic science, where long buried bones have yielded up their secrets, or where innocence or guilt rests upon the chemical analysis of a minute quantity of medicine in the bottom of a glass.

THE FOUNDING OF THE FBI

The badge of J. Edgar Hoover's G-Men, members of a world-famous law-enforcement agency . . . its history bathed in controversy.

THE EARLY years of the twentieth century in the United States were years of greed and corruption. Men were in imminent danger of losing confidence in one another and in many sectors of public life honesty had become a factor of small account. Industrial combines blatantly ignored the antitrust laws and government officials, charged with the stewardship on the nation's behalf of valuable land in the West, lined their pockets by private and illegal selling.

Theodore Roosevelt, who came to the White House in September 1901 after the assassination of President McKinley, was outraged by the moral chaos he saw around him and determined to press with all his energy for a campaign against the lawbreakers.

As his instrument for investigation Roosevelt chose the Treasury Department's secret service, formed in the years

THE FALLEN HERO . . . they loved boxer Jack Johnson as he won bout after bout. But soon Jackson was to fall foul of the F.B.I. and America's vice laws.

following the Civil War to stamp out a large-scale "industry" devoted to counterfeiting United States currency. But this immediately excited the suspicions of Congressmen who, anxious to safeguard the rights of the individual and looking over their shoulders at some of Europe's more undemocratic practices, feared that a secret police force might soon arise.

They took swift action and Congress enacted a law prohibiting Treasury detectives from being employed by other government departments, including the Department of Justice.

Roosevelt was dismayed but not defeated.

He therefore wrote an order to Attorney-General Charles J. Bonaparte — grand-nephew of Napoleon I of France — instructing him "to create an investigative service within the Department of Justice subject to no other department or bureau and which will report to no one except the Attorney-General."

This, too, caused a new wave of anger. "If Anglo-Saxon civilization stands for anything," thundered Congressman Sherley of Kentucky, "it is for a government where the humblest citizen is safeguarded against the secret activities of the executive of the government . . . Not in vain did our forefathers read the history of Magna Carta and the Bill of Rights."

This time, however, the President would not yield. If Congress obstructed his purpose, he warned, it would have to bear the responsibility of encouraging crime and comforting the criminal.

As a result, on July 26, 1908, there came into being the Bureau of Investigation which, 27 years later, was to have the prefix "Federal" added to its title and was to take its place in history as the F.B.I.

In the beginning the new Bureau's contribution to law-enforcement, under its first chief, Stanley W. Finch, was restricted to a limited fringe area — mainly concerned with violations of laws forbidding the inter-state shipment of obscene books, contraceptives, and prize-fight films, and the transporting of intoxicating liquors into "dry" states.

Beating vice rings

But it was the White Slave Traffic Act, introduced in 1910 by Representative James Robert Mann, of Illinois, that gave the Bureau its first real opportunity to operate on a nationwide front and capture public attention.

The Mann Act, stopping prostitutes crossing state lines, arose from public anger over disclosures that, in ten years, a Chicago vice syndicate operated by Alphonse Dufaur and his wife, Eva, had imported 20,000 women and girls into the United States to "stock" their brothels.

The first prominent personality to be arrested under the Act was Jack Johnson, the Negro heavyweight champion who won his laurels by knocking out Tommy Burns on Christmas Day, 1908, in Sydney, Australia. In 1912 he was convicted for persuading a girl, who later became his wife, to leave the brothel where she worked and go with him into another state.

Johnson, who was sentenced to one year — but released on bond pending appeal — disguised himself as a member of a Negro baseball team, fled to Canada,

then moved to Europe, and remained a fugitive for seven years. He returned home in 1920, surrendered to United States marshals and served his sentence.

America's entry into World War I, on April 6, 1917, brought new and larger-scale tasks to the Bureau, and necessitated the first major increase in the number of its agents — from the 300 of the pre-war years to 400. This small force was expected to keep watch on one million enemy aliens, protect top-security zones, including harbours, and pursue draft-evaders and army deserters.

It was not an era in which the Bureau covered itself in glory. Bureau chief Bruce Bielaski, who had succeeded Finch in 1912, accepted a Chicago businessman's suggestion that he should set up an organization of private citizen volunteers to aid the Bureau in its national security work.

Bielaski, however, found himself saddled with a giant that neither he, nor the government, were able totally to control. Within a few months this voluntary organization, the American Protective League, had recruited 250,000 members — many of whom took the law into their own hands in a mistaken sense of patriotism.

Encouraged by a hysterical spy mania, many League members who thought that they had acquired some kind of Federal status, turned their attention to the radical Industrial Workers of the World (the I.W.W.), whose leaders were opposed to the war.

They made illegal arrests, searched private homes without authority, and in Butte, Montana, six masked men kid-

Associated Press

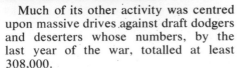

Associated Press

SABOTAGE . . . German agents were blamed for the blast—caused by two million pounds of dynamite—which blasted part of New York harbour in 1916 (above and top). But the German ambassador, Count von Bernstorff (right) had been warned.

Bettmann Archive

napped Frank Little, an I.W.W. leader, and hanged him from a railroad trestle set up as a makeshift gallows.

Such actions as those, and others by other vigilante groups, embarrassed the Bureau. Nevertheless, the situation was complicated by the fact that, whatever illegal action some groups might take, the Bureau was itself officially and legally obliged to move against the I.W.W. and similar groups.

Much of its other activity was centred upon massive drives against draft dodgers and deserters whose numbers, by the last year of the war, totalled at least 308,000.

With the assistance of American Protective League members, roundups were launched in a series of major cities and thousands of innocent citizens were arrested and thrown into jail for periods of up to 24 hours. Although all men between the ages of 21 and 31 were required by law to carry their draft classification cards with them, they, and others of all ages were rounded-up first and asked their draft status afterwards.

One writer recalled: "Some who were dragged into the Bureau's net were physically unfit, crippled, or hobbling on canes, like the 75-year-old man detained in a public square along with others held by the raiders for questioning . . ."

President Wilson called for a full report and Attorney-General Thomas W. Gregory agreed that the raids were contrary to law, and that some Bureau agents had "acted out of an excess of zeal for the public good."

However, the Bureau's record in World War I, when many people in European countries behaved with no less a degree of hysteria, was by no means all black.

Agents, for example, learned that on their departure after the United States declaration of war, the German officials in New York City had left a cache of important documents in the Swiss consulate building on Broadway.

One afternoon, after the Swiss employees had left their work for the day, the agents broke through a wall into the consulate and found boxes and trunks containing around a ton of papers sealed with the Imperial German seal.

The senior agent afterwards reported: "These records disclosed methods by which the enemy was enabled to secure information for delivering war materials and supplies by enemy ships under neutral flags. These papers also furnished the United States government with information as to the identity of methods of codes and enemy intelligence system activities in this country from the beginning of the war."

Even before the United States was involved in the war, British intelligence had warned of the interception of a German General Staff secret message to Count von Bernstorff in Washington which, in preparing him for the likelihood of hostilities, read:

"In United States sabotage can reach to all kinds of factories for war deliveries; railroads. dams, bridges must not be touched. Under no circumstances compromise our embassy."

In the early hours of July 30, 1916.

LYNCH LAW . . . a mob at Marion, Indiana, hang two men accused of murder. But J. Edgar Hoover (right) was soon to clean up America.

an explosion of two million pounds of dynamite wrecked Black Tom Island, the European shipment point and arsenal in New York Harbor.

Six months later a shell assembly plant in Kingsland, New Jersey, was blown up in a second sabotage attack and this, like the first, was financed out of the $150,000,000 budget provided by von Bernstorff for action inside the U.S.

Through some inexplicable ineptitude, details of the intercepted German sabotage signal to von Bernstorff had not been passed to the Bureau of Investigation — which, when the bombing attacks came, was unprepared.

Despite the sabotage, known so-called "enemy aliens" were not as great a problem to the United States as had been expected. But war did add heavily to the Bureau's work.

John Lord O'Brian, a Republican from Buffalo, New York, was appointed as special assistant to the Attorney-General for war work. To head a unit in the enemy alien registration section, he chose a 22-year-old lawyer who had joined the Department of Justice on July 26, 1917.

This young man had received his master's degree in law from the George Washington University Law School, and

was a member of the District of Columbia Bar. His name was J. Edgar Hoover.

As yet the Bureau of Investigation was still very much in its formative stages, finding its way through the labyrinth of law-enforcement by trial and error. So far it had lacked a dominant personality at its head to guide it in positive directions and endow it with a true identity.

With the war's end its agents believed they might at last be free to concentrate upon domestic crime. While the United States had been absorbed in helping to secure the downfall of the Kaiser's German Empire, new problems had arisen. In 1919 prohibition was introduced. The illegal manufacture and sale of alcoholic drink became a highly organized business, bringing gangsterism and protection rackets.

THE SPECIAL AGENTS

Their deeds were glamorous in the eyes of Hollywood, but the men of the F.B.I. worked with discipline and dedication . . . theirs was a scientific war against crime. One of their first battles was over fingerprints . . . and that victory is celebrated in a sign outside their headquarters.

IN ORDER to make its work fully effective an organization with such a wide range of operations as the F.B.I. needs the support of modern science and technology. But the use of science as an aid is a comparatively recent development in law enforcement agencies. And it was not until the late 1920s that the Bureau began to develop one of the finest forensic laboratories in the world.

There were other key elements that contributed to the nucleus of the science and information branches of the service. As far back as 1896 the International Association of Chiefs of Police (I.A.C.P.) had opened a bureau of criminal identification in Chicago, and subsequently moved it to Washington, D.C.

It provided a useful centre through which police departments could exchange information about criminals and their modes of operation. As the importance of fingerprints became increasingly recognized, however, the identification bureau found that it had very few prints.

The majority were held in prisons—the largest single collection at Leavenworth Penitentiary—and consequently there was no proper coordination.

In 1924, just after the close of a convention of the I.A.C.P., Hugh Harper, Chief of Police of Colorado Springs, told Rush L. Holland, U.S. Assistant Attorney General:

"Everything's at sixes and sevens over the fingerprint collection. Some of us think the government ought to take over the whole thing. The job is to make members of the Association a little more enthusiastic about turning over their prints.

"If you had someone who could talk to the Association, and show them all the advantages of a tie-up with the United States Government, it would help."

Holland indeed had someone. "We've got a young fellow here in Washington who's got a marvellous record," he told Harper. "He knows more about fingerprinting than most experts. His name is J. Edgar Hoover and he's in line to be the next head of the Bureau of Investigation. Suppose I ask him to talk to you?"

The invitation was instantly accepted and a few weeks later young Hoover—who shortly afterwards did become the Bureau's acting head—addressed a meeting of the I.A.C.P. urging the need for a centralized fingerprint collection.

77,924,806
FINGERPRINTS ON FILE

Conway

After that speech, and others in which he sought to win further allies, Hoover achieved his first notable success. The custodians of fingerprints, including the I.A.C.P., passed their files over to the Bureau of Investigation. One of Hoover's first tasks, as Acting Chief, was to order the sorting and organizing of nearly one million prints into a properly functioning identification system.

It was a most important start but, despite Hoover's personal efforts, it was not until June 1930 that Congress approved a permanent Division of Identification and Information within the Bureau.

Complacency

Even after that many major cities exhibited either reluctance or complacency about cooperating with the Bureau's identification system. Until 1932, for example, only a trickle of prints reached the Bureau from its own "home" city of Washington, D.C.—even though there was a very high local rate of crime, especially of murder and gang warfare.

In 1929 two wealthy private individuals, a rug manufacturer, and an executive of a soap company, had set up a laboratory at Northwestern University to provide crime detection facilities for the Chicago police. This establishment was among the "inspirations" for the F.B.I.'s own laboratory, which officially came into operation on November 24, 1932.

It was quickly appreciated that almost nothing, from a single human hair to the pieces of fluff in a suspect's pocket, could be disregarded in criminal investigation.

A physics and chemistry section was created dealing, among a variety of other things, with the examination of blood, poisons, fibres, and metals. Handwriting, inks, watermarks in paper, shoe and tyre prints, and examples of forged cheques were studied and most of these items photographed and filed.

As time went on there were very few techniques or materials used in the commission of crime with which the F.B.I. was not familiar.

Firearm Collection

As part of its general research facilities, the F.B.I. also laid the foundation for its collection of every type of firearm. Criminals quickly learned that a bullet fired from a gun carries its own identification marks as unique as fingerprints, and just as incriminating.

For a time, therefore, crooked gun dealers did a brisk business in supplying the underworld with weapons which had interchangeable parts. It was not long before the F.B.I. had the measure of those dealers and their handiwork.

The investigation of "gunprints" is now so routine in law enforcement that it is taken for granted. But in 1936,

Conway

IN THE MONEY . . . Backroom boys were called in to help when F.B.I. men found nearly 2,500,000 dollars and guns and ammunition in the boot of a car.

as this science was still developing towards its high modern technical level, the F.B.I. laboratory proved that it could —as it often has in later years—protect the innocent as well as help to convict the guilty.

In Alaska a prospector was murdered by a shot through the head and his money stolen from his log cabin. Initial inquiries centred upon an ex-convict who was seen by a U.S. Marshal to be wearing bloodstained socks.

"Yes, it is blood," the man agreed. "I shot a reindeer and some of the blood dripped on to my socks while I was dragging it home."

The ex-convict was unable to produce the reindeer's carcass and, as the Marshal found, his rifle had recently been fired. It seemed certain that he was guilty of the murder. In earlier years, and on the evidence available, he might well have been convicted.

The gun, socks, and murder bullet were sent to the F.B.I. laboratory. So, too, was a rifle belonging to an Eskimo who had subsequently come under suspicion because of a sudden and unexplained acquisition of money.

The laboratory proved that the blood on the ex-convict's socks was animal blood. A test bullet fired from the Eskimo's rifle was shown, under the microscope, to match perfectly the bullet that killed the prospector. The ex-convict went free and the Eskimo was sentenced to 20 years.

In the early 1930's, specialized and scientific training for policemen was practically nonexistent. But Hoover, always consumed with the need for constantly improving efficiency and extending the range of Bureau services, began to devise ideas for a properly founded training scheme.

Jointly, he and the Attorney General, Homer S. Cummings, agreed upon the establishment of a police training college—the F.B.I.'s National Academy opened its doors on July 29, 1935, with a 12 weeks' study course for a first batch of 23 police officers.

From that day on there emerged a steady stream of Academy graduates—men carefully chosen by their local police departments not only for a high sense of personal responsibility, but for an obvious capacity to impart the essentials of their training to fellow crime busters.

Apart from the Academy, the F.B.I. also developed intensive specialized training for its own Special Agents—agents who were, increasingly, men of notable ability. Lawyers, accountants, teachers, and others with good educational backgrounds formed a large proportion of Bureau employees.

Their rigorous training involved a broad curriculum from weaponry to a general study of the many Federal statutes with whose violation the F.B.I. was concerned.

Among those laws were some which the F.B.I. had known from its earliest days—including the White Slave Traffic Act and the Antitrust Act—with many more being added as the years passed. Following the kidnapping and murder of Colonel Charles Lindbergh's infant son,

FBI

Conway

in 1932, abduction across a State line became a federal offence, and the F.B.I. was given authority for immediate participation in kidnapping cases.

On the firing ranges the F.B.I. recruits were given exhaustive instructions in the handling and firing of weapons from pistols to the Thompson submachine gun, or "Tommy gun". The minimum score on target was 60%, and those who failed to reach that level were told that their services as special agents would not be required.

The remaining recruits were given written and oral examinations – some of the latter being sprung upon them without warning in order to test their degrees of alertness and observation. As a peak exercise just before the final examination, each man was assigned to take part in an actual investigation.

Important theme

Hoover himself met each class of trainees and talked to them personally about the Bureau, invariably underlining the theme so important to him that the F.B.I. was neither a national police force nor a political arm of the U.S. government.

Discipline was then, and has remained, severe. Men who joined even in the earlier years found that their personal lives had to be sacrificed to the demands of duty. Hoover was an ardent believer in the principle that all agents must be able to rely upon each other totally, and that this kind of "brotherhood" could be welded together only by discipline.

The fact that the Director himself worked long hours, took a direct interest in major investigations, and made the Bureau his life, made the rigorously applied standards acceptable.

Every aspect of training, and the general atmosphere of the Bureau, made

it clear that life in the F.B.I. was far removed from the glamour with which the Press, and later the motion picture industry, were to endow Special Agents.

F.B.I. men were subject to being moved to new territory – often at a few hours' notice.

Behind the scenes, F.B.I. work entailed many hours of drudgery, of patiently wading through mountains of evidence to seek out the one or two decisive facts.

The gold eagled badge with its insignia, "Federal Bureau of Investigation, U.S. Department of Justice", became a symbol to its bearers that they had exchanged personal lives for service to the nation.

Wire-tapping order

One of the most heated of the early legal debates raged around wiretapping (the interception of telephone calls) – a technique in which F.B.I. men were not then instructed.

Even though it was approved of in 1928 by the Supreme Court – which ruled that wiretap evidence was admissible in federal courts – Hoover refused to make use of it, or include it in his training programs.

He was forced to relent in 1931 when Attorney General William D. Mitchell issued an order for the use of F.B.I. wiretaps with the proviso that:

"Telephone or telegraph wires shall not be tapped unless prior authorization of the Director of the Bureau has been secured."

Hoover's first authorization was not issued until a year later – when a series of kidnappings made it essential to intercept telephoned demands for ransom payments.

From that time on increasing attention was paid in the F.B.I. laboratory and training courses to the new and rapidly growing field of electronics.

Nuclear physics

By the time the United States had emerged from World War II, every kind of scientific and technological aid – including nuclear physics – was being employed.

It had become possible to detect even the most "perfect" crime through the assembling by experts of a host of minor and apparently irrelevant factors. Every day the F.B.I. laboratory was looking more closely at clues invisible to the human eye.

The application of science brought new men into the Bureau in ever growing numbers; men who lived among isotopes and photographic processes; men who used chemical and biological techniques to examine worlds that were undetected by the old-fashioned microscopes.

Behind the men who went out to collect the facts that would bring the criminal to justice, stood powerful reinforcements who would evaluate those facts in new and mysterious ways.

THE FBI TODAY

During the 1970's crime figures have soared. New offences, like skyjacking, are being committed; drug trafficking has increased rapidly—these are the challenges faced by the FBI today.

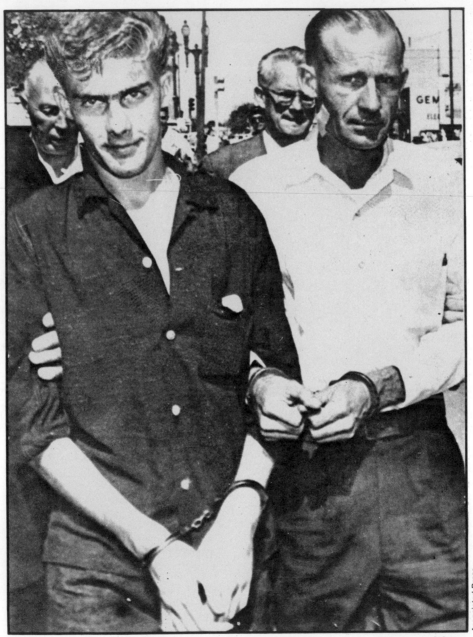

AS THE F.B.I. moved into the early 1970's it was faced with new dimensions of criminology. The top echelons of the international criminal fraternity had concentrated on highly organized plans for developing such attractively lucrative "business" as drug trafficking. At the lower end of the scale violent crime most often perpetrated by small-time amateur hoodlums or drug-taking delin-

THE FIRST skyjackers in America . . . Cody Bearden (left) and his father, Leon, are arrested after ordering a Boeing jet to fly to Cuba.

quents—had escalated alarmingly. This had its effects on the social pattern of life, and had gone far to restricting that personal freedom which is rightly regarded as a vital part of United States citizenship.

In many cities men and women became increasingly afraid of returning to downtown or other inner-city areas late at night. The Judas-hole in the apartment door, the front hall door whose lock could be released only when occupants were satisfied about the identities of callers, became standard equipment.

In the single, five-year period of 1966 to 1971, the F.B.I. index of crimes in-

14

creased by 83 per cent. Within that index, crimes of violence rose by 90 per cent and crimes against property by 82 per cent. During those five years arrests for narcotic drug violations increased by the astonishing figure of 469 per cent, and the enormous worldwide extent of drug-trafficking was demonstrated by the continuing and ingenious efforts to smuggle narcotics into the United States.

Such incidents as the attempts to set up a chain of drug "imports" flowing through European ports into America, and illustrated in the *French Connection* type of operation, using reconstructed automobiles as containers, added to the F.B.I.'s always-rising workload.

Skyjacking became another new menace and, largely because of Middle East conflicts, grew into a worldwide problem. The F.B.I. first experienced this phenomenon in August 1961 when Leon Bearden, an habitué of America penitentiaries, hijacked a Continental Airlines *Boeing 707* over New Mexico. With the help of his 16-year-old son, Cody, he ordered the $55½ million jet to be flown to Cuba – he was tired, he said, of life in the

A NATION MOURNS . . . J. Edgar Hoover is dead. His body lies in state in the Capitol. He left his fortune to his associate, Clyde Tolson (left).

United States, and wanted to spend the rest of his days abroad.

To El Paso, where the aircraft had to land for refuelling, J. Edgar Hoover sent his special agents a clear directive: "Hijackers are to be informed that the government is not going to allow any aircraft to depart if they are in it. We are going to make no promises of any kind to them.

Legitimate journey

"Tell them all the facts will be given to the prosecuting authorities. Tell them their position is desperate, and that if anyone aboard the 'plane is harmed in any way they will be held responsible."

Leon Bearden eventually allowed an F.B.I. man on board the aircraft for a "discussion". While this was going on, other agents quietly boarded the aircraft. Just after Bearden had patiently explained that he could not afford to make a legitimate journey to Cuba "because I've got less than 25 bucks to my name", the agents overpowered him and his son. Bearden was sent to jail for 20 years "for obstructing interstate commerce by extortion". Cody was also imprisoned, but paroled in 1963.

It was, by later standards, a bizarre and amateurish affair. But its importance lay in the lesson it taught the F.B.I. and the

United States. Any kind of individual could, and would, venture into the realms of skyjacking – whether he, or she, was a muddle-headed social misfit, or a highly sophisticated and brutally insensitive political fanatic.

To the public at large this kind of incident typified the work of the F.B.I., and helped to consolidate the romantic image that was conjured up by radio and, later, television. But, gradually and subtlely, the Bureau was being called into question at a high, authoritative level. Hoover had long insisted that under his jurisdiction, the F.B.I. would never be anything other than a fact-finding organization.

Then there came mutterings – and even outright allegations – that the ageing Director was exceeding the bounds of his own self-imposed brief. He was frightened of those he considered too Left-wing, and compiled secret dossiers on citizens who had neither been involved in, nor suspected of, criminal activities.

There were alleged to be numbered files – and some were cited in the press – on such radicals as movie stars Jane Fonda and Paul Newman, and the Negro leaders, the writer James Baldwin and Dr. Martin Luther King. In one of his most ill-advised pronouncements Hoover slated Dr. King as the "most notorious liar in

JOHN F. KENNEDY and Lyndon Johnson. It was said that Hoover passed reports on famous people to Johnson. Below: Robert Kennedy, assassinated by Sirhan (inset). When he was Attorney-General, Hoover refused to speak to him.

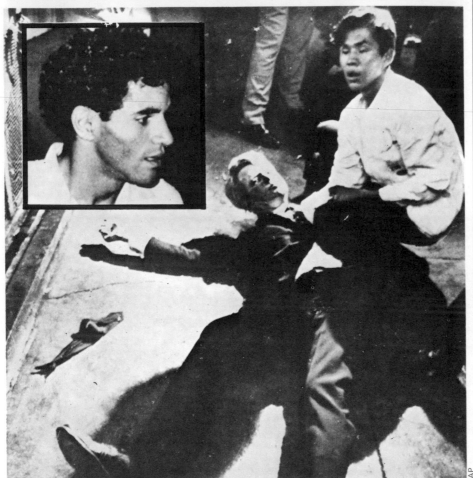

things in this country above criticism – Hoover, motherhood, and the flag."

Many of Hoover's problems arose from the fact that he had begun to feud with politicians. When the late Robert Kennedy served as Attorney General Hoover refused to speak to him (although he was nominally his chief). He did not hide his irritation with those members of Congress whom he regarded as too "Red" in their views. He was angered by the Warren Commission's strictures on the F.B.I. over the assassination of President John F. Kennedy.

In March 1971 a self-styled Citizens' Commission to Investigate the F.B.I. stole some 1200 documents from the local Bureau office in Media, Pennsylvania. The documents were used to bolster charges that the F.B.I. was compiling archives on persons to whom the Director has developed personal dislike. Many people, including President Richard Nixon, believed that the time had come for Hoover to retire.

The Director, however, had no intention of doing so, and continued in his own, eccentric way of life. He lived alone in a Georgian house on the edge of a Washington park, within 15 minutes' drive from his office. In accordance with his lifelong habit, he neither smoked nor drank. He had never married, nor shown any interest in women as far as any one knew, and his only close companion was his 71-year-old deputy director. Clyde Tolson. His only recorded hobbies, long since abandoned by the 1970's, had been occasional night club visits and bets on the horses, which always stopped when he had lost $10.

Behind closed doors

It was undoubtedly a sagging period for the F.B.I. Hoover, who had once been so open-minded and available to all his men, refused to allow certain aides into his private office, and shouted his orders from behind half-closed doors. At night he was driven home with his hat placed conspicuously on the rear window ledge of his limousine as a decoy for the assassins whom he was convinced were lying in wait for him.

His final and most consuming interest centred upon the $150 million new F.B.I. headquarters being built seven blocks down on Washington's Pennsylvania Avenue. He personally photographed each stage of the construction.

J. Edgar Hoover, certainly one of the most colourful and enigmatic figures in modern American history, died in his

the country".

It was said that Hoover ordered detailed reports to be compiled on the sex lives, drinking habits, and other personal affairs of various prominent people, and that copies of these were passed to President Lyndon B. Johnson – who devoured them as bedtime reading. There was no doubt that some of these allegations were embroidered by opponents of the F.B.I. But it was equally clear that there were doubts about the Bureau which would have been considered as being unthinkable in earlier years.

Black and white boss

As the gossip increased, one Bureau agent said of Hoover: "He was never as good as his admirers think he is, nor as bad as his enemies say he is. He is just a very uncomplicated man who sees everything in black and white. He has been the boss so long he can tolerate no criticism. Any criticism of the F.B.I. he sees as a direct attack on him."

Merely to have that kind of thing said publicly, illustrated the vast gap which had opened since the days when a newspaper columnist wrote: "There are three sleep at the age of 77, on May 2, 1972, from a high blood pressure ailment. He had lived well, and in addition to his salary had earned some $250,000 from three books which were published under his name—although there were those who alleged that they had been written by F.B.I. associates assigned to comb through bureau files. President Nixon headed the mourners at the public funeral on May 4.

As so often happens, once the architect of a great and powerful idea has departed it is difficult to find a replacement of a comparable calibre. The first man to take on Hoover's role ended his spell in office ingloriously. Patrick Gray, aged 56, a former naval officer and lawyer, was appointed as acting director and immediately set about introducing reforms—some of which were welcomed by the F.B.I.'s staff.

Rules are relaxed

Hoover had always insisted that agents should keep their hair cut short, should wear white shirts and always, after duty, return their Bureau cars to their office car pools, and make their way home on foot, or by bus or taxi.

Gray relaxed the rules on hair styles and white shirts and, for the first time, F.B.I. men began to assume "outside" fashions in more colourful dress. A new broom seemed to be sweeping clean, but it had little time to penetrate into many corners. For, on April 27, 1973, Gray resigned, himself swept away by the tide of the Watergate affair.

Following the unhappy episode of the burglary of the Democratic National Committee headquarters in Washington, D.C., Gray was alleged to have destroyed files that recorded a ludicrous attempt to discredit the Kennedy family. Patrick Gray himself insisted that he had put the folders into an F.B.I. "burn bag", for incineration, without examining them.

On June 27, 1973, the U.S. Senate confirmed the appointment of Police Chief Clarence Kelley as F.B.I. Director, of Kansas City. Kelley had been an F.B.I. agent for 21 years before joining the Kansas City police department—which he cleansed of its epidemic of corruption. He had earned the nickname of Dick Tracy, because of the electronics innovations he had introduced into police work, and F.B.I. morale revived when he assured the Senate judiciary committee that he would not bow to political pressure from the White House or Department of Justice.

HOOVER'S DREAM . . . The new $150 million F.B.I. building, still being built when Hoover died. He was succeeded by Patrick Gray (above, left) who was followed by Clarence Kelley (right).

So the F.B.I. prepared to grapple with the ever-new problems of crime and criminal investigation that were presented to it. The F.B.I. laboratory and identification division, upon which Hoover laid his mark, had no equal anywhere in the world. The cooperation with local law enforcement agencies by which the former Director set so much store, continued to increase.

Each month of the year the F.B.I. receives crime reports from more than 800 such agencies, and this material goes into computers which help to provide an exacting and detailed record of crimes and criminals. Individual records are available, to those who need them, in hours rather than in weeks, as was once the case.

More than 190,000,000 fingerprints are centrally filed—a far cry from the time when J. Edgar Hoover stumped the country in his campaign to persuade local law enforcement officers to help him compile a national collection. Over the years the Bureau's National Academy has supplied trained graduates for every State of the Union, for Puerto Rico, and for foreign countries as well. Through them the latest techniques on crime prevention and crime detection have been disseminated to thousands of other police officers.

At the request of local authorities the F.B.I. cooperates in other police training schools, gives instruction in such matters as firearms, fingerprint classification, traffic control, and a host of other matters vital to the welfare of law-abiding citizens. At its annual conference with state and local law enforcement agencies the Bureau provides a forum at which common problems are discussed.

Daily, crime becomes ever more complex and the battle against it ever more technical. It calls for the kind of recruits whose brains and ingenuity can match those of the professional criminal. The qualifications required of F.B.I. men necessarily remain high, with emphasis on legal or accountancy training and, above all else, personal integrity and good character.

Buggings, wire-tappings, personal dossiers, talk of political prejudice, the unwelcome events of Watergate—all these things washed against the Bureau's shores in the 1960's and 1970's. But the F.B.I., no less than any other American institution must come, from time to time, under close public scrutiny. The fact that it does, gives it its own special kind of strength in a democratic society. No review of its history can leave anyone in any doubt, that without it, or something very much akin to it, law enforcement in the United States would be an ideal rather than a reality.

SCOTLAND YARD

Scotland Yard's Flying Squad has developed over the years as a highly mobilized "swoop" force whose task is to move quickly onto scenes of crime at a moment's notice. One of the most important advances in the Squad's efficiency was the introduction of a standard telephone link with the public, in case of trouble . . . 999.

Popperfoto, Picturepoint

IN 1850 Charles Dickens captured the attention of the readers of his *Household Words* with an article headed "The Modern Science of Thief-taking", based on his own interviews with the handful of officers who then comprised the staff of Scotland Yard's "detective office".

Dickens was intrigued by the wiliness of nineteenth-century criminals, and fascinated by the clinical yet imaginative minds of the men appointed to search them out and bring them to justice.

Today the detective office is still a focal point of the Yard, the centre of the Criminal Investigation Department, but its work has moved light-years beyond simple thief-taking. The C.I.D. has grown as crime has grown, and its complexities have increased in step with the complexities of law breaking so that now it employs a multitude of specialist squads.

Murder, bank robbery, and housebreaking remain basic ingredients of Scotland Yard's routine. But to those have been added such other criminal activities as forgery, fraud, vice, drug trafficking, subversion and, in the latest period, bombings in large cities by political groups — including the Provisional wing of the Irish Republican Army.

Workless spectres

Few Scotland Yard specialist squads have been endowed with such fiction writers' glamour as the Flying Squad — the original mobile unit launched immediately after World War I to swoop quickly on scenes of crime. Yet there were certain ironic touches about its formation, for the first main targets of the squad were groups of disillusioned front-line veterans who, overnight, found themselves transformed from national heroes into unwanted, workless spectres — and who took to crime with the same dedication they had shown in the trenches.

They launched housebreaking forays throughout the better-off suburbs of London and other large cities. They descended on banks and post offices like a bandit plague, "worked" the London Underground as pickpockets, and emptied dockside warehouses. They hurled bricks through shop windows in main streets in broad daylight, made off with as much of the contents as they could scoop up in a few seconds, and added a new phrase to the language of crime — smash-and-grab.

At first the Yard's new mobile police squad was given a horse-drawn covered van in which a dozen detectives crouched out of sight while observing the passing scene through peepholes. As suspects were spied the officers would leap from the back of the van, one by one, and pursue their quarry on foot. Crude as it now seems, the system worked, and very soon horse and van were replaced by two Crossley tenders — powerful motor vehicles used successfully in the war.

Increasingly ordinary cars were added and, for a time, became known as Q-cars after the wartime fighting "Q" ships disguised as merchantmen. It was the newspapers that dubbed the fast-growing mobile unit the "Flying Squad", and noted the break-up of marauding smash-and-grab gangs as the squad developed in speed and technique.

Despite its speed of movement, what the squad initially lacked was speed of communication with its base. But that drawback began to disappear from the day, in 1922, when patrol cars were fitted with radio and headquarters' messages were broadcast over the London 2LO transmitter of the newly-founded British Broadcasting Company.

Indeed, the two most important additional arms provided for the police in general, and the Flying Squad in particular, were radio and the introduction of the 999 telephone link by which members of the public could pass information directly to the Yard or to local police.

It was a 999 call, received in Scotland Yard's information room one October afternoon in 1955, that launched the Flying Squad on one of its most spectacular pursuits. It came from a young woman who had seen two armed men run from a jeweller's shop in West London's Earl's Court and speed away in a Rover car driven by a third man.

Pistol shots

Sensibly, she had carefully noted the car licence number, and while some of the information room staff were alerting patrol units in the holdup area others checked the stolen-car list and found that the Rover was on it.

Among those who heard the radioed alarm call were the three crew members of a Flying Squad car cruising sedately through Hyde Park on a routine patrol — Detective-Sergeants Albert Chambers and Ernest Cooke, and Police Constable Donald Cameron. At the very instant in which they acknowledged the Yard's message they saw the "wanted" car, travelling fast through the park and sweeping past them in the opposite direction. P.C. Cameron, the crew's driver, brought the squad car around in a frantic U-turn and throttled to full power on the tail of the Rover.

Strollers, out to observe the autumn leaves in London's most famous park, gaped at the sight of two cars plunging at nearly 80 miles an hour over the Serpentine Bridge, and at the two men who leaned out of the Rover's rear windows firing bursts of pistol shots at the careening squad car.

At the park exit on the busy Bayswater Road the surge of traffic forced the gunmen's car to stop and, even before the Flying Squad car had slithered to a halt behind it, Sergeant Cooke leaped out and was battling to drag the Rover's

HORSE POWER used to place a severe limit on the possibilities of the police taking quick action in emergencies!

driver from his seat. However, before he could complete the capture, a blow from one of the men sent him spinning to the ground, and the Rover sprang forward into a temporary gap in the traffic.

The chase continued down Park Lane — where another of the gunmen's shots shattered the squad car windscreen and destroyed all visibility as P.C. Cameron fought his own nerve-stretching duel with double-decker buses and taxis. With his bare fist, and apparently oblivious of the blood-letting lacerations, Cameron beat out the obscuring glass and sped after the getaway car along Mayfair's Curzon Street. There the Rover slammed into a parked car, ricocheted from that into another, and slid unevenly across the street to a final stop.

The holdup men ran from the wreckage, pursued on foot by the three Flying Squad men. Sergeant Chambers was shot in the forearm but, despite his wound, managed to leap on to the back of one of the escaping men and pin him to the ground. Another officer, P.C. Evans Wood, who had joined the hunt in Curzon Street, was hit in the stomach· and in the general confusion the other two gunmen vanished.

Within hours one of the two was found in a hotel in Tottenham Court Road and two days later the third member of the trio was captured, asleep in bed, in a house in South London. To the surprise and relief of the Flying Squad men, who were prepared for a final shoot-out, his only comment was the tired old cliché "I'll come quietly."

The three men subsequently received sentences totalling 42 years and Lord Goddard, the Lord Chief Justice, told the Flying Squad officers: "I give the thanks of the community for your gallant and devoted sense of duty."

As in all British police forces, such spectacular events are still comparatively rare, and most of the C.I.D.'s energies are devoted to the long, complex, and often wearying routine of detective

THREE robbed men! All were victims of the raiders who held up the London jeweller's. A crowd gathers (top) to see the bandits' car after the chase.

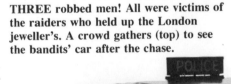

STEP BY STEP, police mobility improved. The car (left) was radio equipped. Right: the 1938 model.

work. But Scotland Yard's international reputation for patient and dogged investigation has been responsible for the arrest and conviction of criminals in countless cases where the prospects at first seemed discouraging.

There was a notable example of the rewards for that patience following the murder, in a Soho street in April 1947, of Alec d'Antiquis—a motorcyclist who was shot down as he attempted to block the escape of a car carrying two men who had just held up a pawnbroker.

Onlookers' descriptions of the men, whose faces were covered by scarves, differed widely. But an office boy told the police that within minutes of the murder two men had pushed past him and run into the block of offices where he worked. A short while later they had dashed out again and the boy noticed that one of the men had discarded the raincoat he was wearing earlier.

Two days later a painter working in the same office building reported the discovery of a raincoat hidden behind a disused counter on an upper floor. On examining it at Scotland Yard the detective in charge of the case saw that the coat's name tag had been removed. But when he ripped open the lining he found a makers' tag marked with indelible code numbers.

From a translation of the code the makers were able to show that the coat had been one of a batch delivered to three shops in the London area. Teams of detectives were sent to check the order books of the shops' managers, and then embarked on the tedious chore of calling upon all those people whose addresses had been noted in the sales records.

It seemed to be a fruitless search until finally one C.I.D. man knocked at the door of a flat in the riverside district of Deptford where, according to the sales sheets, lived a Mr. Thomas Kemp who had bought such a coat.

There Kemp agreed that he was the owner and first insisted that he had lost the coat in a cinema. Later, however, he said his wife had loaned it to her brother, Charles Henry Jenkins. Jenkins was already "known" to the police and was on their current list as a suspect in a recent £5000 London robbery. Eventually, Jenkins and two other men, Geraghty and Holt, were tried at the Old Bailey and convicted of murder. Jenkins and Geraghty were hanged on September 19, 1947. But Holt, who at 17 was too young for the death sentence, was sent to prison for an indefinite term.

The crudities of petty hoodlums, like Jenkins, are balanced in the modern fight against crime by the sophistication of those who have used the enormously increased complications of finance and business methods to make a "killing" through fraud. Today while many of the

C.I.D.'s senior officers study the new techniques applied to "traditional" crimes such as housebreaking and bank robbery, others spend their working lives searching among ledgers and balance sheets for the hidden clues that will lead them to the big-money swindlers.

The Fraud Squad came into being, as a branch of the C.I.D., in 1946. One of its most notable features was that, for the first time, it brought about a formal link between the Metropolitan Police and the City Police—the separate law enforcement agency which covers the square mile of the City of London, the capital's financial centre.

Highly involved

Demarcations were so rigid at the time that City officers had no power to exercise their police authority outside their own area. To make the new squad operative, a group of City detectives were specially sworn in as Metropolitan policemen. For the squad, as a cohesive body, it was an irritating situation which was later ended by Act of Parliament.

While patience is regarded as a major virtue in the C.I.D. as a whole, it amounts almost to sainthood in the Fraud Squad. Many of its cases are so highly involved that they may take two or three years to unravel and require the production of evidence of the most specialized character. Often only the experts (and the criminals themselves) can understand the nature of the fraud and the methods employed in it.

Automobile theft is as much a prime occupation for criminals in Britain as it is in any other industrialized nation. And, since the most professional practitioners have also become extremely knowledgeable about their trade, the Yard's C.I.D. has evolved its own counter measures through its stolen car branch.

At their own London workshop the detectives of this branch spend much of their time, covered to their elbows in grease, minutely studying pieces of automobile ranging from complete engine blocks to small sections of chassis.

A considerable amount of their detection work is concerned with unmasking "ringers"—the car thieves, or their mechanics, who interchange parts between a series of stolen cars to destroy the identities of the original vehicles. Cars are easy to steal, easy and profitable to dispose of, and comparatively simple to disguise.

But in their detection work the men of the stolen car branch are concerned almost as much with criminal threats to life as with theft. For the work of the car ringer—on parts not visible to the innocent secondhand bargain hunter—is often sub-standard, and many "doctored" cars with faulty welding have broken apart at speed, with fatal results.

In one of their biggest single hauls in the car ringing racket officers of the stolen car branch helped to bring to court one group of 28 men who, at the time of their arrests, had cars worth a total of £300,000—or nearly a million dollars. Evidence against them was supplied by 300 witnesses, but none would have been found if the C.I.D. men had not spent long and tireless hours at their workshop detection bench.

It takes experts to catch experts, and as science and technology continue to tempt the criminal into new and promising fields, Scotland Yard will follow with improved skill.

POLICE MECHANIC works on a stolen vehicle. Sub-standard welding on such cars can cost the lives of purchasers.

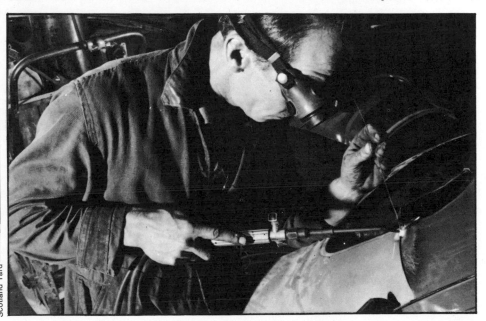

Scotland Yard

L BRANCH

anch have always had to combat acts of
sh bomb attack is just another job.

NO Scotland Yard department walks a more delicate tightrope than does its largest—the 400-man Special Branch originally formed in 1884 to combat attacks, including one on the Yard itself, by Irish dynamiters. Its main areas of activity cover such offences as treason, sedition, breaches of the Official Secrets Act, and rioting.

It is also charged with responsibility for the protection of government ministers, visiting foreign dignitaries, and the general surveillance of non-British citizens entering the country.

Balance of power

The delicacy of its position in the law enforcement system arises from the fact that while its duty is to protect the state from external and domestic enemies, it has neither rights nor powers to behave in ways which characterize secret or political police in some other countries.

In most cases its work is confined to investigation—and the tasks of acting upon its information, of making arrests and charging subversives and others, devolve upon other branches of the police. Apart from occasions when direct action is called for against specific law breakers, the day-to-day routine of the Special Branch centres largely upon the build-up of detailed knowledge of how potentially threatening groups work, and who the principal planners are.

Undercover work

All extremists, whether on the Left or Right of the political spectrum, are carefully observed and so are their associates. To many people in a democracy such surveillance sometimes appears distasteful. But in Britain there is general agreement on the need for protection against forms of extremism likely to move from mere expression of off-centre views to positive subversion or sabotage.

The law itself confers the same rights on the arrested spy as on the offending motorist, and there are no torture chambers at Scotland Yard, or in any other British police force.

In order to do their department's job some Special Branch men are required to infiltrate certain potentially dangerous organizations, to "mingle" with workers in industrial plants engaged on secret government contracts, and even to march with apparent enthusiasm in the more excitable public demonstrations.

But the extent and nature of this undercover work is far less sinister than some police critics suggest—largely due to the fact that, despite their awareness of possible threats to their security, the British people are not given to hysterical reactions, and do not approve of such reactions in their public servants.

Life for the Special Branch, founded in

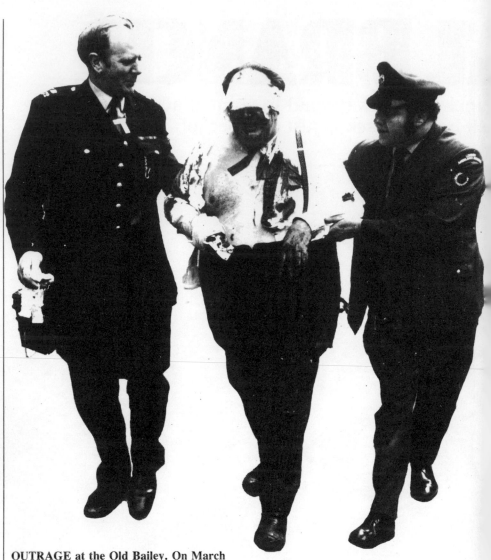

OUTRAGE at the Old Bailey. On March 9, 1973, a bomb blast shattered the court badly injuring lawyer James Crespi.

dynamiting days, has come full circle in recent years with bombing attacks in London by activists belonging to the Provisional wing of the Irish Republican Army, or one of its associated groups, and by an anarchist contingent calling itself the Angry Brigade. But although the attacks have been regarded as an unbelievable outrage by a new generation of Londoners, they are by no means the first the Special Branch have had to contend with in modern times.

Young bride

In August 1939 a young Edinburgh University lecturer, Donald Campbell, who had just returned with his wife from their Paris honeymoon, paid a visit to the luggage office on London's King's Cross station. As he stood talking to the attendant there came a streaking flash and a roar as a bomb, concealed in a suitcase beneath the office counter, exploded with shattering effect.

Both Campbell's legs were blown off

and he died within a few minutes in the ruins of the office. Among the 15 injured men and women scattered around his body lay his young bride.

This was the worst attack, up to that time, in a reign of bombing terror launched in Britain by the Irish Republican Army seven months before. It came in a week in which Parliament had accepted a Prevention of Violence Act which gave the Special Branch power—along with other Yard squads and police forces—to round up I.R.A. suspects.

So dramatically intense was the swoop by Scotland Yard and its associates, that the day the law received the Royal Assent the Dublin boat train was increased by threefold, carrying worried Irishmen away from Britain.

It was the discovery by the Special Branch of a sabotage plan that led directly to the introduction of the Act. The plan had been drawn up by the I.R.A. Chief of Staff and, in disclosing some of its contents to the House of Commons, Sir

Popperfoto

POCKET BOMBS and letter bombs, bombs in Bibles and shopping bags; the Provisional I.R.A. has produced many variations on the same deadly theme. Sir Samuel Hoare (above) is the man who pushed through the Anti-Violence Act.

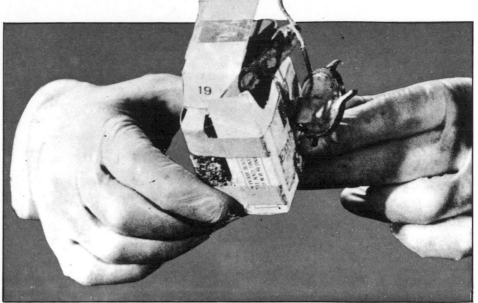

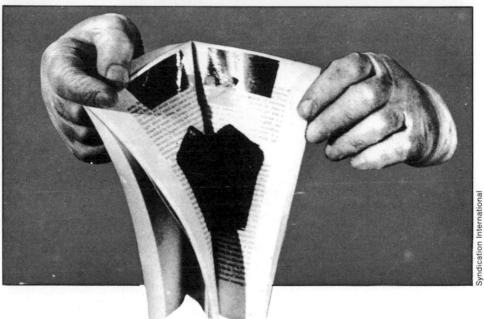

Syndication International

Samuel Hoare, the Home Secretary, said: "It is a remarkable document. It is not the kind of irresponsible, melodramatic document that one sometimes discovers in searches. It is a very carefully worked out staff plan setting out the way in which an extensive campaign of sabotage could be successfully carried out against this country."

Sabotage plan

Britain was then only a few months away from war with Nazi Germany, and the plan had been designed to take advantage of the nation's preoccupation with the forthcoming conflict. Aircraft factories were to be attacked, radio stations destroyed, and public utilities – gas, electricity, railways, and sewage systems – were to be put out of action.

Although the campaign failed to achieve those objectives, people in London and other cities suffered death and injury until the Special Branch men and their colleagues scooped up the ringleaders, and the courts consigned them to prison.

The war itself brought new and complex tasks to Scotland Yard, not only as the result of operations by criminals flourishing in the blacked-out streets, but by the German Luftwaffe air raids which came close to crippling London. The Yard doubled the strength of the Metropolitan force to nearly 46,000 men and women by recalling pensioners and bringing in reservists and special constables for full-time duty.

Policemen helped with the evacuation from London to safer country areas of thousands of children, and the Yard secured the lease of a large school near Wimbledon Common – a few miles beyond its riverside headquarters – in which to house its extra administrative staff.

During the heaviest of the Luftwaffe's attacks – between January and July 1941 – 67 Metropolitan policemen were killed and 389 badly injured. In May of that year a bomb fell on Scotland Yard itself, plunging through the southeast turret, wrecking 15 rooms, including that of the Commissioner, and scattering a million index cards among the rubble.

Invasion threat

Incredibly, no one was hurt and the Commissioner, Sir Philip Game, was out on his regular rounds, visiting other bomb sites. At the same time as she was bearing up under such air raids, Britain also faced the threat of invasion. Accordingly, the traditionally unarmed Yard men ordered 25,000 revolvers and 300,000 rounds of ammunition from the United States under lend-lease arrangements.

The abandonment of Hitler's invasion plans, and the scourging of the Luftwaffe by the Royal Air Force, brought a brief lull to the Yard. But new problems arrived with the unleashing of flying bombs (the V-1) in July 1944, and by rockets (V-2) in the following September.

When the last rocket out of a total of 1050 fell at Orpington, in Kent, in March 1945, the final wartime death roll of the Yard's men and women officers was 200, and another 2000 had been wounded. To members of the force were awarded 150 medals for bravery — most of them earned in the rescue of bomb victims — and the Yard emerged from the war with its relations with the public much enhanced.

Different enemy

In the final period of the war, and in the austere, shortage-ridden years that immediately followed, the men of the Yard found themselves battling with a different kind of domestic enemy — the black marketeers. These were a fresh breed of criminals — some of them petty operators known under the general title of "spivs and drones" — and others more skilfully organized.

They created an industry out of the theft of ration books — books in which coupons were exchanged for food, clothing, and petrol. They found no shortage of purchasers, even among normally respectable citizens whose greed and self-indulgence impelled them to seek more than their fair share of the meagre supplies.

Crime figures, which had fallen as the war reached its peak, soared alarmingly and reached a record level in 1945 — with 128,954 indictable offences in the Metropolitan Police District. Among those arrested were a motley collection of deserters on the run: others who had gone hopefully into the black market as a quick means of acquiring peacetime capital; and still others who, from their jobs in various forms of transport, supplied the "dealers" with pilfered goods.

Later the crime rate fell, only to rise yet again as the post-war years advanced. One of Scotland Yard's continuing problems has been the shortage of sufficient manpower to meet all the demands made upon it. In its recruitment drives the Yard has suffered from the competitive pay and regular hours offered by industry and commerce. Many Yard men, particularly detectives, work long and irregular hours, and generally only those with a strong sense of dedication — and who are prepared to sacrifice their home and private lives — stay the course.

False alibis

British criminals have also learned, long after their United States counterparts, the value of understanding the law and hiring good lawyers. Scotland Yard, while recognizing the need to protect the innocent citizen, has become increasingly frustrated in recent years by what it sees as the ability of some clearly guilty crooks legally to defeat the ends of justice.

In November 1973, in a controversial television lecture, Sir Robert Mark, Scotland Yard's Metropolitan Police Commissioner, accused a minority of criminal lawyers of being "more harmful to society than the clients they represent". In a television speech he told the B.B.C.'s viewers:

"We see the same lawyers producing, off the peg, the same kind of defence for different clients. Prosecution witnesses inexplicably change their minds. Defences are concocted far beyond the intellectual capacity of the accused.

"False alibis are put forward. Extraneous issues damaging to police credibility are introduced . . . If the prosecution evidence is strong the defence frequently resorts to attacks on prosecution witnesses, particularly if they are police.

"They will be accused, as a matter of routine, of perjury, planting evidence, intimidation, or violence. What defence is there, when found in possession of drugs, explosives, or firearms, than to say they were planted?

"Lies of this kind are a normal form of defence but they are sure to be given extensive publicity."

Sir Robert gave an example of the kind of "bent" legal trickery with which, he said, the police had to contend: A hardened criminal burgled a flat and seriously wounded one of the elderly occupants. He was arrested, denied the offences, and was remanded to prison. Later his solicitor said the man had a complete alibi — on the night of the break-in, he was playing bingo at a club, and his signature was plainly to be seen in the club's visitors' book.

When the Yard examined the book they found that the man had indeed signed the book, on the right date, at the foot of the page. But, unfortunately for him, a group of four other people had also individually signed in, writing their names one after another. The suspect's name appeared in the middle of that group of names, indicating that it must have been entered later.

The investigating detectives realized that there was only one place in which the man could have made that late entry: in prison. It was not possible to prove who had taken the visitors' book to the man behind bars. But as Sir Robert stated:

"The prison authorities pointed out drily that only a visit by a lawyer or his clerk would be unsupervised!"

EVACUEES from London arrive at their new homes in the country, shepherded by police. The date — September 1939. It was all part of an officer's job. Sir Robert Mark (below) is the man whose speech about "criminal lawyers" caused a sensation throughout the profession.

Popperfoto

THE FIRST FRENCH CRIME BUSTER

A master of deception and disguise, Eugène Vidocq employed discharged convicts and formed a new French Criminal Investigation Department.

THE residents of the Paris district paid no serious attention to the little old eccentric with the pigtail and three-cornered hat. Wrinkled and bearing a gold-knobbed cane he shuffled through the streets staring into doorways, peering through windows, looking into court-yards. He was regarded as a harmless crank—especially when he knocked on a tailoress's door and told the woman he was looking for his runaway wife. He described the man the wife had supposedly gone off with and asked if such a person had been seen in the vicinity. On learning that he had—and, what was

THE JAILBIRD and galley slave who fled to become a famous crime buster ... and the decree appointing Eugène Vidocq head of the famed Paris Sûreté.

more, had only just moved to a new address—the old man started to sob. Taking pity on him, the tailoress helped him to obtain the address and sent him gratefully on his way.

A few days later the "crank"—minus his pigtail and now wearing the garb of a coalman—went to the house and loitered outside until the man he was looking for entered his apartment. The coalman waited until night fell. Then, together with a number of gendarmes, he burst into the upstairs apartment and surprised the man in bed with a woman. While the gendarmes secured and gagged the woman, the coalman grabbed the alleged lover and hurriedly tied him up. Once again François Eugène Vidocq—a master of deception and disguise—had got his man. By posing as an eccentric and then a

27

coalman, he had captured a notorious thief named Fossard, who had previously frustrated all attempts by the Paris police to arrest him. Not only that, he recovered jewellery and 18,000 francs hidden in the apartment and added to the growing legend of Vidocq—the detective who had been on the wrong side of the law himself, and still strayed across the narrow criminal borderline.

Vidocq believed in the infallibility of setting thieves to catch thieves, and wrote: "During the twenty years I spent at the head of the *Sûreté* I hardly employed any but ex-convicts, often even escaped prisoners. I preferred to choose men whose bad record had given them a certain celebrity. I often gave these men the most delicate missions. They had considerable sums to deliver to the police or prison offices. They took part in operations in which they could easily have laid hands on large amounts. But not one of

them, not a single one, betrayed my trust."

But Vidocq was not, as he has so often been called, a reformed crook. He never *was* a crook in the strict sense of the word. Up to his middle thirties he had been a soldier in Napoleon's armies, a show man and puppeteer, a frequent dueller, and admittedly rather a swashbuckler—not to say a womanizer. In 1789 he severely beat up a man who had seduced one of his girl friends, and was sent to prison for breach of the peace. He promptly began a series of spectacular prison escapes, each one leading to recapture and an increased sentence.

This irrepressible man was finally sentenced to eight years in the galleys, and his next escape accordingly took longer to arrange. But in 1799 he was free again, went to Paris and set up shop as a second-hand clothes dealer which he then ran successfully for years. Eventually the

underworld found out who he was, and they mercilessly blackmailed him until at last he went to the police, declared himself, and offered them a bargain.

If they got the threat of recapture and longer imprisonment removed from his life, he would provide them with priceless information from his acquired knowledge of "the criminal scene". They agreed, because crime had broken all bounds and the back streets of Paris had become, since the revolution of 1789-95 inaccessible to any party of less than four or five men armed with swords or pistols. So Vidocq began his job as a "police informer", and in his first year of operation he put more than 800 men behind bars.

The following year, 1810, he was made head of the Paris *Sûreté*. To "legalize" his position the authorities arrested him once more and then discharged him with a clean sheet. He set up his new organization on the then revolutionary principle that serious crime can best be fought by criminals. He employed 20 discharged convicts and developed them into the nucleus of a brand-new French Criminal Investigation Department. He planted his men in prisons by having them arrested on sham charges; and got them out again when they had learned enough from the current gossip inside, by pretended escapes or even by bogus deaths and burials. He was the greatest enemy the criminal classes have ever had, and probably the greatest and most methodical of all detectives. His files and archives were colossal and his memory unfailing, and the surviving mystery of his 23 years as head of the *Sûreté* is that he was never assassinated by his underworld rivals.

As it was he lived another 24 years, set up a private detective agency (the first in the world and the inspiration for many a writer of who-dun-its), and himself became a prolific author. He compiled a work of reference on the criminal classes of France, a book about the rehabilitation of criminals, and two immense but undistinguished novels about criminal life. There is a much-quoted book called *The Memoirs of Vidocq,* which he did not write and which he utterly repudiated for its dishonesty. He became friendly with the novelist Honoré de Balzac, and supplied him with the material for countless stories, becoming himself in due course the basis of Balzac's famous detective Vautrin in the *Comédie Humaine*. In his old age he became a counter-espionage agent to the Emperor Napoleon III. Napoleon III's destruction of the Republic and his reckless foreign adventures got the country into its disastrous war with Prussia in 1870.

By then Vidocq, who had shared the general worship of the power-drunk Emperor, had been dead for 13 years: he was perhaps lucky not to see his Emperor's downfall and execration. But in France his name is remembered as vividly as that of the fictitious Sherlock Holmes in Britain or the real life Alan Pinkerton in the United States.

Contempt and hatred

Although he was a colourful character, he was accounted an honest man. And though he was drawn into the "crime war" by an acquired contempt and hatred for the criminals he came to know, he was also the first to recognize that ex-prisoners are better able than anyone to bring about the reform of an ex-prisoner; a belief which has recently been revived both in the United States and in Britain, where ex-prisoners' organizations (such as Recidivists Anonymous, based on Maidstone Prison in Kent) maintain a rehabilitation service with considerable success.

No other country ever had anyone like Vidocq. A century earlier, an English highwayman and truly squalid crook, named Jonathan Wild, secret "organizer" of the London underworld, was induced in 1715 by the available government rewards to turn "thief-taker", and sent many of his old accomplices to prison or the gallows. He was a dandy in his dress, always carried a gold-headed cane, and kept an office in London and an estate in the country, each with a big staff of servants. But the offenders he turned over to the authorities were those who refused to submit to his criminal organiza-

SET A THIEF to catch a thief . . . although Britain had its own informer Jonathan Wild (left), Eugène Vidocq was the greatest practitioner . . . he was the inspiration of artists (below, left) and playwrights (below, right).

ROYAL COBURG THEATRE,

UNDER THE SOLE MANAGEMENT OF MR. DAVIDGE.

First Night of New and most peculiar Drama, which has been many Weeks in Preparation, giving a comprehensive glance at the Crimes, Police, and Manners of the French Metropolis.

FIFTH WEEK of that Unequalled Display of Splendour, the LORD of the MAELSTROM!!!

MONDAY, JULY 6th, 1829, and During the Week,

At Half-past 6 precisely will be presented, an entirely New Melo-Drama, in Three Acts, of peculiar interest, written by Mr. J. B. BUCKSTONE, founded upon Incidents in the Life of *Eugene François Vidocq*, the Secret Agent of the French Police, and which will be produced, with entirely New Music, Scenery, Machinery, Dresses and Decorations, to be called,

Vidocq, the French Thief-Taker!

Music by Mr. T. Hughes.—Scenery by Mr. Danson & Assistants.—Properties by Mr. Eallett.—Machinery by Mr. Durson.—Dresses by Mr. Saunders & Mrs. Follett.

The above Drama is offered to the Public as combining features of entire Novelty & singular Interest. The manners & peculiarities of our Neighbours & Rivals, the French, have always excited, in an intense degree, the curiosity of our Countrymen, and have, therefore, frequently been exhibited for their amusement on the Stage. The present production, however, penetrates into those remote recesses of Society, those dark, mysterious, and sometimes appalling transactions, which are only impervious to ordinary means of observation, but which possess features of the most thrilling interest, the most harrowing pathos. The Hero of the Piece, is himself one of the most singular and interesting characters, that have, in this eventful age, appeared on the Theatre of public affairs in Europe. After an adventurous career as CONVICT, BANDIT, SOLDIER, and CITIZEN, he became the principal and confidential Agent of that formidable body the French Police; at once the Defeater of a Burglary, the Detector of mighty Conspiracies. Such opportunities of diving into the mysteries of LIFE IN A GREAT CAPITAL have fallen to the lot of few; no rank so elevated as to be beyond his access, none so humble as to be unworthy his notice, none so concealed as to elude his penetrating vigilance. The Memoirs of no Hero that ever lived, are, perhaps, so pregnant with information, interest, and amusement; and it is believed, few Dramas have ever been more remarkable for the same qualities than the present. It has been produced with the most scrupulous anxiety to place before the Public a LIVING PICTURE OF THE EVENTS IT DELINEATES.

Colonel St. Jean, of the French Infantry, Mr. MORTIMER. Raymond Delzeve, a young Officer of French Infantry, Mr. COBHAM. De Villers and Julius, Officers, his Friends, Mr. WOOD and Mr. WORRELL. Monsieur Henry, Chief of the Police, Mr. JAMESON. Coco Lacour and Yvrier, Police Agents, Mr. SAUNDERS and Mr. CRADDOCK. Eugene François Vidocq, an escaped Convict, Mr. H. WILLIAMS. Roman, Captain of Banditti, Mr. KING. Bisson de Tretz, his Lieutenant, Mr. FRANKS. Terrier & Coquelle, Bandits, Mess. H. GEORGE & J. GEORGE. Fanfan, a Rogue and ci-devant Pastry Cook's Apprentice, Mr. DAVIDGE. Debenne, a Soldier, and pordoned Galley Slave, Mr. M. CORRI. First Soldier, Mr. NIXON. Second Soldier, Mr. TULLEY. Serjeant Belle Rose, Mr. E. L. LEWIS. Germain & Boudin, Thieves, Mess. ELSGOOD & HERBERT. Lachique, a Jailor, Mr. H. GEORGE. Robert, his Assistant, Mr. SCARBRO. Fossard, a Notorious Thief, Mr. COOKE. Fosse, a Brass-Worker, Mr. PORTEUS. Jacquard, his Son, Master MEYERS, Commissary of Police, Mr. WORRELL. Dubois, Raymond's Servant, Mr. IRELAND. Officers of Gens d'Armes, Bandits, Soldiers, Recruits, Mob, Lemonaders, Currant Wine Sellers, Gamblers, Thieves, Gens d'Armes, Bailiffs, &c. Rosine, devoted to Raymond, Mrs. BAILEY. Annette, Vidocq's Mistress, Miss WATSON. Mademoiselle Maria, a Humpbacked Lady, Mrs. WESTON. Cecile & Babet, Fruit & Flower Women, Mesdames LEWIS & MORRIS. Jenny, the Brass-worker's Wife, Mrs. DANSON. Louise, a Milk Woman, Mrs. DAVIDGE.

Act 1.—Scene 1.—Mountainous View AND APPEARANCE OF ROMAN's BAND. Vidocq a Fugitive Convict,—Attack of a Diligence, Vidocq a Brigand.

2.—EXTERIOR OF A RUDE HUT. Arrival of the Robbers with Booty,—a Rogue's Soliloquy

3.—*Interior of Hut, and Retreat of the Banditti.* Robbers carousing,—a Song,—Vidocq accused of Robbery,—his denial of the Charge and Recital of his past Life,—how to detect a Thief,—generous Bandit, Vidocq's departure.

4.—DISTANT VIEW OF LYONS, with MILITARY ENCAMPMENT! Recruiting during the Consulship,—a Rogue enlisted, Vidocq a Soldier.

5.—THE CAMP NEAR LYONS. The Female Duellist,—all for Love,—a Discovery,—Duelling the rage,—a Pupil in the Art of Fencing,—mind your Guard,—a Comic Duel,—Interference of Vidocq,—a Duel in earnest,—Malice of Vidocq's Antagonist,—Arrival of the Gens d'Armes with orders for his Arrest. VIDOCQ DENOUNCED AS AN ESCAPED GALLEY SLAVE.

Act 2.—Scene 1.—Interior of a Prison. Vidocq a Prisoner,—the Galley Slave's Complaint, they Plunge into the Scrape, and SECOND ESCAPE OF VIDOCQ.

2.—THE ENVIRONS OF PARIS. Where's my Bounty Money?—Where's Vidocq?—Fortunate Drunkenness,—Narrow Escape of Vidocq, Thoughts of a Rogue,—Song.

3.—AN APARTMENT. The Female Duellist married,—Appearance of a Notorious Thief, THE ROBBERY! Escape of the Thief with Papers and valuable Booty, the Suspicion,—the Arrest.

4.—ROOM AT ANNETTE's Vidocq's Mistress,—Vidocq at Home,—Thoughts of a better course of Life,—the Gens d'Armes,—the Disguise, the Stratagem,—the Gens d'Armes secured, and THIRD ESCAPE OF VIDOCQ.

Act 3.—Scene 1.—A SQUARE IN PARIS. REJOICINGS FOR THE *Victory of Marengo!* Vidocq's new line of Business,—the Thieves,—the consequences of bad Connections,—Vidocq a Tailor, the ruin of his Establishment,—again denounced,—the Gens d'Armes in pursuit,—the Garret Window, Escape on the Roof.

2.—THE BRASS-WORKER's GARRET. General search for Vidocq,—his concealment in a Bed, Gens d'Armes in the Garret,—their Departure,—Surprise of the Brass-Worker and his Wife,—a Disguise, a Lame Soldier,—and Fourth Escape of Vidocq.

3.—*PARIS.* Who'll buy an Apple Tart?—no being honest among Rogues,—the Thieves disappointed,—Catching a Tartar. THE BATTLE OF THE WOODEN LEG! Victory of Vidocq,—Flight of the Thieves.

4.—*POLICE OFFICE.* The Police Reprimanded,—Vidocq is not to be taken, his Appearance in the Office,—he devotes himself to the Service of the Police,—Fossard Denounced,—Vidocq undertakes to find him,—a Word of Advice from the Chief Magistrate,—a Batch of Thieves apprehended, Reward of Roguery,—Vidocq appointed *The Secret Agent of the French Police.*

5.—THE RUE THEVENOT. Any new Milk or Cream,—the Hump-backed Divinity, Vidocq a respectable old Gentleman,—the Stratagem.

6.—*The Lodgings of the Thief Fossard.* Apprehension of Fossard,—the Jump from the Window, the Pursuit.

7.—A LANDSCAPE. Condemnation of an Innocent Victim,—Procession of Death,—Pursuit of Fossard.

8.—*EXTENSIVE VIEW of the COUNTRY,* WITH THE Ceremony of a Military Execution! The Hunted Thief,—the Word given to Fire,—the Execution suspended. *Death of the Thief Fossard, & Triumph of Vidocq.*

To conclude with, for the 25th, 26th, 27th, 28th, 29th, and 30th times, the encreasingly attractive and unprecedentedly magnificent Legendary Spectacle, in Three Acts, with entirely New Music, Extensive Scenery, Splendid Dresses, and Decorations and altogether unequalled and unattempted Aquatic and other Scenic Effects, founded upon the celebrated Tales of the *Wild & the Wonderful,* and Called, The

LORD of the MAELSTROM!

Or, The Elfin Sprite of the Norwegian Seas.

Otho, ...(King of Denmark and Norway,) .... Mr. MORTIMER. Fredegond, ... (a Scandinavian Prince,) .... Mr. COOKE. Valschiolf, Foster-Father of the Princess Urilda,) Mr. KING The Unknown Knight, (*****) High Priest of Odin, Mr. FRANKS. First Conspirator, ... Mr ELSGOOD. Second Ditto, ... Mr. SCARBRO. Gundulph, ... (Pilot of the Royal Galley,) ...... Mr. E. L. LEWIS. The Princess Urilda, (Daughter of Otho,) Miss WATSON. Elrica and Elswitha, (her Attendants,) Miss HAMMERSLEY and Mrs. MORRIS. High Priestess of Freya, ... Miss MEARS. Lok, Sunter, Midgard, ... (Evil Divinities,) ...... Messrs. WILMORE, JONES, EDMONTON. Knights, Lords, Courtiers, Ladies, Priests, Priestesses, Sprites, Guards, &c. &c.

Asgard, - *the Elfin Sprite of the Norwegian Seas,* - Mynheer Von Klishnig, The Astonishing Gymnasiast, who is the first Professor of the Art of Posturing of the present day.

The Three Valkyries, Mrs. LEWIS, Miss PHAROAH, and Miss H. BODEN. Brandomann, (the Lord or Monster of the Maelstrom, Mr. COBHAM.

Act 1.—GRAND VESTIBULE OF THE PALACE OF THE KINGS OF NORWAY AT SANDAAL. *Tremendous Ravine in the Rocks by Moonlight, with Falling Stream of Real Water.*

Act 2--STUPENDOUS CATARACT of the Maelstrom, formed by REAL WATER! Rushing and Foaming from the Roof of the Theatre to beneath the Stage, comprising various Torrents falling with terrific force in different Directions, constituting the most Tremendous effect ever produced by a simulative Waterfall, and comprising upwards of 17 Tons, a larger Body of Water than was ever before introduced into a Theatre.

Act 3--The Temple of Fifty Fountains in the Mystic Regions of Valhallah! The whole of the Magnificent Effects in this Scene produced by Real Water.

Doors open at Half-past Five. Second Price at Half-past Eight. Romney, Printer, Lambeth.

Harlingue-Viollet

tion, and in this respect he was the ancestor of the two London gangs headed by the Richardson brothers and the Kray brothers; the forerunner of the American gangster boss such as Al Capone; and the prototype for the present-day Mafia. In 1725 he was himself convicted and hanged for robbery, and his odious story is satirically told by the eighteenth-century author Henry Fielding in his *History of the Life of the Late Mr. Jonathan Wild.* He had turned his knowledge of crime to good account—the reward for the conviction of a highwayman was £40 (worth about £500 or $1500 today) plus the man's horse, weapons, and property.

Informers available

While there was much about Vidocq that was flamboyant, there was nothing odious—although the *Sûreté* came to disown him, and subsequently played down the comparative lack of success achieved by the recruiting, from 1833 onwards, of none but respectable citizens as its new detectives, all of whom it called "inspectors".

From then onwards, however, in France, Britain, and the United States, the "hidden force" of the police-minded thief was indispensable. Each of those countries relied, and now all countries rely, on the availability of informers by the thousand, and sometimes they act as *agents provocateurs*; not always willing ones, certainly not always paid ones. The "picking up" of ex-prisoners for questioning, moreover, is especially easy in France, where there is a long-established system of subjecting the discharged prisoner to an *interdit de séjour,* a document listing a number of cities and towns in which, for the next five years, he may not "live or appear". To be found in any of them means arrest and imprisonment without trial. But in all countries, an ex-prisoner needs to live a very careful life if he values his freedom, and he will certainly never again live a carefree one. In the growing number of countries operating a parole system—which often involves long post-prison periods under supervision and a freedom which is specially precarious—the supply of potential informers is not diminishing.

"In the United States the F.B.I. relies on informants," states William W. Turner, who was an F.B.I. agent for ten years. "Payments are made from confidential funds, the total being one of the F.B.I.'s best-kept secrets. By purchasing information rather than obtaining it through other investigative techniques, the F.B.I. gains a measure of protection

THE GREATEST ENEMY the criminal classes ever had, Vidocq was perhaps the greatest and most methodical of all detectives.

against embarrassment to the Bureau. Should a case backfire, the informant can be piously disowned." In the United States, as in England, journalists have actually gone to prison rather than divulge their sources of information: but police officers, New Scotland Yard Special Branch men, and F.B.I. agents are never pressed about it.

Sometimes the police in all countries will actually use an experienced and co-operative ex-crook in setting up a crime—a robbery, an assault, a break-in—by way of an ambush. He is arrested with his accomplices, "offers" to give evidence for the prosecution, and is therefore himself acquitted. The English High Court Judges will have none of this, and if it comes to their notice the other men are also acquitted, and there is trouble for the police for using an *agent provocateur.*

To catch criminals it is not enough to know what an artful man would do in given circumstances. You must more often know what a stupid man would do. And to do this it is necessary, not so much to be naturally stupid as to be capable of stupidity. In setting a thief to catch a thief, the one you set should be chosen with this in mind. But the system has two built-in dangers, one of them old and recognized, the other new, growing, and sinister.

The first is that the informer may be a liar, concerned either to pay off an old score or to distract police attention from something else; the second is that he can (and does) use bugging devices and phone tapping techniques not always accessible to the police, whom he will then feed with the results—in which event all the statutory safeguards are ignored.

In the long run, however, even this abuse of the law may be preferable to living in a country where the police are hobbled by unrealistic rules and regulations, and where the villain is king.

THE FIRST PRIVATE DETECTIVE

The Pinkerton National Detective Agency were asked to break up the Mollie Maguires—a gang of men who were liable to kill.

Pinkerton's Detective Agency

PINKERTON agent James McParland infiltrated the Mollie Maguires.

FOR months officials and workers of the Philadelphia and Reading Railroad had been worried by the "terrorist acts" of the Mollie Maguires—the secret society formed by Pennsylvania miners to protect their rights against the bosses. But like the original organization (founded in Ireland to intimidate absentee landlords, and so-called because the men had worn women's clothes while hiding from the police), the members had turned into brutal thugs.

In October, 1873—in desperation—railroad executive Franklin B. Gowen called in the services of America's first and leading private eye: the Scottish-born Allan Pinkerton. He told the detective that the state police were helpless,

and that the mines and railways were being "put out of business" by the Maguires. Could Pinkerton break up the gang?

Pinkerton believed that he could, but on one condition—that he was able to infiltrate one of his own men into the society. He found the man he wanted on his return to Chicago, when he came across one of his former operatives working as a horsecar conductor. Twenty-nine-year-old James McParland was eager to return to sleuthing, no matter how dangerous or unorthodox the assignment. He knew that discovery would mean

death, but he also realized that Pinkerton—who at one time had been Chicago's only full-time professional policeman—would use all his power to protect him.

Since opening the Pinkerton National Detective Agency in 1850 (with the motto: "We Never Sleep"; and an open eye as a trademark) Pinkerton had achieved nationwide success and worldwide fame. His agency was known as "America's Scotland Yard"; he was a master of disguise; and the first detective to use women on some of his toughest cases; he had foiled an attempted assassination of Abraham Lincoln; he had worked behind the Confederate lines as America's first-ever Secret Service agent.

In addition to this, he had "ridden shot-gun" against the outlaw gangs of the Wild West—including those of the Reno Brothers and Frank and Jesse James—and believed that a wrongdoer's crime "haunts him continually . . . [until] he must relieve himself of the terrible secret which is bearing down on him".

With this in mind, McParland, dressed in tramp's clothing, took the name of James McKenna, and set off for the mining towns of Pennsylvania. For the next few weeks he wandered from Port Clinton, to Middle Creek, to Tower City, making free with his Irish accent and broadcasting his dislike of the "tyrant railroad chiefs, the devilish mine-owners". He noted down the descriptions of everyone he talked to, recorded their conversations, and posted his reports to Pinkerton.

One night in Pine Grove he was actually mistaken for a Mollie Maguire, and learnt that the society's password was: "The boys who are true." A short while later, in a saloon in Tower City, he got into a backroom fight over a game of euchre. He caught the dealer cheating, felled him, and then proposed a toast, "To make English landlords tremble! And to bring confusion to the enemies of old Ireland!" He then moved to Shenandoah, where he met the bodymaster of the local branch of the Maguires, and posed as a pedlar of counterfeit money. He was near to penetrating the core of the society, and his reports came directly from the bodymaster's house, where he was a boarder.

Before long, as more and more mines closed down, and the Mollies faced long-term unemployment, there was a call for a new bodymaster—one who would deal even more severely with the bosses. By then McParland had been appointed secretary of the Shenandoah lodge, and was a "natural" for the even more important job. He had memorized all the society's toasts, passwords, codes, signs, and symbols, and was aware that—even as secretary—his own room was searched on occasion. There was nothing there to betray him, and certainly nothing worth stealing. But his large supply of stamps would have aroused suspicion if discovered—so he hid them in the sheepskin lining of his one pair of boots.

As the dissatisfaction with the current bodymaster grew—he was "too weak", "too timid"—it appeared inevitable that McParland would be asked to take his place. This, however, meant that he would have to plot and carry out assassinations. His year among the miners had taught him that anyone who opposed the Mollies or stood in their path was liable to be killed. McParland could not be a party to this, and he wrote to Pinkerton telling him that he had decided to become

a "drunk". Hour after hour, and for day after day, he consumed cheap, gut-rotting whisky. The unaccustomed liquor had such a bad effect upon him that his hair fell out and he was driven to his bed.

Eventually, he recovered enough to buy a wig and resume his duties as secretary. But it was obvious to the society members that he was too much the drunkard to ever be their bodymaster. In April 1875 —his file in Chicago bulging with intimate and damning details about the gang—he travelled to Philadelphia to meet Pinkerton and Gower.

The two men, the detective and the railroad chief, were delighted with the operative's efforts, and more agents were assigned to the case. Within a few weeks there wasn't a mining town in Pennsylvania that didn't have its own undercover Pinkerton detective working there. But not all of them were as inconspicuous as McParland.

Word soon spread that the society and its activities was being spied upon, and every member was suspected of being "untrue". One by one the Mollies were able to clear themselves until only McParland was left. By now the Irishman

SCORES OF MOLLIES (like the four above) were found guilty and sent to prison—or hanged. McParland's work earned him a Pinkerton promotion.

was a physical and mental wreck. The crude, raw alcohol he was still consuming was turning him blind, and his nerves were splintering. Only his smooth and rapid tongue saved him from an execution squad, and he begged Pinkerton to have him "arrested". Before this could happen, however, he said that his sister in Chicago was dying and that he had to be with her. He arrived at Shenandoah railway station minutes ahead of a group of assassins, and safely made his escape.

Later, when the Mollie Maguires were rounded up and put on trial, McParland's evidence—and the months he had spent with the gang—proved vital. Despite the $30,000 raised by the members to pay for their defence (and to have McParland murdered), scores of Mollies were found guilty and sent to prison. Two Pinkerton marksmen guarded the former spy throughout the courtroom proceedings, and McParland was afterwards appointed head of the Agency's branch in Denver.

THE PURSUIT OF THE NAZIS

From his office in Vienna a lone Jew spreads tentacles to the farthest quarters of the earth in tracking the former persecutors of his people. His name is Simon Wiesenthal, and his organization, the Federation of Jewish Victims of the Nazi Regime, exists to bring survivors of the notorious Gestapo to justice. Below right, Nazi youth and the infamous Auschwitz.

RUDOLFPLATZ is a secluded square of rather humdrum buildings in Vienna's first district. Nothing remarkable distinguishes it from a hundred similar squares in the Austrian capital or elsewhere — except, that is, for the sparsely furnished offices on the fourth floor of number seven. The entrance to them is heralded by a small, discreet sign which reads DOCUMENTATION CENTRE, followed by the letters B.J.V.N. — *Bund Jüdischer Verfolgter des Naziregimes* — Federation of Jewish Victims of the Nazi Régime.

The director of this unusual organization is perhaps the best known — and most feared — Nazi-hunter to have emerged from the horrors of World War II. His name: Simon Wiesenthal. Born in Poland of Jewish parents, Wiesenthal was an obvious target for persecution when the Germans overran his native country, and he was hounded through more than a dozen concentration camps during the war. But while six million of his fellow Jews died in gas chambers, Wiesenthal miraculously survived, to become one of the most outspoken witnesses of the atrocities committed by the dreaded German S.S. whose task it was to carry out Hitler's "Final Solution of the Jewish Question" — the extermination of the entire race. When he was at last liberated by the Allies in 1945 Wiesenthal immediately began work on what was to become a lifetime obsession — the pursuit of Nazi criminals.

Apparently without trace

It was an exceedingly difficult task. There was no money, after the war, to finance a professional investigative centre with full-time staff, so he started alone by collecting and collating all the information he could lay his hands on concerning the activities of former S.S. men. Gradually he developed a series of files and card indexes detailing names, crimes and possible witnesses. These were already of value to the Allies during the preparation of the Nuremberg trials, and they were used extensively by the American Military Court at Dachau during proceedings against S.S. concentration camp guards.

Wiesenthal, however, was not satisfied. He realized that many of the worst Nazi criminals had escaped Allied justice and disappeared, apparently without trace. Among these were Adolf Eichmann, the man charged by Hitler to organize the Jewish extermination programme, Franz Stangl, former commandant of the notorious concentration camp at Treblinka, and the horrifying Dr. Josef Mengele, whose "mission" at his Auschwitz surgery was to perform genetic experiments on "inferior" races.

As sympathizers learned more about

AP, Popperfoto, Camera Press

Wiesenthal's work they began to send contributions — usually small sums of money but also useful information — and in 1947 he was able to establish a small Documentation Centre at Linz, in Austria. Lack of funds and interest forced it to close down in 1954, but later, in 1961, it was reopened in Vienna, and still operates under the tireless direction of its creator.

The Odessa trail

Wiesenthal understood immediately that the first task of the new centre was to discover, if possible, how the fugitive Nazis had escaped. A chance meeting with an expert on Nazi affairs gave him the answer: ODESSA. The word has since become a legend. This complex escape network had already been organized by the S.S. well before the end of the war, and financed with vast quantities of gold spirited out of Germany into foreign bank accounts by Nazis who had foreseen the defeat of their country.

Along ODESSA's carefully concealed highways some of history's greatest

THREE KILLERS brought to justice. Clockwise, Franz Stangl, commander of the Treblinka camp, Adolf Eichmann of Auschwitz, and his colleague Dr. Josef Mengele.

criminals have travelled in safety to Spain, the Middle East and South America. Their documents were always in order, their identities brilliantly disguised. Most of them left Germany in the confusion after the war and then vanished into apparent obscurity. No one, any longer, seemed to know who they were, or where they were, or what they had done.

It was a dispiriting situation for Wiesenthal, but he stuck to his work, slowly compiling dossiers on S.S. fugitives and piecing together, thread by thread, the pattern of their escape routes along the ODESSA lines in the hope that one day the information would be useful. Sometimes it was, as the case of Franz Stangl amply proves.

Even by the gruesome standards of the S.S., the record of the commandant of Treblinka was particularly horrific; at least 400,000 Jews were either shot or choked in gas ovens under his orders alone; some estimates reckon the figure to be nearer double that number. And for this contribution to Hitler's extermination plans he had been awarded a special Cross of Merit for what was euphemistically known as "causing psychological discomfort". In Nazi terminology this meant "special excellence in the technique of mass murder".

Ghastly inventory

In 1948 Wiesenthal came across a fascinating document. It was a list of items recovered from Jews at Treblinka —both before and after death. The sheer size is staggering:

25 goods vans of women's hair
248 goods vans of clothing
100 goods vans of shoes
22 goods vans of sundries
46 goods vans of drugs
254 goods vans of blankets and bedding
2,800,000 U.S. dollars
12,000,000 Soviet roubles
400,000 pounds sterling
140,000,000 Polish zloties
400,000 gold watches
145,000 kilograms of gold wedding rings
4,000 carats of diamonds
120,000,000 zloties in gold coins and pearls.

The goods were consigned to the Interior Ministry of the S.S. to be ploughed back into the war effort—or the emergency escape fund. But it was not so much the figures that captured Wiesenthal's attention as the signature which lay at the bottom of the list. It was Franz Stangl's. Here then was irrefutable evidence of his involvement in the extermination programme; evidence which would stand up to the closest scrutiny in a court of law. But where was the killer?

Waiting and watching

Wiesenthal learned that he had, in fact, been captured at the end of the war and automatically imprisoned by the Americans as a former S.S. lieutenant. He was given a routine investigation and acquitted himself well. No one imagined that he could be the notorious Treblinka commandant. Later, however, it was discovered that he had once worked at Castle Hartheim, the Nazi training school for scientific human extermination, and on these grounds the Austrian government made preparations to try him.

Their plans were suddenly cut short. On May 30, 1948, Stangl slipped away from a prison working party and vanished under cover of darkness. At the time it seemed relatively unimportant—he was just another insignificant war criminal— and as a result the news was not officially reported.

Months passed before Wiesenthal discovered the truth, by which time Stangl had been carried by the ODESSA network to the safety of the Middle East, from where it was unlikely that he would be extradited even if he were found. Soon afterwards his wife and three daughters disappeared in the same direction. There was nothing that Wiesenthal—or anyone else—could do about it except shelve the file and wait.

It was 10 years before any further information came to light. One day, in 1959, a German journalist burst into Wiesenthal's office in a flurry of excitement. "It's Stangl," he blurted out breathlessly. "I've seen him—in Damascus."

Wiesenthal was cautious.

"How do you know it's him?" he asked.

"I've checked," came the reply. "It's him for sure."

There was still nothing Wiesenthal could do directly, but it meant that the man could be watched in case he ever attempted to leave his country of refuge. In the following year, however, the picture changed dramatically. Adolf Eichmann was seized in Argentina and later extradited to Israel for trial—an event in which Wiesenthal played a significant role. Stangl took fright. Supposing the Israelis decided to send someone over the border to get him as well? He decided to make a break for it—and once again he succeeded in vanishing.

There was another long pause in the saga. Over five years passed without any

further news of the Treblinka killer. Then, on February 20, 1964, Wiesenthal gave a routine press conference at which he listed a number of wanted Nazi criminals. Deliberately he singled out Franz Stangl for particular attention and gave a vivid account of some of the crimes which the latter had committed. One day later an Austrian woman arrived at Wiesenthal's office in floods of tears.

"Herr Wiesenthal, I feel so ashamed," she sobbed. "I had no idea my cousin Theresia was married to such a terrible man. I can't believe Franz is a mass murderer."

A U.S. cent for each victim

"Where is your cousin now?" interrupted Wiesenthal casually.

"They all went to Brazil . . ."

With a start the woman realized she had revealed too much. She had come to check on the press stories, not to give the game away.

As it turned out, however, her evidence did not betray the whereabouts of her cousin's husband as effectively as Wiesenthal's next visitor. This was a shifty-eyed, nervous-looking character who had also read the press reports on Stangl. Wiesenthal noticed immediately that the man was unsteady on his feet and his breath smell-

DEATH OVENS at Auschwitz. The bodies were taken from gas chambers to be cremated here. Eichmann, the commander, was tried in Israel and hanged.

35

ed of alcohol. Motioned to a chair, he sat down heavily and mumbled for a few seconds incoherently. Then, suddenly, as if coming to a decision, he began to speak.

"I used to be in the Gestapo," he blurted.

Wiesenthal waited and said nothing. The visitor watched anxiously for the reaction. Then, having ascertained that all was well, he went on.

"I didn't do anything bad. I was just the little fellow who got pushed around."

Again there was silence.

"I read the story in the papers. About Franz Stangl. Because of men like him we little fellows have had nothing but trouble since the end of the war. The big men, the Eichmanns, the Stangls—they had all the help they needed. False papers, money, new jobs. But look at me. No one will give me a job because I've been in the Gestapo. I've got no money. Can't even afford a little drink."

Wiesenthal hesitated between throwing the stranger out and listening a while longer. He chose the latter course.

"Look," the man continued, "I know where Stangl is. I can help you find him. He never gave me any help, so why should I cover up for him?"

Suddenly interested, Wiesenthal leaned forward.

"Where is he? Come on, man. Where is he?"

The stranger grinned.

"I can't tell you just like that. Information—good information—is worth a lot of money . . ."

The whole purpose of the visit was now clear.

"How much?" Wiesenthal snapped.

"Thirty thousand dollars."

It was an absurd amount to demand from a man whose organization had always been run on a shoe-string. Since there was no way to raise such a sum, the price would somehow have to be lowered. Sensing this, the visitor, now in his element, offered to accept less.

"Tell me," he rasped. "How many Jews do you think Stangl managed to exterminate?"

The reply came quickly: "As many as 700,000."

"Very well. I'll take one U.S. cent for each victim. That makes 7000 dollars. A bargain!"

Wiesenthal half-rose from his seat, for an instant blinded with rage, and reached out to grab the man. Seconds later he controlled himself and sat down. The information was too important.

"I agree," he muttered.

Immediately the man responded. "He's a safety officer in the Volkswagen plant in São Paulo, Brazil."

Hurriedly, Wiesenthal arranged for secret checks to be made before paying

his informant; it was true. Stangl was in São Paulo. The problem which now remained was how to bring him to justice. Wiesenthal handed over all the details to the West German authorities so that arrest warrants could be prepared. But there were difficulties; the Brazilian government had to be persuaded to take action, firstly by having the criminal arrested and then by extraditing him back to West Germany.

Meanwhile the entire negotiations had to be kept secret in case ODESSA got wind of the discovery and enabled Stangl once more to elude his pursuers. At last, however, in February 1967, Franz Stangl was arrested by the Brazilian police. Subsequently, he was transported back to face trial in a German court and sentenced to life imprisonment, officially for the murder of 400,000 men, women and children. He died in a Düsseldorf jail on June 28, 1971. Painstaking effort and patience had forced him to end his life where he belonged—behind bars.

For Wiesenthal the capture of Stangl was an undoubted triumph. But he knows that the task he has set himself will only end with his own death. There are 22,000 names on his card indexes, and it is in-

THE WARTIME DIARIES of Gestapo victim Ann Frank shocked the world. Simon Wiesenthal traced and caught the man who had arrested her.

conceivable that all these men should be found and brought to justice. Nevertheless he believes his work is of value not just in terms of punishing the guilty but of periodically reminding the world of what took place during the terrible years of Nazi power, so that a repetition of those events can be avoided.

For this reason publicity is vital to Wiesenthal—which is why he once set about the seemingly impossible task of finding the S.S. officer who arrested Ann Frank, the young Jewish girl whose diary of life under the Nazis shocked the world. In this, too, he succeeded.

The officer himself turned out to be small fry and was officially exonerated of any criminal guilt for the girl's death. But the hunt still proved worthwhile; many people had claimed, before, that Ann Frank's story was pure invention designed to discredit the Germans, and that she hadn't existed at all. Now, thanks to Wiesenthal the Nazi-hunter, they know the truth.

INTERPOL

The organization whose probing arm stretches round the whole world.

INTERPOL, after Scotland Yard and the F.B.I., is the police organization most popular among film producers and fiction writers, and its cosmopolitan image has launched dozens of mystery movies and books. Yet, surprisingly, Interpol in its present form is less than 30 years old.

The International Criminal Police Commission—to give its full title—was originally launched at an international police congress in Monaco in 1914, but was reconstituted in 1946 when its headquarters were switched from Vienna to Paris.

The first Article of the "new" statutes reads:

"The purpose of the International Police Organization is to ensure and officially to promote the growth of the greatest possible mutual assistance between all criminal police authorities within the limits of the laws existing in the different States, to establish and develop all institutions likely to contribute to an efficient repression of Common Law crimes and offences to the strict exclusion of all matters having a political, religious or racial character."

Three years later, in 1949, the Secretary-General, M. Ducloux, re-stated

RECORDS . . . but with a difference. One of the most important aspects of Interpol's work is the filing system giving details of international crooks.

Interpol's official policy thus: "To establish rapid liaison among all criminal investigation branches so as to speed up the identification, arrest and trial of delinquents who have sought refuge abroad, enlighten fully courts as to the true personality of professional criminals, and to provide legal experts, sociologists and scientific experts of all nations with the benefits of the discoveries made by the police through their direct contact with Common Law criminals."

In 1951 Ducloux handed over to his successor as Secretary-General, the brilliant Sûreté detective, M. Marcel Sicot, a staff of 40 detectives and the nucleus of a well-run organization. Nowadays, thanks

to Sicot and to Richard Leofric Jackson, then head of Scotland Yard's C.I.D., who was President in 1961, Interpol is now housed in impressive modern buildings in Paris suitable for its importance.

Today Interpol spans the world with a permanent staff of around 100 men and women, most of whom work at St. Cloud, on the outskirts of Paris. It does not employ—as is sometimes believed—thousands of top scientists and research workers, but it can and does avail itself of the discoveries made by university laboratories, industrial research groups and individual scientists of all categories consulted from time to time by a criminal investigation department, as well as the work of all forensic laboratories maintained by member States. Thus it can command a far wider pool of expertise than any one Ministry of the Interior.

Interpol's nerve centre is its radio station 30 miles outside Paris—its fantastic efficiency depends on the speed of its communications. Paper-work and time-wasting correspondence have to be cut to a bare minimum. The Paris staff are almost all former detectives of the Sûreté or Prefecture: women staff act as interpreters and make on-the-spot translations so that no time is lost in sending off messages. Interpol holds files on 200,000 people, but the policy is to file only the records of the top criminals.

INTERPOL CHIEF R. L. Jackson of Britain's Scotland Yard. Top: The general headquarters of the organization situated in a quiet suburb of Paris.

These records are contained in two index systems—one phonetic, the other alphabetical. There are, however, also card indexes containing the names of ships in which drugs have been found, registration numbers of cars, the numbers of certain passports, reports on mysterious deaths and details of unidentified stolen property.

Like every other police organization in the world, Interpol relies for positive identification on fingerprints, but also employs one system which is unique in police work. This is the Portrait Parlé, or Speaking Likeness, developed to an astonishing pitch of perfection by M. Beaulieu, chief of Interpol's photographic and fingerprints section. He has devised a system of facial measurements which cannot be altered. In his files there are sometimes as many as 20 pictures of the same man who, to the untrained eye, looks like 20 different men, but not to the expert in Portrait Parlé.

If a man is suspect or under surveillance in a country 10,000 miles from Paris, Interpol can transmit all its pictures within an hour to facilitate his arrest. The system is based on a series of coloured tags, each corresponding to a factor in the description. Thus a synoptic index is built up based on information obtained from police forces which complete a descriptive Form S, a document which lists 177 different characteristics of the subject in the following 17 groups:

(1) Nationality. (2) Place where com-

COMMUNICATION is the whole basis of Interpol. Pictured (below) is the radio-communications room which is in operation day and night through the year.

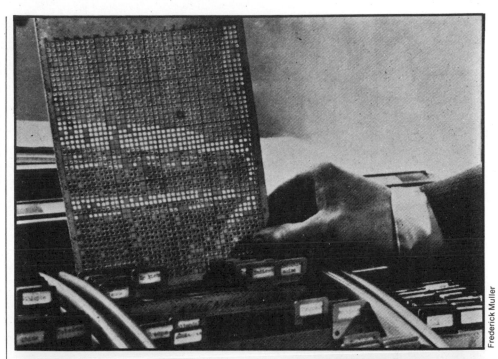

Frederick Muller

Interpol, AP

mitted. (3) Probable race. (4) Apparent height. (5) Face. (6) Complexion. (7) Colouring. (8) Teeth. (9) Voice. (10) Gait. (11) General demeanour. (12) Traits of character and vices. (13) Visible scars. (14) Moles and other marks. (15) Tattoos. (16) Deformities and amputations. (17) Habits and peculiarities.

Interpol uses three categories of "circulation"—now an internationally recognized document—to further the ends of justice. The red-cornered circulation spells urgency or top priority and is a request to the police force of the country receiving one to seek out, hold and hand over the subject named in it. A blue-cornered circulation is a request for information or particulars, say, of a person's present whereabouts or his movements on a certain date, his mode of

SPECIAL INDEX . . . Interpol's rapid reference library (top) allows instant criminal identification. Above: The second Secretary-General, Marcel Sicot.

life, real name and aliases. The green-cornered circulation is a warning: "Keep an eye on X."

In the course of tracking down a wanted man, half-a-dozen countries may be involved, and the work in each is carried out by its Central Bureau who are representatives of Interpol but not on its permanent staff. These detectives are seconded from their own police force for this specialized task and are the field workers who make the arrests.

There are three official languages for Interpol—English, French and Spanish—but, because some countries have trouble in sending accurate messages, a filing system based on purely phonetic spelling has been adopted. All names are filed according to their French pronunciation, which avoids the danger of breakdown in communication through confusion.

Almost all original messages received and transmitted by Interpol pass through the radio station outside Paris, and the traffic reaches 80,000 a year, arriving at the member countries within minutes. Interpol insists on real evidence being provided before it sends out a circulation, except when:

the offence is a crime against Common Law; a warrant has been issued for the suspect's arrest; the country requesting an arrest produces evidence and seeks extradition as soon as the wanted man is detained.

Britain became a member of the reconstituted Interpol in 1946 and the office of Interpol, Great Britain, was set up in June, 1949 and incorporated as a separate unit within Scotland Yard by Sir Ronald Howe, who for many years was Interpol's representative for England, Scotland, Wales and Northern Ireland. Interpol GB is sited on the third floor of the seven-storied white stone block over-looking the Thames Embankment which houses New Scotland Yard.

Here, with desks set at right angles to each other and the walls well charted with diagrams of Interpol's radio links and maps of member nations, sit two Yard officers, the office staff of Interpol GB. They deal with inquiries from all points of the compass that may involve, at any hour, a drug-runner of British nationality held in Los Angeles or a Briton on the run tracked down in Australia.

Indeed, any British citizen who is ever tempted to get up to mischief abroad might be interested to know what can go on concerning him behind the scenes. Local police report all troubles caused by a British national to Her Majesty's Consular officials in their area. If these cannot be cleared up by British representatives on the spot then full particulars are requested about the Briton concerned through the Foreign Office's Consular Service—and the inquiries often land on a desk at Interpol GB. What happens then should

OVERVIEW of the criminal records office. It is the most comprehensive international documentation centre ever set up to help the fight against crime.

certainly act as a deterrent to all would-be mischief-makers in a foreign land.

Take the case of Rex Macclesfield, a British national who came to the notice of Interpol in Paris, where he was using a fraudulent passport in the name of Louis Max. He was apparently on a racketeering tour of Europe—he spoke French and German well and had a smattering of Scandinavian languages. He was arrested by the Oslo police for petty theft in July 1954, and his trail of trickery left traces in France, Germany, Denmark and Sweden. The Norwegian police decided to pack him off home and reported this decision to the British Consulate in Oslo, who contacted Interpol GB.

It was quickly established that he had a dossier in the Yard's Criminal Records Office with his true name and favourite aliases. Further, he was listed on the Yard's files as "wanted" for petty thefts and frauds in Sheffield, Barrow, and Stratford-on-Avon. He was returned to Newcastle-on-Tyne docks on July 26, 1954, where he found a police reception committee waiting to take him in hand. He was tried at Sheffield and sentenced to a year's jail—because of eight international police telegrams.

INTERNATIONAL CO-OPERATION

A vast communications room, a powerful radio station, and the personal details of hundreds of wanted persons lie behind the wall plaque on the Interpol building in Paris. Together they act as a trap for unwary villains.

IT is doubtful if any villain has caused Interpol Great Britain more trouble than the totally conspicuous Arthur French, 6 ft. 2 in. tall, scarecrow-thin, with ears sticking out of his head like huge question marks. He had an American partner named Norman Krebs, another six-footer, and together they played the "false cheque caper" under dozens of aliases. They were the subject of an Interpol circulation as wanted men as far afield as Curaçao, the Dutch possession in the Caribbean.

Hardly had Interpol GB filed this international circulation when they received news that French planned to apply for a British passport from an address in Christchurch, Hants. It seems he had lost the passport originally issued to him. Now the British Home Office does not allow their police to arrest a man merely on receipt of an Interpol circulation—as do many other countries. He may, of course, be put under surveillance or even held if he is known to be a man of violence; otherwise a provisional arrest warrant must be obtained from a magistrate's court before he can be taken into custody. That procedure eats away time which is often precious. But it protects the suspect's right to know the charge against him.

The Bow Street magistrate to whom application was made for a provisional warrant of arrest for Albert French raised no objection. But French's antennae must have warned him that he was tempting fate by applying officially for anything— and particularly for passport renewal. He took to his heels.

Phoney cheques

Detectives traced a girl-friend of French and tried, without success, to persuade her to talk. Then Interpol GB got wind of the arrival in England of French's partner, Krebs. So both men, wanted by the police of the U.S.A., Mexico, Venezuela, the Cuban Republic and the Dutch West Indies, were now in the Yard's territory. And Interpol GB got a break just when it badly needed one. Krebs was reported to have left Manchester Airport on May 28, bound for Paris—and at once Interpol GB radioed the information to International Bureau in Paris.

Now it was up to Interpol HQ to run Krebs to earth. But he moved fast—it seemed he spent only five hours in Paris, in and out of night clubs cashing phoney cheques like a man with four hands. The Sûreté picking up the complaints after

him, totalled his proceeds at 450 dollars, and there must have been several clubs which, for diplomatic reasons, preferred not to report their losses.

In the money once more, Krebs flew to Lisbon. The Portuguese police missed him, for he stopped off at Lisbon for only ten minutes before flying on to Madrid. This time Interpol's radio message had the Spanish police waiting for him. They picked him up as he was trying to board a transatlantic airliner—he had a first-class ticket for New York in his wallet.

Missing link

With the much-wanted Norman Krebs now languishing in a Spanish jail, Interpol Spain notified their Paris HQ, and later officials in several countries looked at their extradition treaties. Interpol GB was as relieved as all the others, but for them one important question remained unanswered: where was his partner in crime, Arthur French? Seeking the missing link, one of the Yard's Interpol officers decided to revisit French's girl-friend. And this

BORSTAL BOY Brynley Fussel had read books on flying but never been in a real aeroplane. He stole an Auster, below, and flew to France before being caught.

time he found her eager to talk! It seems the fickle French had ditched her for a new girl-friend—and she willingly supplied the Yard man with details.

The Yard man found the new girl-friend also willing enough to talk—because, she said, she had heard from him the previous day. He had written to her from prison—in Madrid. She produced his letter to prove it: French's handwriting, beyond doubt. Now Interpol GB had to forward all details of French, including fingerprints and pictures, to Interpol HQ, which then asked Interpol Spain to compare the fingerprints. The man was the Briton French, not the American Krebs!

Slender clue

As French had used Krebs' identity to leave England, it was obvious that he had entered England in the same way. So Interpol GB had to go back to French's girl-friend number one to discuss his movements immediately after his arrival in England. She remembered that they had dinner together in a Strand hotel, and that he had left her for a short time to send off a telegram. It was to a country she had never heard of, and she could only remember that it began with "An—"

With the help of this slender clue and the hotel's efficient administration the Yard established that French had sent cablegrams from this hotel to an accommodation address in Antigua. He had sent them in the name of Krebs—and that was how he had signed the hotel register.

Elusive partner

It now seemed to the police that the telegraphic address used by French offered a clue to the real Krebs' hiding-place, so a further message was drafted to the International Bureau in Paris, in which it was suggested that the Antigua address should be investigated in the search for Arthur French's elusive partner. The chief of Interpol's Department of Police Documentation sent a cablegram in English to the Police Commissioner, Antigua, stating that, on information supplied by Scotland Yard, it seemed likely that Norman Krebs, for whom there was a warrant of arrest, was hiding on the island. He asked for Krebs to be arrested, if discovered.

No one could even feel confident that such a tiny island in the British West Indies had even heard of Interpol. Yet, 48 hours later, came an answering cablegram to report that the wanted man had been identified, arrested and was now held pending further orders. When all the evidence was collected it was found that the two swindlers had 1000 false cheque forms manufactured for them at a counterfeiter's premises in Haiti!

Interpol GB were called in twice in three years to take over two remarkable cases involving youths of 18. The first was nothing less than the theft of an aircraft in the early 1950s when "skyjacking" was an unknown word. It happened on an R.A.F. airfield at Sywell, Northampton, where a boy of 18 jumped into the cockpit of an Auster, got the plane in the air and headed for the south coast. He travelled in a series of hops, as the Auster carried no navigational instruments. So he had to land—and ask passers-by for his bearings.

Airborne

He landed first in a meadow off the Great North Road near Daventry and asked a lorry driver: "Am I all right for London?" Then he took off again, crossed the Channel and put down near Dieppe.

THE GLITTERING facade of the Interpol headquarters at St. Cloud, on the outskirts of Paris. Interpol answers calls from world-wide police forces every day.

Here a farmer gave him food and water, and he was airborne once more until he ran out of petrol—the Auster was fuelled for 300 miles—and was able to land in one piece outside Orleans.

So far the plane was undamaged, but now, as he tried to taxi towards a clump of trees for shelter, he had the bad luck to hit a rabbit-hole, and the Auster's nose dipped sharply, buckling the propeller tips. As soon as the plane was plotted across the Channel Interpol GB reported the theft to their International Bureau, and, unknown to him, the 18-year-old made police history by becoming the youngest-ever subject of an Interpol circulation.

Extradition formalities

Not that he was difficult to trace, with the Auster stuck fast in a foreign field. The boy had the sense to give himself up at once to the French police. He was held for entering France illegally, and some weeks elapsed before extradition formalities were completed, but, on March 9, 1951, officers of Interpol GB called for him at the Santé prison in Paris.

On the drive back from Dover one of his police escorts, himself a former R.A.F. pilot, was so astonished by the boy's grasp of aeronautical technicalities that he refused to believe he had had no training. In fact his previous flying experience was limited to one seaside hop. He had read all the flying manuals he could put his hands on and was clearly a "natural", as he subsequently proved when taken on by a major aircraft company who were impressed by his enthusiasm and gave him a chance to make good.

The second case of a boy in trouble came in the summer of 1953. An 18-year-old Spaniard was alleged to have plundered the Chapel of the Virgin of the Kings in the Cathedral of Seville and removed precious stones and gold pieces valued at 700 million French francs—a fantastic haul. The boy's home was in the Calle de Julio Cesar, and he had become friendly with a verger in the cathedral in order to familiarize himself with the layout and routine. Then he bided his time until he saw the chance of hiding himself among the treasures in the chapel on the night of April 14.

Stolen treasure

All doors were locked and the lights dimmed. Alone in the Holy Shrine, he wrenched gems from their sockets, defiling the Image of the Virgin. Then, in the morning, he sneaked unnoticed out of the cathedral, his pockets stuffed with sacred symbols worth at least half-a-million pounds—if they could be sold.

In the hue-and-cry that followed, the boy was never a suspect. Indeed, on May 7 he left Seville for Paris, travelling with

a properly authorized passport. After spending some days in Paris he made for London. Meanwhile the Seville police, combing through all local jewellers and silversmiths in an urgent hunt for the stolen treasures, came on an expanding gold bracelet studded with 17 diamonds, and another relic consisting of a single diamond mounted on gold.

The Spanish Chaplain-Royal and the Keeper of the Treasury identified these items as part of the stolen treasure, and the silversmith who had them in his shop said the boy had handed them over and asked him to sell them—the silversmith claimed the boy's mother confirmed that her son had bought the jewels at the government pawnshop.

Meanwhile Interpol GB learned from the International Bureau in Paris that the boy was thought to be in London. The Scotland Yard men who were put on the

BOY PILOT Fussel was extradited by Interpol and later received one month's jail for his joy ride. But a major company was so impressed by his expert aircraft knowledge that they gave him a job.

case found that he had made no attempt to hide himself, but was staying at an address in Regent's Park Terrace which he had left in Paris as a forwarding address for his mother.

Sacred symbols

They called on him there, but he denied any part in the robbery—and no gems were found in his possession or at his address. Again the extradition formalities took some weeks, but, in the end, he was sent back to Spain. As all the sacred symbols were found intact, he was sent to the Spanish equivalent of an approved school.

INTERNATIONAL FORGERIES

There is one sure way of always having enough money—whenever you wish you just go ahead and print some. Of course you need a little skill and a good printing machine. And how could police ever find you out?

AS counterfeiters present a threat to the economies of all nations, they co-operate much more readily in running down these criminal-technicians than in dealing with, say, drug-traffickers. Fortunately for law enforcement the illicit business of counterfeiting calls not only for exceptional skills but for a heavy capital outlay on printing presses. The whole process inevitably involves a team of conspirators who must meet from time

to time before the coup is perfected, thus offering the men from Interpol a better chance of infiltrating and eavesdropping. Then such teams must be recruited from the ranks of habitual criminals, and most of their records are on file at Interpol H.Q. in Paris.

It must be emphasized that Interpol—full title, International Criminal Police Commission—is *not*, despite glamourization by films and T.V., a world police

Guy Williams, Keystone

force. It is a clearing-house of crime on behalf of its member-states, and it represents the federal police systems of those countries, co-ordinating their efforts and acting as an information centre and records office, with powers to transmit requests from one country to all countries, if need be, to run wanted law-breakers to ground.

As well as bank notes, counterfeiters may forge credit cards, travellers' cheques, Giro cheques, letters of credit, and similar documents. The problem is often that of realizing the fruit of their forgeries without attracting suspicion. Obviously it would be dangerous for a forger to pay a large number of brand new bank notes into his bank account, or to make a substantial purchase with a bundle of freshly printed notes. Usually he will release his forgeries through a number of distributors, who "buy" a few notes at a time at a substantial discount. Through the uncovering of such a distribution network the chief forger is often arrested.

The counterfeiter, of course, is no respecter of nationalities — he switches from one country's paper money to another whenever he sees an opportunity for high profit. In recent years a Japanese ring was discovered at work in Brazil running off cruzeiros; in the West Indies another

PERFECT COPIES (above) . . . Or are they? Usually there is some kind of flaw even in the most apparently perfect forgery, but it sometimes takes the authorities a long time to find out. The most innocent-seeming people may be forgers, like the four-family Brooklyn household who faked the bills (left) . . .

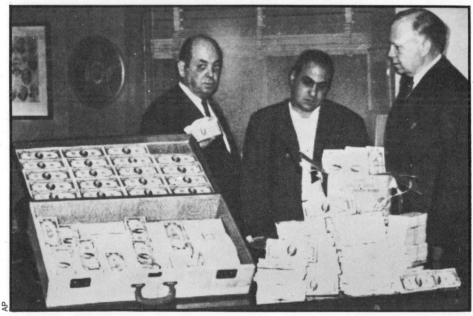

gang was caught in the act of flooding black markets in South America with fake 50-peso notes of Colombian currency.

So much of Interpol's daily business is taken up in dealing with this menace that the General Secretariat has sponsored a film, *False Money and its Repression*, to help national police forces understand how dangerous this crime can be to their country's economic health. The film drives home the point that, unless the police can raid the counterfeiters' secret press-room while printing is actually going on, thus seizing the plotters *and* the proofs of their conspiracy, then it is extremely difficult to collect strong enough evidence for a conviction.

Phoney banknotes, whatever the currency, often give themselves away by the very feel of the paper — and the trained eye is ever on the look-out for tiny imperfections, some false swirl or scroll or even a minute flaw in lettering. The expert can usually tell whether a gang

has been at work or a solitary crank; the gangs prefer small denomination notes — the 20 Deutschmark or the five-dollar bill — whereas the crank will slave for months to copy a note of high value, feeling that the small ones degrade his art!

The craftsmanship of the counterfeiter is usually of an extremely high order, and he is often prepared to go to great lengths and expense to get as near perfection as possible. One gang even raided the State Bank of France, stole several reams of the specially processed 1000-franc paper and then used it for counterfeiting 1000-franc notes.

In another case the gang's master technician confessed to the police after capture how he had stripped a 50-dollar bill in two, using special liquids, and then studied the structure. With the front of the note separated from the back, he said, he was able to examine the arrangements of the red and green filaments, distinguishing each side, and he set himself the task of faithfully reproducing the colouring pattern.

The counterfeiters went to their work

46

immediately after World War II and copied currency issued by the Allied military authorities. They followed this up by forging the banknotes of the "hard" currencies—Swiss francs, dollars, pounds sterling, German marks in the Western Zone, Belgian francs and Spanish pesetas.

During the years 1947 and 1948 the International Bureau of Interpol at The Hague identified 127 different types of counterfeit, among which only 24 concerned coins. This is because the technical improvements in printing methods have made counterfeiting easier. No longer does the counterfeiter have to make use of cumbersome material, nor does he need the services of an expert engraver—photo-mechanical processes are as easily available to the criminal as to the honest man.

Interpol has been campaigning for many years now—discreetly, of course, for it has no power to coerce its member-governments—for more frequent currency changes, for designs and colours on notes to be made more intricate, and

INTERPOL radio stations are located in many unlikely places, such as the humdrum attic (below), but they provide a vital crook-catching service.

for a specialized type of paper—all of which would make the counterfeiters' job very much more difficult.

The United States suffers more than any other country at the skilled hands of these forgers. The Treasury Department of the U.S. Government is mainly responsible for tracking them down, and the Secret Service is also involved in this tricky work.

Jet travel has opened up fast and easy avenues of communication and escape for the big-time criminals, but in a bid to counter such opportunities Interpol now operates 20 radio stations covering the main cities in Europe, the Middle East, Iran and the Americas. These stations are grouped around the central one outside Paris, and their coverage is being extended to equatorial Africa and the Far East. All messages are sent by Morse in the Interpol code which cuts down sending and receiving time.

However swift air travel becomes in the Space Age, it cannot match radio, and many a runaway criminal has been held thousands of miles away from the scene of his crime and only a few hours after he committed it. Murderers, bank robbers, gold and diamond smugglers, drug-runners and forgers all use jet travel

either to escape or to find a market for their loot, and might well get away with their crimes were it not for Interpol's radio network which is now serving well over 70 countries who are subscribers to the police organization.

In the 1960s a gang stole a large number of travellers' cheques from New York's First National City Bank—the cheques were in transit from the U.S. to Montevideo, Uruguay, when they disappeared. They were all blank and worth 700,000 dollars when cashed.

Commissioner U. E. Baughman, then chief of the U.S. Secret Service, radioed Interpol, which at once circulated the numbers and other details of the cheques to all affiliated police forces. Within days news came that some of the cheques had been cashed in Cologne, Düsseldorf, Bonn and Wiesbaden by a Robert Castille, holding a passport issued in El Salvador. Other cheques turned up in Monaco, cashed by Isaac Gutlieb, using an Argentinian passport. Then the trail switched to Milan, where a man giving the name of Helmuth Kender ran off, abandoning his German passport when the cashier became suspicious of the cheques. Another man in the name of Joseph Decker tried to cash some of the cheques

Interpol

AP

in Paris, but he, too, ran off when challenged, leaving behind an Argentinian passport.

When the abandoned passports were scrutinized it became clear that they had been used by one or two people. An Interpol circular went out with all available information about the men involved. A month later a man named Fischer was arrested in Bad Naheim, Germany, trying to cash one of the stolen cheques. He turned out to be the one who had used the passports in the names of Kender and Decker.

Within a month another man was arrested 3000 miles away in Buenos Aires—he was identified as the one who had used the passport in the name of Isaac Gutlieb. When the Argentine police checked his fingerprints with their files and those of the F.B.I. his real name was found to be Salem Karngalder who had been on Interpol's wanted list since 1948.

Every fake currency seizure sent to Interpol by any of its member-nations is passed to the Paris section which deals with the counterfeiting of banknotes and coins, cheques and securities, false passports and other forgeries. There comparison is made with genuine notes. The detectives in this department, with wide experience of every type of forgery, can often tell the author at a glance—so many of them tend to repeat their mistakes. In this section are filed specimens of thousands of forged notes and hundreds of dud

CROOKED LAWYER Joel Lee (far right) was seized at Kennedy airport. His bags contained over four million dollars in forged $100 bills. It was one of the biggest counterfeit jobs of all time. Above left: Interpol's forgers' file . . .

coins. Here, too, is stored the apparatus seized in raids on counterfeiters' dens.

More than 6000 cases of currency forgery have been notified to Interpol since the end of World War II, with notes of almost every known denomination involved. Detection is an exact business —the men in that job have studied the composition of the inks used, types of paper and watermarks and all the intricacies of design and lettering.

These experts do much more than detect—they also prevent by producing Interpol's *Counterfeits and Forgeries Review* so that banks, insurance offices, hotels and travel agencies can be kept up-to-date with the activities of the known gangs. Scotland Yard reserves one corner of its notorious "Black Museum" to immortalize the work of celebrated forgers. Here Adolf Hitler and Jim the Penman share a showcase— the £5 and £10 notes printed on German Treasury apparatus lie beside the notes made by London's most infamous counterfeiter.

Another case holds a bundle of Post Office savings books and car log-books, examples of the work of an extremely

talented criminal family. Mr. and Mrs. Arthur Pierce occupied a semi-detached house in Norwood, London, with their son Harold, aged 24, and their daughter Janet, 18. All did respectable jobs during the day, but at night Harold made ready forgery implements while father brought up the treadle-operated printing machine from the basement. Janet organized inks and chemicals and mother sat down to pedal the machine.

Every evening for four months the Pierce family printed Post Office savings books until they had a stock of hundreds. They burned any books which showed the slightest imperfection. They chose names from the telephone directories, entered them into the forged savings books, gave them a modest balance—between £20 and £30—and embossed the books with a beautifully forged rubber stamp. This done, the family took a day off, raced from one Post Office to another withdrawing £2 from each of their books.

Eventually the family decided to make a final killing of around £1000, but on the great day Janet got her savings bankbooks mixed and presented one with a man's name on it. When challenged, she panicked and ran back to the family car. Later all four Pierces were arrested—they had 170 forged bankbooks in their possession, and Mrs. Pierce had £488 in her handbag. Mr. Pierce got seven years, his wife 18 months, son Harold 12 months, and Janet was bound over.

DRUG TRAFFICKING

Perhaps the most lucrative of all "businesses" is the dope trade. Hard drugs which find their way from the East to the United States can be sold for up to 200 times the original cost. For that kind of profit almost anyone might be tempted to run the risk — which means one big headache for narcotic squads.

FEW would deny that, war and pollution apart, the greatest menace to the health, wealth and happiness of mankind as our species approaches the twenty-first century is drug trafficking. The growth of this social evil over the past two decades has been so stupendous that there are grounds for the suspicion that certain countries are actively promoting it either as a political or an economic weapon against others.

Despite the lip service paid by many of the guilty countries to the ideals of the United Nations, Interpol finds itself fighting a losing battle against the world-wide gangs — including the Mafia — which are cashing in on the multi-million-dollar business of selling narcotics.

The third floor of Interpol's headquarters in Paris has a room well charted with the routes used by the traffickers.

A COOL MILLION dollars was in these small bundles in the form of 50 pounds of raw opium. The three Chinese seamen were seized as they tried to smuggle the drug from Baltimore docks . . .

Popperfoto

CHOCOLATE CREAM TRICK . . . The idea of concealing opium—and other drugs—inside chocolates is a clever one. There is no way of detecting this method . . .

That room also contains some revealing statistics. The invidious distinction of being the main supply source of opium goes to the Lebanon, followed by Kuwait, Turkey, India and Germany. For morphine—a derivative of opium—the Lebanon again heads the League of Shame with the favourite routes used by the dealers in human decay listed as: Lebanon-Italy-France-U.S.A. and Iran-Egypt-Italy-France-U.S.A.

Obviously the United States is the prime target for illicit narcotics dealers since it offers the highest rewards for the dope and the widest market for its distribution. Drug addiction is now one of the major social problems in the U.S.A. In tackling it, the U.S. Bureau of Narcotics has had to develop a world strategy. Interpol's role—remembering that it is pledged to political neutrality—is to keep the Bureau posted with information and to alert all its member-nations with the names of the traffickers, the ships and aircraft they use and the routes of supply and distribution.

The heroin, which fetches a dollar a grain in a New York street, has probably crossed the world to reach the addict. After the resin from poppies is collected in the spring it is smuggled from the country of origin and sold at around 50 dollars a lb. It is then taken to secret laboratories to be processed into morphine which increases its value to 500 dollars a lb. But there is a further process to come which turns the morphine into heroin, and the price accordingly soars to 1500 dollars a lb. Even that fantastic profit is not enough for some traffickers, who mix the white drug with bicarbonate

of soda and kitchen salt and get an even greater rake-off.

An equally complex problem is created by drugs derived from the Indian hemp plant, Cannabis, which is grown in the Far East, Middle East, parts of Europe and South America. From its leaves and flower when dried comes the cigarette known as the "reefer" which can be bought easily in most major cities.

Hashish comes from the resin of the same plant and is generally smoked in a pipe known as a "kif". The traffickers in

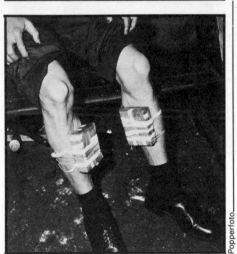

MARIJUANA often reaches the U.S. in truckloads (top). Heroin can be carried in smaller quantities and still be highly profitable to the dealer . . .

this drug make vast profits, and as they pay their agents well it is difficult for the police to find an informer—unless it is someone who has watched a friend or relative go down the slippery slope to the hard drugs from the softer cannabis.

A further complication with Indian hemp is that many countries cultivate it as part of their economy and sell it quite legitimately for medical supplies. In China, Burma, Laos and Thailand, where opium is in common use as a stimulant,

peasants cultivate the poppy, so the authorities tend to turn a blind eye to any *extra* cultivation—and it is this, sold to the traffickers, which is creating the world's narcotics problem. Morphine is from six to ten times more addiction-forming than opium, and heroin is from 30 to 80 times more potent.

These two killer drugs—morphine and heroin—are in greatest demand in North America, where more than 200 million dollars are spent annually by addicts, including many thousands of teenagers. Hashish claims a million addicts in Egypt, and Iran has half-a-million hooked on opium. Cocaine is most popular in South America, where it is produced—four million Indians chew the coca leaf, which is supposed to help them survive the rigours of the Andes.

Traffickers use every conceivable dodge for smuggling opium for refining. It has

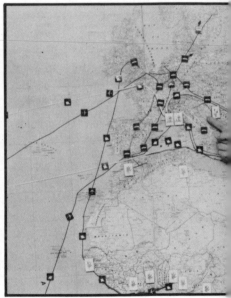

been packed into small tins and forced down the throats of camels which are given a purgative when they reach their destination; it has been concealed in fish or in snake-skins which are made to look alive; it has been picked up in bags by small aircraft which then drop the bags by parachute at the required destination. But the vast majority of the supplies are sent by sea, the carriers being sailors who find it fairly easy to smuggle it ashore.

Italy and France are the countries most plagued by the evil men involved in this sickening trade, both as transit centres and for setting up the secret laboratories for processing opium, and naturally it is on these two countries that Interpol and the U.S. Narcotics Bureau concentrate. Working together, Interpol officers and U.S. agents have smoked out and closed down a dozen illicit drug laboratories in recent years. They have attacked heroin supply sources in Italy, France and

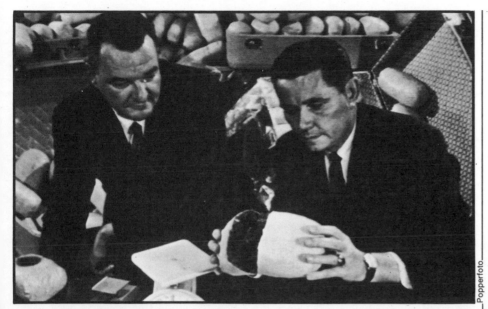

LOAVES OF BREAD specially baked were discovered by perspicacious New York detectives to contain marijuana. The "baker" and his wife were arrested . . .

carried a blackjack, and whenever the women grabbed at Jarrin he clouted their wrists with his cosh. Still he and Col. Guerra, the police chief, were having a bad time of it from the women when reinforcements arrived in the shape of the colonel's men, bundled the women out and restored the dignity of the law.

Jarrin's villa was a storehouse of narcotics—raw opium, heroin, morphine, cocaine and marihuana. Police also unearthed a secret laboratory used by chemists in Jarrin's pay to process the opium into morphine. All the supplies were destined for the U.S. market.

White next crossed to Europe on

NARCOTICS NETWORK . . . Police have succeeded in mapping out the major drug traffic routes, but there are still problems. Marijuana is a common weed . . .

Jarrin's sumptuous mountain hideout near Quito. He was posing as a big-time dope purchaser. Jarrin, 65, small and sly-looking, seemed satisfied that he was on a good deal. "Three pounds of raw opium for cash" was his offer—and he pulled a brown-paper package from a drawer. White opened the package, confirmed it was dope, then nodded to his "chauffeur" who turned out to be chief of the National Police of Ecuador.

As they closed in on Jarrin he yelled for help. At once his powerfully built wife, a bunch of her women relatives and the servants poured into the room. It was useless to threaten them with guns. White

another drug suppression trip and, on advice from the Sûreté, decided to smoke out traffickers in Marseilles. He played the part of a loud-mouthed American businessman with plenty of dollars in his pocket and wandered into an Indo-Chinese café in the Old Quarter. There he struck up a conversation with the proprietress "Zizi" and arranged a further meeting to pass over the "stuff" for good American dollars. Zizi eventually led White (backed up by the U.S. Vice-Consul and a squad of French police) to her main supplier, and another major operator was stopped.

By patient investigation the French police traced and closed down a large-

HEROIN FACTORY . . . This photo, taken in New York City, shows a large consignment of the drug being prepared for sale. Above: the opium trade mark.

Turkey. In one case illicit factories, closed down in Yugoslavia, moved to Istanbul, but—thanks to an American undercover agent's intervention—an international gang 30 strong was broken up and its clandestine laboratory demolished.

These undercover men, known in their dangerous profession as "tightropers", must be ready for any situation. One of them, George White, a district supervisor at the Narcotics Bureau, has several times pulled off arrests by masquerading as one of the trafficking gang. His most embarrassing assignment was when he won the confidence of a drug-runner in Ecuador by the name of Manuel Jarrin. White, with "chauffeur", drove up to

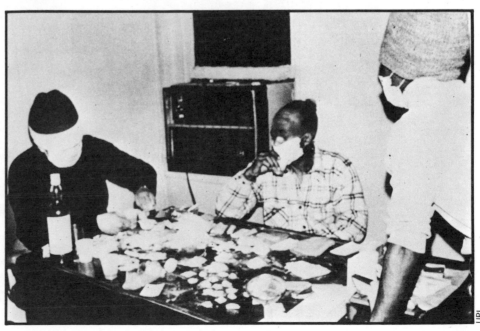

scale clandestine heroin factory at Montgeron, 20 miles south of Paris. They started out by shadowing the mistress of one of their suspects, Marie Poteau, who proved to be an expert driver and "lost" her tail in the Paris traffic. One day, however, they managed to hang on to her slick Peugeot, and she led them to Montgeron, where she disappeared into an isolated villa standing in its own grounds.

Detectives set up an observation post in the small upper room of a railwayman's cottage. For six months they photographed and registered everyone who visited or left the villa. When they were sure they knew the identities of the gangsters they pounced on the villa. Every room, except for the kitchen and bedrooms, was packed with dope or manufacturing equipment. Even the garage had a plant for purifying morphine and converting it into heroin. They also picked up five automatic pistols and a load of Swiss watches.

Sometimes the whole network of law enforcement can be badly shaken by the discovery of corruption in areas of society that might be assumed to be above such evil practices. Such a case shook Italy—and, indeed, the whole of western civilization—in the 1950s when it was found that a major chemical firm there had been responsible for an appalling leakage of heroin in a racket of global dimensions.

The company was licensed to sell substances containing drugs, and its technical director, a professor at an Italian university, proved to be the master-mind of the conspiracy to dispose illicitly of a ton of the deadliest dope. Most of this was shipped through the well-known routes to dope syndicates in the U.S., where it was ingeniously distributed under the guise of lawful medicine to the wretched addicts for whom it was always intended —at sky-high prices.

The unpalatable fact must be faced: until all member-states of Interpol display the same ruthless determination to stamp out this revolting traffic as do the U.S., Britain and France, the grisly business of getting the shot to the addict will remain what it is today—Interpol's No. 1 problem.

A score of years have passed since the United Nations Narcotics Commission approved (in May 1954), with none opposing, the following resolution:

CONFISCATED . . . Millions of dollars' worth of hard drugs, along with a small arsenal of weapons. Traffickers are playing for murderously high stakes . . .

"The Commission notes that the magnitude of the illicit drug traffic is still disquieting; considers that, owing to the international aspect of this traffic, close international collaboration should be established for the purpose of effectively opposing it; requests governments to coordinate their efforts in this field by making use of all existing means; directs their attention in this connection to the work of the International Criminal Police Commission which, by the immediate circulation and use of the information at its disposal, is in a position to provide help in the suppression of this illicit traffic; requests governments to provide this organization with as little delay as possible any information relative to persons implicated in cases of illicit drug traffic which might be of international interest."

It is a commentary on the social condition of our world that, since the date of that resolution, the traffic in illicit drugs has doubled, not diminished. Some countries have made no effort to pressurize their legislators or police forces to get to grips with the problem. They allow crops of drug-yielding plants like opium and Indian hemp to be grown without restraint in their territories, and the international gangs deal openly for their supplies.

CONFIDENCE TRICKSTERS

Confidence tricksters abound in the files of Interpol. Edward Johnston-Noad —seen below and left—was just one. Interpol also checks on stolen paintings.

Associated Newspapers, Mirrorpic, Keystone Press/Quartet

THE files of Interpol offer a rich variety of confidence tricksters, from the smooth, handsome rogues who batten onto wealthy widows to the quicksilver swindlers who deceive dealers in precious gems. All have one thing in common – the gift of the gab. And usually one aim in common too: to live in idle luxury.

Edward Johnston-Noad had most of the advantages. Early in life he inherited £100,000; he became a successful solicitor; he was extremely popular with fashionable women; he threw lavish parties at his home in Mayfair. He became known to his wide circle of friends as "The Count", a title he felt suited him so well that he used it to further his career of fraud.

In the 1950s he launched his first swindle from a small office in Kensington. He advertised two flats for sale at a time when Londoners were suffering an acute accommodation problem. The Count not only let the flats several times over but sold the furniture to different people. He took deposits from the professional classes—barristers, doctors, civil servants—and in all tricked 70 people out of £20,000. Whenever an impatient depositor complained, Johnston-Noad immediately offered him his money back, mentioning that the choice flat would at once go to the next person on his list. So desperate were people for decent accommodation that the threat was usually enough to silence objectors.

Count's luck was out

The Count knew very well that he could not stall them for ever, so he had planned to retreat to Paris as soon as his victims called in the police. He talked himself into a job in the British Embassy in Paris just as Scotland Yard were called in to clear up the flat swindles. Chief Inspector James Callaghan, of the Fraud Squad, was assigned to the case, and when he had heard that his bird had flown he sent a "Wanted" noticed to Interpol.

Chief of Interpol's Central Bureau in Paris was a conscientious young detective, Roger Ravard, who put a small photograph of The Count in his wallet. He did not, of course, realize that the wanted man was, in fact, in the same city. But The Count's luck was right out—because Ravard's wife also worked at the British Embassy in Paris.

Even then he might have escaped notice had not Madame Ravard needed some money to pay a tradesman at her door while her husband was still asleep. Rather than waken him she opened his wallet to take out a note—and Johnston-Noad's photograph fell out. She recognized the man as another employee at the Embassy. But she was in a spot, for she knew that the man must be wanted by her husband, yet she was reluctant to tell him she had "raided" his wallet. In the end duty overcame scruple, she told her husband, and the Count was arrested next morning.

Lightning switch

Edward Johnston-Noad was sentenced to four months for possessing false papers, but the Yard's extradition proceedings took one year to complete. At last it was all clear for Chief Inspector Callaghan to go to Paris and bring his man back to London. The Count wound up in the dock at the Old Bailey and got 10 years' in jail for his flat frauds.

Prime targets for the slickest fraud-sters are the jewellers and diamond merchants who, naturally, will go to all lengths to avoid offending a valued client, and thus lay themselves open to every kind of trickery. The usual ploy is for a buyer to spend a long time examining a selection of stones, choosing several and then asking the dealer if he minds if the chosen stones are sealed in an envelope and left with the jeweller overnight. The buyer promises to return the next day to make his final selection. If the jeweller agrees, an envelope is produced, and the stones are sealed and locked in the safe.

Only when the appointment is not kept does the jeweller realize he has been the victim of a lightning switch, and he has been left with worthless stones. There were so many variations on this switch technique that Interpol allocated a team of three to track down the international gang of jewel thieves who were clearly behind the rash of incidents. All the victims were interviewed and all paid tribute to the skills of the thieves—some did not even know how they had been robbed.

Worthless diamonds

In Zurich one of the gang, calling himself Wyeder, got away with 30,000 Swiss francs by "selling" a worthless packet of diamonds. Another, called Chande, paid 20,000 counterfeit dollars for jewels from a Lisbon merchant. Neither of these men appeared in the records of Interpol, but the "method" was circulated.

Later the Israeli police arrested a Pedro Cambo and sent his detailed description to Interpol in Paris. It was found that

MASTER FORGER Hans van Meergeren was one of the most successful fakers in art history. His "Vermeers" and "De Hoochs" fooled art-loving Nazi Goering.

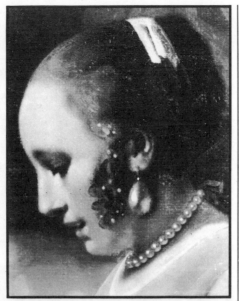

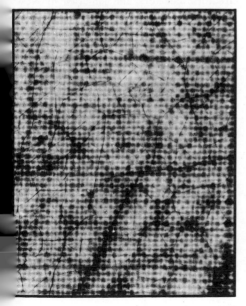
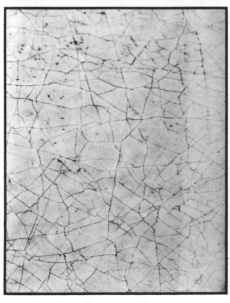

FORENSIC SCIENTISTS pin van Meegeren down. Left, a genuine Vermeer as compared with a superb fake by the forger. Centre, forged signatures by van Meegeren showed up only under microscopic examination. Bottom, radiograph photograph of picture "Disciples at Emmaus" by van Meegeren at left shows fewer genuine age cracks than the ordinary macrograph photograph on the right. To scientists this evidence was conclusive and helped convict the Dutchman, who died in jail.

Cambo was identical with Chazan, an international crook known to deal in forged bankers' orders and counterfeit. A full description of him was radioed, and the Portuguese recognized him as the Chande who had defrauded the Lisbon jeweller. He served a sentence in Israel, but after his release he teamed up with Wyeder, first in New York, where they got away with 4000 dollars, then in Geneva, where they picked up nearly 9000 francs' worth of jewels and watches; two months later they swindled three Paris jewellers; so to Amsterdam, where they took tea with their jeweller dupe and left fingerprints on the tea-cups.

"Arrest them"

These were sent to Interpol, where Chazan was quickly identified, but, as there were no prints of Wyeder, his were sent out on all-world photo-transmission. Several days later a cable arrived from the Federal Bureau of Investigation in Washington to say that Wyeder's prints were in their records under the name of Simonetti—he had once applied to the U.S. Embassy in Mexico for a visa which involved leaving his "dabs".

Two months after that Interpol got a radio message from Pretoria, South Africa, to say that a Kimberley diamond merchant was the latest victim of the switch technique. His two swindlers had given the names of Benjamin Shapiro and John de Rabinovich, but this time they were identified by photographs as Chazan and Wyeder. It was soon established that they had fled to Australia, and "Arrest them" messages were sent off to all airports and seaports en route. As a result Chazan was picked up at the airport of Port Louis, Mauritius.

The hunt for the elusive Simonetti was now on, in a big way. It was learned that, instead of heading for Australia, he changed direction towards Europe. All flights were watched without success. But Interpol kept on the alert for a full year until at last the Central Bureau learned that their quarry was flying into Paris! He booked—with Interpol's knowledge, of course—into a fashionable hotel in the Avenue Pierre Premier Serbie near Christian Dior's salon.

Three detectives were waiting for him in the foyer as he emerged, dressed to kill, carnation in button-hole, for a stroll on the boulevard. Instead he was taken for a drive in a police car to the Quai des Orfèvres, police headquarters. When they searched him they found four gems valued at 10 million francs and three diamond rings in his pockets. He also carried many sheets of plain paper cut to the size of U.S. 100-dollar bills. Under questioning it was discovered that he was already in contact with a jeweller in the Rue de la Paix, who was obviously to be his next victim.

Simonetti proved to be Berl Fareas, Austrian-born, and the head of a gang far more widespread than even Interpol had realized. In the next two years they caught up with and arrested 49 fraudsmen working the same racket.

Within recent years a new scientific technique has come to the aid of law enforcement—the laser beam, which can be used to cut through a diamond, perform eye surgery, match paint flakes and test the authenticity of a painting. Many art forgers are so brilliant that only the analysis of the paint itself will reveal whether or not the painting is a fake.

Selling "Vermeers"

The greatest art forger of them all was surely Hans van Meegeren of Amsterdam, whose astonishing career of selling "Vermeers" which he had painted himself was exposed when the art treasures of the Nazi warlord, Hermann Goering, were captured in 1945. Among those paintings was a supposed Vermeer, Christ and the Adulteress, for which Goering had paid 1,650,000 guilder. The Dutch are deeply concerned to preserve their art heritage, and when the sale to Goering was traced back to van Meegeren he was suspected of collaborating with the enemy by selling them Dutch masters which, in Holland, amounts to treason. Van Meegeren broke down under police grilling and confessed that he had painted Christ and the Adulteress himself. What art-lover Goering had bought as a Vermeer was, in fact, a van Meegeren. . . .

Sensation

At first the Dutch police regarded his confession as the desperate device of a cornered criminal to evade punishment. But van Meegeren made statements that sent art experts scurrying round the museums to re-examine a number of Vermeers. Scientists were experimenting with a new X-ray technique in this post-war period and this was tried on the suspect Vermeers. Sensation! Some of the precious paintings were exposed as forgeries—and Goering's prize was among them. The charge of treason against van Meegeren was reduced to swindling and forgery, and, instead of a life-sentence,

he got one year in jail. Even that short sentence was too much for him, for he died in prison a few months after the trial. It is a sign of our times, perhaps, to record that today, only a quarter of a century after van Meegeren's death, the master forger's own work is fetching increasingly high prices.

The 1960s was the decade of the great art robberies. Goya's portrait of the Duke of Wellington was stolen from London's National Gallery in August 1961 and was not recovered until May 1965. But the Goya theft sparked off many others, until paintings were disappearing at a rate of a million dollars' worth a week. Even Russia was not immune—in 1964 Moscow police reported that "rare and priceless articles" had been stolen from the city's Historical Museum.

Police forces of the world, finding themselves confronted by what was becoming an art-theft epidemic, had to reorganize their procedures for dealing with such crimes. Now, when a major art theft is reported, Interpol is called in at once to notify all its member-nations. The F.B.I. has greatly intensified its efforts in the last decade to track down art thieves and has recovered hundreds of works by Van Gogh, Klee, Cezanne and Picasso worth a total of many millions of dollars.

The F.B.I. crime-records section in

THE RETURN OF THE MONA LISA. The famous picture was stolen by Italian Vincenzo Perruggia. He got seven months.

Washington now houses a dossier of art thefts throughout the world, regularly analyses any trends in this field and keeps in touch with the special investigator of art thefts, frauds and forgeries, an official who maintains contact with all the major directors, curators and galleries in New York.

The F.B.I. is now under orders to intervene in every case in which the value of the stolen art is 5000 dollars or above. Most countries, the U.S. included, abide by international agreements requiring the return of stolen goods. Thus, in countries which are parties to such agreements, the legitimate buyer of a stolen work of art never gets title to it.

Honour disgraced

Surely the daddy of all art thieves remains the Italian, Vincenzo Perruggia, who, on August 21, 1911, walked out of the Louvre in Paris with Leonardo da Vinci's masterpiece, the Mona Lisa. He claimed, when caught, that his country's honour had been disgraced by France's possession of this greatest of all paintings. Perruggia was let off lightly with a seven-month prison sentence.

POISON

"I am dying before my time," wrote Napoleon—and, more than a century later, traces of arsenic in hairs from his head suggested that he might have been right. His case will never be solved, but the modern arsenal of poisons guarantees an endless supply of mysteries. . . .

Popperfoto

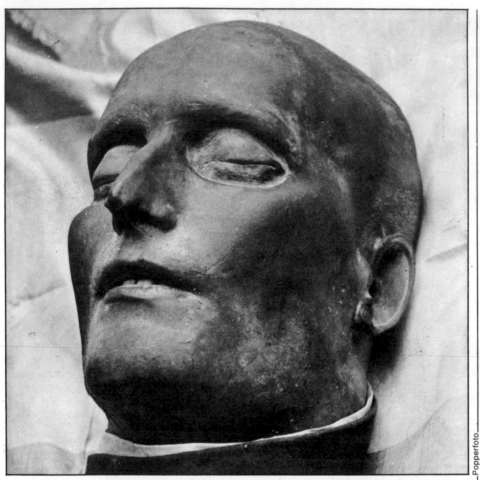
Popperfoto

WAS Napoleon I murdered by the British on the island of St. Helena to which he was exiled after his final defeat? Officially he died of cancer of the stomach—the diagnosis of an Italian doctor who conducted a post-mortem. But a remarkable new space-age technique known as Neutron Activation Analysis has recently been used to cast doubts on the "natural causes" verdict.

Neutron activation is a by-product of modern atomic research and has now reached an advanced stage both in the United States and in Britain. It uses properties of radio-active decay to detect and measure accurately a trace of arsenic one thousand times smaller than can be detected by any known chemical test.

Napoleon's body lay for a score of years in a grave on St. Helena before it was moved, with due pomp and ceremony, to its present resting-place in Les Invalides in Paris. The French have always been uneasy about the circumstances of the death of their great warrior-genius, and when the fantastic possibilities of neutron activation analysis became known to them it was agreed that samples of hair from the head of Napoleon should be subjected to it—almost a century-and-a-half after his death.

The result of the neutron activation test was that Napoleon's hair was found

ALWAYS UNEASY about how their great warrior-genius died, the French subjected hairs embedded in Napoleon's death mask to neutron activation analysis.

to contain 13 times the amount of arsenic normally contained in human hair. This discovery was quickly claimed as evidence that he was poisoned—especially by historians who reminded the world that Napoleon had written in his will: "I am dying before my time, murdered by the English oligarchy and its hired assassin"—an obvious reference to the English Governor of St. Helena at that time, General Sir Hudson Lowe.

Arsenic as stimulant

There are, of course, other possible explanations for the discovery of such an amount of arsenic in the hair. Arsenic from the soil of St. Helena could have infiltrated into it during his long interment there. It is also possible that, during his years in exile, Napoleon could have taken small quantities of arsenic as a stimulant; so it is likely that the case of Napoleon's hair will remain one of those insoluble mysteries so favoured by authors of historical romances.

But the discovery of neutron activation analysis does illustrate dramatically the capabilities of modern forensic science;

by using this new technique it is possible to detect the most minute traces of certain metals contained in hair—gold, silver, lead, cadmium. When analysis shows that the percentages of these elements are identical in two hairs, the chances that both have come from the same person are clearly increased.

This breakthrough by the nuclear scientists has come at a time when the headlong growth of the pharmaceutical industry since the mid-twentieth century is threatening to overwhelm forensic toxicologists —they now have to cope with a host of new synthetic poisons and medicines which can kill as well as cure those who take them. The alarming fact has to be faced that technological progress is making scores of previously unheard-of poisons available to millions and thus supplying new means for murder, suicide and accidental death at a rate which is far outrunning the techniques of forensic detection.

World-wide craving

Take the barbiturates alone: alphenal, amytal, delvinal, evipan, nembutal and seconal are a few that have become household names. World War II, followed by the strains and tensions of the Atomic Age, produced a world-wide craving for drugs which would make life more bearable.

By 1954 the number of known suicides from barbiturates in England was 12 times the number in 1938. But it was not until 1955 that the death of a child taught England that barbiturates were not only an easy way out for suicides—they could also be an effective murder weapon.

The scene of this first murder by barbiturate poisoning was set in Gosport, near Portsmouth. John Armstrong, a 26-year-old nurse at a nearby naval hospital, and his wife Janet, 19, were a nondescript couple whose married life was punctuated by three children, a load of petty debts and a series of rows. At 1.20 p.m. on July 22, 1955, Armstrong called the family doctor, Bernard Johnson, to report that his five-month-old son Terence was very ill.

Dr. Johnson knew the family background—their oldest boy, Stephen, had died suddenly the previous year. He reached the Armstrong bungalow at 1.30 to find the baby dead. Dr. Johnson did not suspect foul play, but as he could not establish the cause of death, he notified the Gosport coroner who at once sent two of his staff to the Armstrong bungalow. They took away the dead baby's bottle, the pillow he had vomited into the previous day, and had the little body removed to the mortuary.

That same afternoon Dr. Harold Miller, a pathologist, carried out an autopsy. Examining the larynx, he found a shrivelled red shell that reminded him of the skin of a daphne berry—and there were more of these shells in the child's stomach. Dr. Miller put the shell from the larynx in a bottle of formaldehyde, placed the stomach's contents in another bottle and stored both bottles in a refrigerator.

By now Dr. Miller suspected that death must be due to some form of food poisoning. The coroner's men went back to the Armstrongs' home to ask whether the child had access to daphne berries—and they were startled to find the couple watching TV as if nothing untoward had happened. There was, in fact, a daphne tree in the garden, and it was fruiting. Armstrong remembered that the baby's pram had stood under the tree and its fruit could have fallen within reach. Daphne berries are highly poisonous.

When this was reported to Dr. Miller he thought his problem was solved, but when he opened the refrigerator the red berry shell in the bottle of formaldehyde had vanished—it had dissolved and coloured the formaldehyde red. The shells in the other bottle had also vanished overnight and deepened the red colouring of the stomach contents.

Unusual substances

So Dr. Miller sent both bottles, as well as the pillow and the baby's feeding bottle, to a chemical laboratory which regularly performed investigations for the coroner. The lab. report stated that there was no sign of any known poison and no trace of daphne berries. The only unusual substances in the stomach were a very small quantity of cornstarch and red dye, eosin. The cause of the baby's death was still unexplained.

At this point Inspector Gates, in charge of the inquiries for Gosport police, decided to have a last look round. He went to see the Armstrongs and asked a few questions. John Armstrong made such a bad impression on Inspector Gates that he was unwilling to close the case. Gates discussed the baby's death with Dr. Miller who, it turned out, had been giving some thought to the disappearing "berry skins". He now suggested they could have been coloured medical capsules—for instance, seconal. He experimented with seconal capsules in gastric juices and found a red discoloration similar to that in the baby's stomach. Gates asked about the effects of seconal and was told that a few grains would be enough to kill an infant, but there was no precedent for murder by barbiturate.

Gates now felt he was getting somewhere, and he reported his misgivings to his superior, who decided to call in Scotland Yard. Superintendent L. C. Nickolls, Director of the Metropolitan Police Laboratory, at once asked for all materials relevant to the baby's death. Gates was asked to collect them and found, to his annoyance, that the Gosport chemists had only remnants left after their analysis—the best preserved was the pillow stained with the child's vomit. But he took all he could to the Yard.

Nickolls spent five days on tests and at last found that the vomit traces on the pillow contained 1/50th of a grain of seconal, and then he succeeded in isolating another 1/3rd of a grain from the

A NONDESCRIPT COUPLE with three children and a load of petty debts, the Armstrongs were charged with plotting to murder their baby son. Their daughter Pamela (right) also fell ill suspiciously, but later recovered in hospital.

Popperfoto

Syndication International

stomach contents. He now applied for an exhumation of the child's body which was granted on September 6. While Nickolls was carrying out a meticulous examination of the tiny body, Gates went to the naval hospital because, assuming the child had died of seconal poisoning, it was important to discover how Armstrong had obtained supplies of the drug. After the most painstaking inquiries he tracked down a nurse who had been in charge of the drugs on Armstrong's floor—and remembered a mysterious theft of 50 one-and-a-half-grain seconal capsules from a cupboard to which Armstrong had access. Of course this was not proof that Armstrong was the thief, but at least Gates had his nose to a strong scent.

Blue in the face

Now Inspector Gates, the indefatigable, looked into the death of the Armstrongs' firstborn, Stephen, in March 1954. He found that the death certificate had been made out by a doctor aged 82 who had never previously attended the family. Further, Gates learned that Stephen's symptoms were similar to those shown by the baby—blue in the face, drowsiness, difficulty in breathing, then sudden death. More striking still, the Armstrongs' daughter Pamela, then aged two, had been taken to hospital in May 1954. Symptoms: gasping for breath, discoloured face, drowsiness. She made a swift recovery in hospital.

At last Nickolls delivered his long-awaited analysis to the Gosport police—he had extracted 1/20th of a grain of seconal from the baby's organs, and he concluded that the child must have been given between three and five capsules for such a quantity to be left in the body: a fatal dose.

The police chiefs were now certain that the Armstrongs were guilty, but how to prove it? They got an order to exhume the body of the firstborn. John Armstrong had to go with Gates to the cemetery for this macabre procedure. At the gates he said to the inspector: "After all, there won't be much left of him by this time, will there?" He was right. All efforts to detect poison in Stephen's remains had been defeated by time.

Everything now hinged on the baby's death. But there was an added problem for the police. Gates was convinced that husband and wife had planned together to kill their baby and be free of a tiresome and expensive burden. But which of them had administered the fatal dose? Nickolls got down to work again, visiting the makers of seconal until he found one

A SORDID TRIAL, in an atmosphere of hatred and lies, followed special hearings (right) at the apartment of witnesses in the Armstrong murder case.

which had, for three years "for commercial reasons", used a different type of material for its capsules, which were made of methyl cellulose dyed with eosin. In addition to the seconal, the capsules contained a small quantity of cornstarch. The methyl cellulose absorbed the stomach fluids, and when the fluids penetrated the interior of the capsules the cornstarch swelled, bursting the capsule into two parts, thus releasing seconal into the stomach. The halves of the capsule later dissolved and their colour disappeared.

Suddenly it became clear why the Gosport chemists had found cornstarch in the stomach of the dead baby. Nickolls now resumed his experiments with capsules made of methyl cellulose. He found that, in some cases, they opened swiftly, but in others they took as long as 90 minutes before the two parts separated. These findings, while confirming that the baby had been murdered, made it impossible to rule out either parent as the one who gave the child the capsules. The police knew, too, that they must prove the Armstrongs were in possession of seconal on the day of the murder—and strong suspicion was not proof.

Inspector Gates decided to play a waiting game and kept both John and Janet Armstrong under observation for a year. He was beginning to despair when, on July 24, 1956, Janet applied to the Gosport Magistrates' Court for a separation and maintenance order against her husband, alleging that he beat her up again

and again. The court refused her the order, but Gates contrived a meeting with her and found that, at last, she was ready to talk. She admitted she had lied and said that her husband had brought many capsules of seconal from his hospital. Three days after the baby's death he had ordered her to throw all the capsules away. She claimed she asked him: "Did you give baby any?" and said he replied: "How do I know *you* haven't?" She had not told the police all this because she was afraid of what he would do to her.

Gates knew full well that the woman was acting out of spite, but, whatever the whole truth of the matter, he now had an admission that the Armstrongs had seconal in their possession on the day of the baby's death. Four months later, on December 3, 1956, the Attorney-General of the day, Sir Reginald Manningham-Buller, Q.C., personally prosecuted both John and Janet Armstrong on the charge of jointly planning to commit murder by poisoning their own baby, Terence.

It was a sordid trial, with charges and counter-charges between husband and wife in an atmosphere of lies and hatred. An astute defence, throwing doubts on the time it took seconal to discharge its poisonous content into the stomach, achieved an acquittal for the wife, but John Armstrong was found guilty of murder.

The importance to society of this, the first trial for murder by barbiturates, lay in the complexity of the problems set by new and rapidly proliferating poisons.

DEADLY DRUGS

A welcome teabreak meant death for two workmates of poisoner Graham Young. He had tried to kill two other men and had given poison to two more, and as a boy he had poisoned his father and sister.

SISTER

SURVIVOR John Williams

SENT BALD Jethro Batt

FATHER

MURDERED Frederick Biggs

DIED IN AGONY Bob Egle

"HOMICIDE BY poison is rare," opined Keith Simpson when Professor of Forensic Medicine at the internationally-known Guy's Hospital, London, England. "The Maybricks, Seddons, Crippens, and Merryfields are famous only because they are of rare interest. On the contrary, suicide by poison is more common than ever, and the rapid rise in the figures of the barbituric acid drugs makes one doubt the effectiveness of the regulations which were designed to control their sale; overworked doctors may too readily prescribe these drugs for the many psychosomatic disorders of 'civilized' life. . . ."

It is certainly true that homicide by poison is rare, and equally true that forensic pathologists and others in the world of toxicology have a high successrate in the cases of poisoning which do come into the laboratory. Nearly 90 per cent of all homicides are committed by close relatives or friends of the victim, and as most incidents of poisoning necessitate elaborate preparation, forensic examination of the human aspects of the case as a whole usually pinpoints one or more immediate suspects.

Small man's weapon

The late Sir Bernard Spilsbury, responsible for a large number of triumphs in forensic toxicology, caused his biographers Douglas G. Browne and E.V. Tullett to comment: "Poison would seem to be the small man's weapon—not only, perhaps, because small men are not given to violence, but also because they suffer from a sense of inferiority. The remote and generally prolonged action of poison gives them a feeling of power. They can sit back, like gods, and watch it work."

Psychiatrists probing motives for poisoning may agree or disagree with legal findings. However it is sometimes wise of prosecution counsel to accept notguilty pleas "with intent to cause grievous bodily harm", and therefore to hear a judge accept the lesser charges of "administering poison with the intent of injuring, grieving or annoying". This is a distinction now possible in English courts, but not in the United States.

This merciful provision enabled, for example, an 18-year-old boy to walk out of the Manchester (England) Crown Court in July 1973, after telling the judge, Sir William Morris, of his practical joke which could have killed an entire works staff.

As a boyish prank, he poured cyanide into the milk used for the cafeteria tea at a Lancashire factory. Before the tea was actually poured, a cafeteria worker stooped down and gave some of the milk to two kittens. They died in agony. Fortunately this prevented harm to the two immediate intended victims of the practical joke, the woman in charge of that

POISONERS AND VICTIMS

CAUGHT . . . Crippen (top right) who poisoned his wife, Belle (top left), and buried her mutilated body in a cellar . . . Florence Maybrick (centre left) who served 15 years in jail for giving arsenic to her husband James (above). But he is thought to have taken it himself as an aphrodisiac . . . Frederick Seddon (left) who, with his wife, poisoned his old lodger, Eliza Barrow, and took the £200 in gold she had with her.

section of the factory and a 17-year-old workmate.

Giving the boy a six-month prison sentence, suspended for two years, the judge said: "It was a wicked thing you did, and you might have been standing here on a very serious charge of killing."

This is typical of the foolish practical jests and complete misunderstanding of the seriousness of poisons, equalled perhaps only by another Lancashire case a few weeks later. Here a student nurse became critically ill and later died after a hospital party at the Wigan Infirmary.

Again, no complex forensic examination was necessary, since others who had attended the hospital party gave evidence that a bowl of punch had been placed in the recreation room, and near it were bottles containing methanol, ethanol and surgical spirits. As the party progressed and the level in the punch bowl went down, the alcohol was added.

Ethanol added

Commercial products such as Ethanol are misused in this way to lace drinks—chiefly because they are easy to obtain. This is why the various types of cyanide feature in a high proportion of poison attempts. Almost the only person to benefit is the pathologist, since the hydro-cyanics can usually be detected at once by the smell of bitter almonds (although Dr. H. J. Walls, B.Sc., once said that 20-30 per cent of people can *not* smell it), and the U.S. oleum amygdalae amarae ("oil of bitter almonds") can contain up to 10 per cent of hydrocyanic acid.

Would-be poisoners able to get access to it have been known to misuse the solid cyanide used to kill vermin and wasps; but when poison attempts are reported in factories, shops and among people with access to chemical stores, it is more usually the commercially-pure potassium cyanide which is administered. This is in common use—and therefore does not create immediate suspicion—in photographic laboratories, plating works and process engravers.

Graham Young, the poisoner who killed after being freed from Broadmoor, avoided suspicion for a time because he used thallium, an insecticide which was virtually unknown as a poison at that time.

Toxicologists always hasten to stress that while even five grains of cyanide constitute a fatal dose, it deteriorates when stored and is not necessarily a certain killer—provided a doctor is called in time to carry out cleansing by stomach

THE MAD MONK . . . Rasputin was poisoned by Russian noblemen. But why did he take so long to die? Modern science may have the answer . . .

tube, and to administer a stimulant such as methyl amphetamine, plus a detoxicant of the sodium thiosulphate nature.

It was Professor Keith Simpson who first pointed out that cyanide is more or less harmless until it comes into contact with the ionizing acid in the gastric juices, so its action in the body may be delayed by carbonic acid gas.

He declared from this a surprising explanation to the events of the last hour of Grigori Rasputin, the Russian peasant monk who gained an evil influence over the court of the Czar Nicholas II. As the result of a conspiracy among a group of noblemen, Rasputin was assassinated, presumably with cyanide.

His death in 1916 was long delayed, however, causing the assassins to dread that in his dying ravings, Rasputin would be able to unmask his poisoners. "Should the victim suffer from chronic gastritis as Rasputin probably did," asserted the blunt Keith Simpson, "he may swallow many times the fatal dose and escape the fate an ordinary subject would quickly meet . . ."

Another odd case of homicidal poisoning occurred some years later in New York State. The body of a woman who had apparently leaped to her death from an upper floor of an office building was taken away for a post-mortem. The Chief of Homicide and the Chief Medical Examiner arrived almost simultaneously, because what might have been a straightforward case of suicide proved to be one

of murder. A brief examination by the toxicologist disclosed that the woman was in the early stages of a pregnancy, and that she had been doped with an anti-cholinestarse poison (in fact a systemic insecticide with a well-known trade name) before the body was thrown out of the window.

Just how low down in the Crime Index scale of the United States are poisoning cases? In any typical year, handguns are the weapons used in 51 per cent of cases, knives and similar cutting weapons in 20 per cent, shotguns in 8 per cent, rifles in 6 per cent, and personal weapons (such as "putting the boot in") in 9 per cent. Poison is used in the smallest group of all, far less than 6 per cent.

In real life (as in fiction) it is always easier to identify and bring a poisoner to trial than it is to get the bandit before a jury for the dollars stolen from a bank. Poisoning is usually a personal affair, with a motive like a shining beacon. This is why the clear-up rate for poisoners, indeed for murders in general, is far higher than with *any* other type of crime.

In any one typical year, from F.B.I. Crime Index figures, the proportion of murders solved is 84 per cent—and this includes all poisoning cases—compared with only 19 per cent burglaries, and 16 per cent auto thefts.

Some of society's problems are concerned with the difficulty of isolating involatile organic poisons, and the metabolism (change of cell or organism struc-

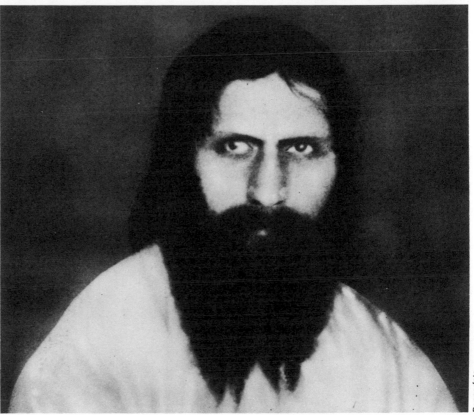

Popperfoto

63

ture) which some of these involatile poisons undergo in the body. Dr. H. J. Walls, a former Director of the Metropolitan Police (New Scotland Yard) Forensic Science Laboratory warned: "What is extracted post-mortem may not be what was taken."

In addition to this, there are other factors, such as lack of international uniformity of drug names, which makes for hazards in a poison emergency. In European usage drugs ending in "one" (such as phenobarbitone) usually, but not always, correspond with similar American drugs with names ending in "al" – such as Seconal (quinalbarbitone) and Nembutal (pentobarbitone).

Accidental death

In Britain in any typical year 400 suicides result from barbiturates, with 192 accidental deaths from the same cause, compared with only 11 deaths (4 accidental) from corrosive acids and 8 (2 accidental) from phosphorus compounds such as what was formerly Rodine, a rat poison. While barbitone (and American equivalents such as Soneryl) are slow to metabolize, Nembutal and Seconal are metabolized quickly, and the forensic worker may be faced with a time problem.

As Dr. Wall put it: "In a death from a rapid-acting barbiturate, especially if the deceased had lived for some time after taking it, very little of the unchanged compound may be left in the body. Unfortunately we are still extremely ignorant of the reactions involved

and compounds produced in these metabolic processes.

"Time of death" was important to Sherlock Holmes, to Father Brown and Agatha Christie; still more so to a chemist in the forensic poisons laboratory. Britisher, Dr. A. S. Curry carried out forensic work which helped in solving a number of barbiturate-poison problems where the time factor was critical. He found, to put it briefly, that the longer the poisoned victim lives after taking the barbiturate, the lower will be the blood/liver concentration rate when it comes to the post-mortem stage. The ratio may be anywhere from unity to five or six; if for example, it is greater than four, in all probability death occurred in under five hours.

Three workers in the United States, Umberger, Stolman, and Schwartz, have greatly helped toxicologists the world over with their development of an alcohol-distillation system to test body slurry where poison is suspected. It operates on a distillation and recycling principle. Boiling alcohol is passed continuously through the body slurry (the "goo") which is mechanically agitated, compounds are recovered from the gaseous stream, and then the alcohol is recycled back to the boiler after condensation. Naturally the toxicologist has to consider not only the time of taking the poison, but also what constitutes a fatal dose in the particular circumstances.

It is common knowledge that alcohol consumed at about the same time as

barbiturates acts as an adjuvant or potentiator, greatly increasing the effect of the poison. There have been many cases on both sides of the Atlantic where addicts have taken compounds such as Oblivon to achieve the same effect more economically and quicker than a slug of alcohol. Normally with barbiturate compounds the minimum lethal dose is about twenty times the therapeutic (sedative) dose. But toxicologists become tired of cases where it is said on behalf of the victim that: "Only a few tablets were taken, but of course that drugged her mind and she didn't then realize she was swallowing the rest of them."

Popular belief

On this, Keith Simpson states firmly: "It has become a popular belief that a state of partial narcosis from barbiturates introduces a liability, because of mental confusion, to the taking of another dose, or 'a few more tablets', so accounting for many deaths as 'accidents', or misadventures rather than suicides. The possibility clearly exists . . . but there is usually no evidence whatever to justify taking such a view. It is upon such conveniences that erroneous views may become accepted as common truths."

THE CAUSE and the cure . . . Nineteenth century scientists boiled stomach contents in the flask (far left) and watched for poison deposits in the tube and flask, right. Below, a snake liver stone is given to a poison victim.

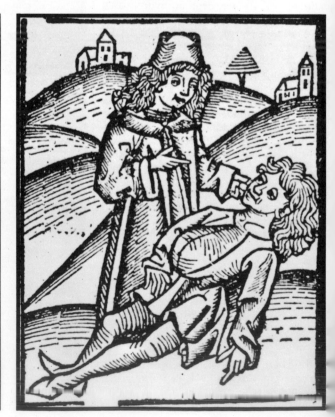

STRYCHNINE

If a grim, rigid smile fixed the features of Betsy Frances as she drew her last breath, it betrayed nothing less than murder at the hands of her smooth-talking boyfriend George Hersey, whose choice of strychnine was as cruel as it was effective. The picturesque New England town of South Weymouth had never seen anything like it; but worse was yet to come as the grief-stricken parents voiced their suspicions.

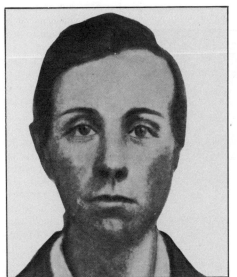

STRYCHNINE is an alkaloid extracted from the seeds of the East Indian tree *Strychnos nux vomica*. It was discovered in 1818. It has an exceptionally bitter taste and is used in tonics and animal poisons. Whether given orally or by injection, strychnine rapidly enters the bloodstream; it affects the central nervous system and in medicinal doses acts as a stimulant. The senses are made more acute and mental powers are heightened — there is a general feeling of well being.

The *British Pharmacopoeia* contains several strychnine preparations, including Tincture of Nux Vomica and Easton's Syrup. These contain very small amounts of the drug and are used as tonics in cases of convalescence after weakening illnesses. Strychnine is also used by veterinary scientists for killing moles and seals. No strychnine preparations are listed in the *US Pharmacopoeia*.

Strychnine comes out of solution in an alkaline mixture and accumulates at the bottom of the medicine bottle, and failure to shake the medicine properly has resulted in cases of accidental overdosing, while suicidal use of the drug was common before the laws relating to poison were made stricter.

In overdoses there is a twitching of the muscles and difficulty with breathing within about five minutes. The chest feels tight, and as respiration is further affected there is a feeling of suffocation.

The victim is suddenly seized by violent convulsions. As the motor areas of the spinal cord react to the drug, the back arches dramatically. The muscles are stiff and rigid and only the head and heels of the feet touch the ground. This condition is known as opisthotonus. This violent contraction of the spine may also bend the body forward or laterally.

The chest is also fixed so that cyanosis results and the face becomes congested. The muscles of the face contract in a tetanic spasm, clamping the jaw and producing a grinning effect; this grim "smile" is called "risus sardonicus". The pupils of the eyes dilate and the eyes have a wild, staring look; the fingers are clenched tightly in the palms of the hands.

This spasm lasts for anything up to two minutes and then the body relaxes, leaving the victim gasping for breath. Then, within a few minutes, there is another convulsion; this may be triggered off by the slightest thing, such as touching the victim in an attempt to give assistance. During the convulsions the victim is conscious and suffers intense pain. In the relaxed periods between convulsions he is calm but weak. The pattern of convulsions followed by relaxation may be repeated several times before death intervenes. Death may occur within an hour from respiratory paralysis or exhaustion.

Strychnine poisoning closely resembles the symptoms of tetanus or lockjaw. A distinguishing feature is that fixation of the chest does not occur in tetanus, and whereas the clamping of the lower jaw is one of the earliest symptoms of tetanus, it is only part of the condition of strychnine poisoning and relaxes between spasms.

Popular poison

A fatal dose of strychnine is considered to be 100 mg by oral administration, but fatalities with doses as low as 30 mg have been recorded. Individual variation is wide, and symptoms of poisoning can result from absorption by external application of the drug. A small dose of 5 mg of strychnine in the eye has been reported to cause effects of poisoning within four minutes.

There are no typical post-mortem characteristics of strychnine poisoning, although the lungs, brain and spinal cord usually appear congested. The drug may be found in the tissues and fluids but only in small quantities. Analysis is usually made of the urine, brain and spinal cord.

Urine	7.7 μg/ml
Brain	0.4 μg/g
Spinal Cord	1.8 μg/g

Chemical tests for strychnine are simple. Suspected residues, normally colourless crystals, are treated with a drop of sulphuric acid. The crystals go into solution, and the edge of the solution is touched with a yellow crystal of potassium chromate. In the presence of strychnine, a purple colour forms immediately and changes to crimson before fading completely.

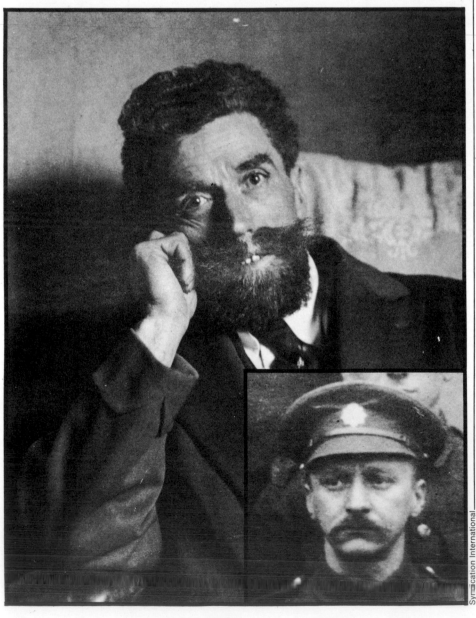

STRYCHNINE cured the landlord's hangover — permanently. Bearded poisoner Jean Pierre Vacquier said he wanted it for "wireless experiments", then fed the "remedy" to his victim (inset)

Syndication International

Strychnine was a popular poison in the latter half of the nineteenth century, and two infamous exponents of this form of murder were Dr. William Palmer and Dr. Thomas Neill Cream. Because of its extremely bitter taste, strychnine has to be disguised; Palmer found the answer by administering the poison in brandy, but Cream preferred to "doctor" real medicine with it.

Another problem confronting the strychnine poisoner is obtaining the poison itself. This posed little difficulty for the doctors, but others have gained access to it ostensibly for the killing of dogs and rats. Jean Pierre Vacquier, murderer of the landlord of the Blue Anchor Hotel at Byfleet, Surrey, in 1924, had a novel excuse. He bought his strychnine from a local pharmacy, explaining that he wanted it for wireless experiments; he subsequently disguised the poison in a hangover remedy which the landlord took with fatal results.

George Hersey was a young man who had had the misfortune to lose his wife early in their marriage. He lived and worked at South Weymouth, Massachusetts. In January, 1860, the young widower became engaged again, but his fiancée, Mary Tirrell, died soon after the announcement. The girl's parents, distressed by his grief, offered him a home. He accepted and soon became friendly with the eldest of the remaining daughters. Betsy Frances was 25 years old, plain and unmarried.

Just a melancholy girl

Betsy Frances looked after George, mending his shirts and caring for his appearance. George was morose and did not work for a while, but he studied chemistry and could talk knowledgeably about poisons. At about this time family friends thought that Betsy Frances' health was not what it should be for a young woman. Unmarried women of her age were subject to moods, and in the phraseology of the time she was thought to be just melancholy.

Subsequent events showed that Betsy Frances' otherwise dreary life was lightened by sexual intercourse with George. The opportunity was afforded on occasions when the family were away visiting. Eventually George went back to work. He seemed to have a new lease of life, and in no time at all he was secretly

HIS AUTOPSY showed the victim was three months' pregnant. And that wasn't all Dr. Charles S. Tower found out about the dead Miss Tirrell. . . .

engaged to a girl called Loretta Loud. He told her that he did not wish to upset Betsy Frances' parents, and he ventured the opinion that he did not think Betsy Frances would live long if she did not soon get better. Perhaps George moved too quickly for Loretta's liking. At any rate she broke off the engagement.

Meanwhile Betsy Frances' "melancholy" got worse. George thought that she would not last long. It was a prophecy that he intended should be fulfilled. He went to Boston and bought some strychnine from a pharmacy. The chemist warned him about the dangers of the substance—George said he wanted it to put down a dog. On May 3, 1860, George took Betsy Frances out for a ride in a horse-carriage. They returned home about 8.0 p.m. and George went to bed immediately, complaining of a headache. Betsy Frances sat with her family for a while and read aloud to them from the evening paper. Then she too retired for the night.

Betsy Frances went to the room which she shared with her 12-year-old step-sister, Louisa. She spoke to the younger girl, undressed and got into bed. Half an hour later, Louisa called for her mother in a terrified voice. Betsy Frances was thrashing about on her bed. She was twitching and convulsing and screaming, "I shall die. I shall die." Her back was arched and she was in terrible pain.

George appeared and was sent to fetch the doctor; her convulsions exhausted

her, and her face was covered in blood where she had bitten through her lip. She was dead before the doctor reached the house. The family were frightened of food poisoning, and they decided to boil all their water. An autopsy was suggested, but George objected to the mutilation of a loved one. He was overruled by the family, whose belief in coincidence after three sudden deaths must have been wearing a little thin.

In spite of his professed horror at the thought of an autopsy, George asked if he could be present when the doctors made their examination of Betsy Frances' body. No objection was raised. He was therefore right on hand when the doctors discovered that the dead woman was three months pregnant. In answer to his questions, the doctors told George that they thought Betsy Frances had been poisoned. They notified the coroner of their findings, and parts of the body removed for analysis revealed the presence of strychnine.

The revelation that Betsy Frances had been pregnant was too much for her parents, and they ordered George to leave their house at once. Meanwhile a search was made of the dead woman's room, and on a spoon—found in the fireplace—were traces of jam, which analysis showed to contain traces of strychnine.

George Hersey's arrest was not long delayed. He was put on trial on May 28, 1861—he pleaded not guilty. A Boston doctor testified that George had approached him regarding an "operation" for a woman friend who was pregnant. The doctor would not listen and also refused a request for some strychnine to kill a dog. A former room-mate remembered George producing a small vial and telling him, "There is something to kill young ones."

A fatal spoonful of jam

The conclusion drawn was that on learning of Betsy Frances' condition, George decided to rectify the matter and "help" the girl out of trouble. No doubt he told her that if she took the medicine which he would get for her, all would be well. On the fatal night Betsy Frances took the strychnine-loaded spoonful of jam in the hope of getting rid of her baby. She had probably been well primed to hide the spoon in the fireplace after swallowing its contents.

The defence argued that Betsy Frances committed suicide, but the shadows of George Hersey's wife and fiancée cast their sinister spell. The jury brought in a verdict of first-degree murder and Hersey was sentenced to death. Before meeting his end, he confessed to causing Betsy Frances' death but denied killing his wife and fiancée.

Another case which involved the forensic chemist's skills was the murder of Carroll Rablen in Tuttletown,

California. Carroll Rablen was deaf, due to an injury received during World War I. His attractive second wife, Eva, liked dancing, and although her husband did not dance himself, Carroll took her to dances and stayed on the sidelines while she danced with other men.

On April 29, 1929, the Rablens attended the regular Friday night dance in the school-house at Tuttletown. Eva wanted to dance, and Carroll unselfishly let her enjoy herself while he stayed outside in his car; about midnight Eva pushed through the crowd with a cup of coffee and some refreshments for him.

Writhing on the floor

She handed the refreshments to her husband and then went back into the dance. Seconds after swallowing some of the coffee, Carroll was writhing on the floor of the car in great pain. His distressed cries brought people running to his aid; among them was his father. Carroll complained to him of the bitter taste of the coffee. A doctor was called, but Carroll was dead before he arrived.

Eva appeared heartbroken. Although the possibility of suicide was mentioned, the police had no real idea of what caused Rablen's death. The contents of his stomach were analyzed by a chemist from a neighbouring town, but no traces of any poison were found. There was a good deal of gossip, and a lot of the talk was uncomplimentary to Eva. Carroll's father told the police that he thought Eva had

BITTER COFFEE killed Carroll Rablen (right), and its traces on the clothing of a witness helped convict his wife Eva (arrowed, at trial) of murder.

poisoned his son for the insurance money. There were two policies worth $3000.

The police had already made a search of the school-house area and found nothing of significance to the case. Their second attempt was more rewarding; under a broken wooden stair a police officer found a bottle—its label bore the menacing word STRYCHNINE. The supplier, whose name was on the label, was a pharmacist in a nearby town. The pharmacist traced the poison sale in his register. It had been made on April 26 by a Mrs. Joe Williams, who said she wanted the poison to kill gophers. Eva Rablen was later identified as Mrs. Joe Williams, but she denied buying the strychnine and said the pharmacist must be mistaken. Protesting her innocence and claiming that her father-in-law was behind it, Eva was arrested.

The police case was weak by virtue of the failure of analysis to show any poison in Carroll Rablen's stomach. But Dr. Edward Heinrich, an eminent chemist and criminologist, was called in to help; with an experienced forensic expert on the case the evidence began to turn against Eva Rablen.

Heinrich found traces of strychnine in the dead man's stomach, but more importantly, he also found traces of the poison in the coffee cup. With excellent co-operation from the police, Heinrich was able to back up a hunch with forcible results. He reasoned that Eva, pushing her way through the dance crowd with some sandwiches in one hand and a cup of coffee in the other, might have spilled some of the coffee on the clothing of someone in the crowd. An appeal brought forward a woman who remembered bumping into Eva Rablen that night. Yes, some coffee was spilled on her dress. The stains contained traces of strychnine.

Fittingly, perhaps, Eva Rablen's trial was held in an open-air dance pavilion. Only by doing so was it possible to accommodate the throng of people who wanted to be present. Confronted with Heinrich's evidence, Eva Rablen changed her plea to guilty. The court sentenced her to life imprisonment.

CORROSIVE POISONS

Hideous disfigurement, an overpowering acrid smell—and the absence of a corpse . . . these are some of the effects of corrosive poison. But even the most vitriolic substance leaves a trace, as John Haigh learned to his cost.

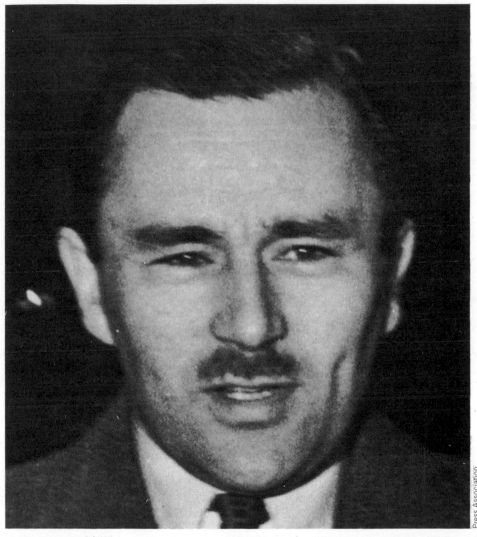

Press Association

THE swallowing of corrosive poisons—acids, alkalis and metallic salts—causes a particularly unpleasant kind of death. These agents erode and destroy the tissues with which they come into contact. Death from corrosive poisoning is commonly the result of suicide or accident. The ready availability of compounds such as metal polishes, bleaches, toilet cleansers and disinfectants make them convenient agents for suicide. The widespread industrial use of corrosive materials

also increases the dangers of accident.

The destructive nature of the mineral acids has led to their criminal use in disfigurement and in the disposal of bodies.

When a corrosive is swallowed the tissues in contact with it are in some measure destroyed; the victim feels a burning sensation in the mouth and throat, and there is intense stomach pain; this is followed by vomiting of shreds of blood-stained material, accompanied by intense thirst. Choking is common, and the air

passages will probably be congested.

There will be signs of corrosion around the mouth and lips—grey or brownish stains. Consciousness is usually maintained, but the victim is drained of colour as respiration breaks down, and death usually follows within a few hours of a fatal dose, and results from a combination of shock, extensive tissue damage and respiratory failure. Post-mortem examination will show the destruction of those tissues affected by the corrosive. The extent and coloration of damage will identify the agent used if that is in doubt.

Hydrochloric Acid }	Grey/black
Sulphuric Acid }	
Nitric Acid	Red/brown
Caustic alkalis	Grey/white
Cresols	Brown
Mercury Chloride	Blue/white

Some corrosive agents have a double effect — attacking the tissues directly and also acting on the central nervous system: such poisons are carbolic acid and oxalic acid. Carbolic acid in its pure form is phenol, and is used as a component in many branded disinfectants. These agents have a corrosive action which is partly modified by their anaesthetic effect — vomiting is therefore uncommon. But they also have a depressant action, and death usually results within about three hours from respiratory or cardiac failure; a fatal dose may be as low as 4 ml. but recoveries have been recorded from much higher doses. Phenol may also be absorbed through the skin.

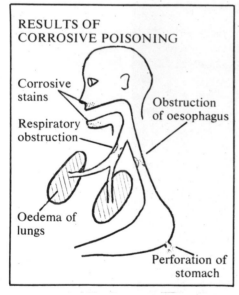

RESULTS OF CORROSIVE POISONING

Corrosive stains

Respiratory obstruction

Obstruction of oesophagus

Oedema of lungs

Perforation of stomach

Sulphuric acid — Oil of Vitriol — is one of the strongest corrosive poisons. It is used extensively in its most concentrated form for industrial purposes and also in laboratory work, but battery acid (30% sulphuric acid) is still sufficiently strong to cause corrosive poisoning. Sulphuric acid acts by extracting water from the tissues and, in the process, generates considerable heat. This has a charring and blackening effect. Perforation of the oesophagus and stomach is likely to follow this.

Hydrochloric and nitric acids give off irritant fumes and therefore involve the respiratory system. Their destructive effects are less severe than those of sulphuric acid.

The principal alkaline corrosive poison

DR. YELLOWLEES, a psychiatrist, was defence witness for Haigh — who was convicted by traces of his victim in the sulphuric acid vat.

is ammonia. It has an intensely irritant vapour and usually involves the air passages; it is commonly used in suicide and is frequently taken by accident. Many cleaning fluids contain ammonia in large proportions. The choking fumes of concentrated ammonia may cause cardiac failure, and they are particularly dangerous when inhaled, as they dissolve in the mucous membranes, thereby prolonging their action.

Caustic soda and caustic potash have a similar effect to the mineral acids, but the damaged tissues are distinctive because of the large quantities of mucus present. The destroyed tissues are also slimy to the touch.

Staining of the mouth

The appearance of corrosion stains on the face may be a guide to the nature of the fatality. The general nature of the vessel from which the poison was swallowed may be ascertained from the staining of lips and mouth; a cup, for instance, will leave wide areas of staining around the mouth whereas a bottle may cause a smaller, neater stain. Dribbling stains down the chin and throat are quite common. Accidental poisoning from supposed doses of medicine often leave no marks — a

spoonful being put straight into the mouth.

The powerful action of the mineral acids has frequently been applied to the problem of disposing of a body. In 1933 a French lawyer, Maître Sarret, concocted a get-rich-quick plan with the help of two girls who were sisters, Katherine and Philomene Schmidt. Sarret was in debt, and he persuaded Katherine Schmidt, who was also his mistress, to help him in an insurance fraud. He set up an elaborate scheme in which a man who was known by him to be in the terminal stage of an illness was insured for 100,000 francs. As insurance companies are not in business to insure people on the point of death, the scheme involved Katherine marrying the sick man and arranging for another party to the fraud, a man called Chambon, to impersonate her husband and get the insurance.

Lured into a trap

This was done successfully, and in due course the sick man died. Maître Sarret and his confederates thus collected 100,000 francs. In no time at all Chambon decided that his share of the spoils was insufficient, and he threatened blackmail; Sarret and the girls pretended to play along with this but lured Chambon and his mistress into a trap. They were shot by Sarret while the two sisters ran a motorcycle engine to absorb the gunshot.

The bodies were put into a bath, and Sarret poured over them 25 gallons of sulphuric acid which he had bought, and the corpses were soon reduced to sludge. The deadly trio tried to repeat these tactics, this time for a larger stake of 1,750,000 francs. But before they could pull it off, one of the sisters was caught; when they were brought to trial, Sarret was sentenced to death, but the two sisters were each given 10 years' imprisonment.

John George Haigh, the acid bath murderer, was the most celebrated user of acid as a means of disposing of the victim. The 39-year-old self-styled engineer was convicted in 1949 of the murder of Mrs. Henrietta Durand-Deacon. His victim was a well-off widow who lived in the same South Kensington hotel. She had spoken to Haigh of her plans to market a cosmetic product. Haigh expressed interest and invited her to visit his "factory".

The factory, which was no more than a store-room belonging to another building, was at Crawley in Sussex. On February 18, Haigh drove Mrs. Durand-Deacon down to his factory premises. There he shot her in the back of the head, stripped her body of all valuables and tipped the corpse into a tank of sulphuric acid. The same day Haigh pawned the wrist watch he had taken from his victim.

Mrs. Durand-Deacon was reported missing from the hotel, and Haigh was among the first to express concern. He went with another resident to Chelsea police station to report her as missing.

The police were suspicious of Haigh's glibness and checked up on him. They soon found that he had a record as a petty criminal. Further inquiries were made, and the Crawley factory was visited. There detectives found some of Mrs. Durand-Deacon's clothes, traces of blood and a recently fired ·38 Webley revolver. Haigh was apprehended. In cocksure mood he told the police, "Mrs. Durand-Deacon no longer exists – I've destroyed her with acid. You can't prove murder without a body." When charged with the murder he admitted to seven other killings, the bodies all being disposed of in drums of acid.

While the acid had reduced his last victim's body to sludge there were sufficient identifiable traces remaining to bring the murder home to Haigh. Twenty-eight pounds of body fat, various pieces of bone and an acrylic plastic denture were among the grisly remains. The denture was positively identified by a dentist as belonging to Mrs. Durand-Deacon. Haigh was executed on August 6, 1949.

Nitric acid was used in 1962 by a doctor in an incredible disfigurement of his wife. Early in August, Dr. Geza de Kaplany and his new bride, Hajna, moved into an apartment block in San Jose, California. About 9.00 p.m. on August 28, fellow residents heard the sound of running water and classical music played at high volume. These noises, which came from the de Kaplanys' apartment, seemed to disguise a kind of wailing sound.

At 10.18 the police arrived at the apartment block. The music stopped, and a disturbing human wail was distinctly audible. Ambulance men were called and shortly afterwards brought out a figure on a stretcher. Siren blaring, the ambulance drove off at full speed to Santa Clara Hospital. The curious onlookers thought they could smell acid fumes.

The patient, Hajna de Kaplany, was a 25-year-old model. She had been married to Dr. de Kaplany for only five weeks. When admitted to hospital, the surgeons

A SMILING HAIGH is driven off after having been sentenced to death for the murder of Mrs. Durand-Deacon, a rich Kensington widow, and seven others.

were shocked to find the appalling state she was in. She had third-degree corrosive burns covering 60 per cent of her body. Her eyes were so burned that the pupils could not be seen; her breasts and thighs in particular had been subjected to the terrible corrosive action of the acid. The woman was choking, and a tracheotomy had to be performed to sustain her breathing. She was not expected to live – the last rites were administered.

Torture chamber

Police meanwhile searched the apartment where she had been found. Retching at the stench of acid hanging in the atmosphere, they took in an incredible scene. The three-roomed apartment had all the appearance of a torture chamber. In the bedroom there was a heap of yellow-stained bedclothes disintegrating into a mess of rags, and there was a large hole in the carpet. A pair of discarded rubber gloves was lying near a leather case containing three pint bottles of sulphuric, hydrochloric and nitric acid – the last one was two-thirds empty.

Other items included acid-sodden

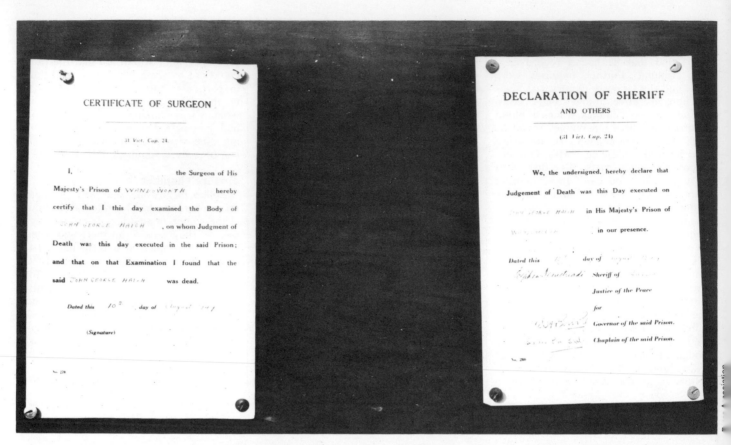

surgical swabs, rolls of adhesive tape, some electric flex and a note written on a medical prescription form. It read, "If you want to live – do not shout; do what I tell you; or else you will die."

Hajna de Kaplany did die, but only after 33 days of agonized suffering. Her husband, Geza, who was a 36-year-old refugee from Hungary and anaesthetist at a San Jose hospital, told the police that he had attacked his wife to take away her beauty and to warn her against adultery. He did not think she would die. The police reconstructed the doctor's lesson against adultery.

After a period of lovemaking, de Kaplany beat his wife and bound her naked body at wrists and ankles with electric flex. He taped her mouth so that she would not scream. Then he put on rubber gloves and applied nitric acid to her naked, unprotected body. Nine doctors fought to save Hajna's life. Her lungs were inflamed as a result of inhaling the acid fumes, and large areas of her body became infected. She was on large doses of pain-killing drugs and had to be fed intravenously. Her condition was so painful that she had to be held upright by two attendants in order to urinate.

The poor woman was put on sterile bedding in order to try to check the spread of infection, and warm air blowers were used to reduce the moisture which oozed from the burns. The skin on her face went hard and turned brown – her near sightless eyes stared out of an inhuman head.

She was disfigured beyond belief and was conscious enough to realize it.

Mercifully, she did not survive her ordeal by acid – she died on October 1. Hajna's condition had been the subject of daily progress reports in the press. Horror and revulsion expressed the public's reaction. Dr. Geza de Kaplany was charged with murder by torture. He recorded two pleas – not guilty and not guilty by reason of insanity. His trial began on January 7, 1963, before Superior Judge Raymond G. Callaghan at San Jose.

Terrible testimony

During the presentation of evidence by the prosecution, de Kaplany seemed cool and detached. But his calm was shattered when a large photographic enlargement was introduced to the court – it showed Hajna's frightful condition soon after entering hospital. De Kaplany leapt to his feet, shouting, "No, no, no! What did you do to her?" He had to be restrained and was then half-carried from the court.

When he returned, the horror story, fully illustrated with photographs, was continued. A procession of witnesses followed. Police officers, ambulance men – who had burned their hands when moving the victim – doctors and criminologists all added their terrible testimony.

Dr. de Kaplany was taken to a special cell and kept under constant supervision so that he might take his own life. In court the following morning, his

"YOU CAN'T PROVE murder without a body," Haigh had boasted. But they could and did – as these execution notices at Wandsworth Prison show. . . .

defence attorney announced a change of plea to guilty. Judge Callaghan asked the doctor if he fully understood that he pleaded guilty to murder in the first degree. De Kaplany nodded and explained, "I am a doctor. I loved her. If I did this – as I must have done – then I'm guilty."

The defence called psychiatric evidence to show that the doctor's love for his wife had been rejected. It also transpired that de Kaplany occasionally posed as Pierre la Roche, a French journalist. This *alter ego* was used to build up a picture of a split personality. One psychiatrist offered the opinion that de Kaplany already considered himself dead, and that whilst he knew what acid would do, his schizophrenia prevented him from understanding the social significance of his act.

On the thirty-fifth day of the trial and after 55 hours of deliberation, the jury reached its verdict. They found that Dr. Geza de Kaplany "shall be punished by imprisonment for life as prescribed by the law". The verdict was greeted by a furious public reaction. The newspaper switchboards were jammed with calls from angry men and women, and some of the jurors were threatened.

Manacled and under escort to the van which would take him to the State prison, Dr. de Kaplany said, "I am dead.

MORPHINE

The poppy's juice is a cocktail of narcotics, the most potent being morphine. The "Big M" can brand a man; it can spell mercy, misery . . . or murder. Among those people who have access to the deadly drug are doctors everywhere . . . they have a ready-made weapon for homicide.

MORPHINE is not readily available to the public, but every doctor carries it in his bag. Because he has rightful access to morphine and controls its use in treatment, the unscrupulous doctor thus has a ready-made murder weapon.

The dried juice of the white Indian poppy, *Papaver somniferum,* produces opium, and opium contains several natural narcotics of which morphine is the most powerful. Narcotics are drugs which kill pain and reduce consciousness; they are also habit forming. The use of opium-derived drugs in Britain is controlled by the Dangerous Drugs Act (1965) and the Misuse of Drugs Act (1971).

Morphine can be given by mouth or by injection, and it is available under a number of pharmaceutical and trade names. Several well-known medicines used for sedation contain morphine, and overdoses of all these can cause morphine poisoning:
Laudanum (Tincture of opium) contains 1.0% morphine
Paregoric (Camphorated tincture of opium) contains 0.05% morphine
Chlorodyne contains 0.18% morphine

Death within an hour

As a pain killer, morphine is usually given by injection. A normal dose of hydromorphine hydrochloride is 2.0 mg. A great danger with giving morphine is that a patient quickly acquires "tolerance" to the drug; patients treated for painful terminal illnesses frequently require amounts far in excess of the normal dose in order to obtain relief. Battle casualties injected with morphine have a large letter M painted on their foreheads to ensure that their treatment is clearly identified and controlled. Addicts have been known to take up to ten times the normal therapeutic dose.

Morphine poisoning causes a deep coma, and this is accompanied by slow respiration, sweating and reduced reflexes; a lethal dose of about 180 mg can cause death within an hour. The tell-tale sign of morphine poisoning is the pin-point contraction of the pupils of the eyes, so that when foul play is suspected, the presence of pin-pointing will always suggest an overdose of morphine to the forensic expert. When death has only recently occurred, opium may be smelled in the mouth, or in the stomach on post-mortem examination.

It is possible to detect morphine by simple chemical tests on drug-containers, syringes or residues found at the scene of death. These usually apply only in cases of suicide or accidental death. Morphine gives a blue colour with ferric chloride and dry residues instantly turn purple when treated with a solution containing equal parts of concentrated sulphuric acid and formaldehyde. Where homicide is suspected, the presence of morphine in the body will be determined at post-mortem by analysis of blood, urine and bile.

A case which illustrated how the unscrupulous doctor can use his position of trust for criminal purposes was that of Dr. Robert Clements. On the evening of May 26, 1947, Clements, a 57-year-old Fellow of the Royal College of Surgeons, called a doctor to his Southport home to attend his wife. The fourth Mrs. Clements was unconscious. Two doctors, Brown and Homes, examined her and transferred her immediately to a nearby nursing home, where she died the following morning. Her husband said she had mycloid leucaemia, and that was entered on the certificate as cause of death.

A post-mortem was performed by a third doctor, Dr. Houston. He confirmed that the dead woman had been suffering from mycloid leucaemia. Drs. Brown and Homes voiced their suspicions of Mrs. Clements' eyes, the pupils of which were pin-pointed, though Dr. Houston said he was satisfied with the cause of death. However, the other two doctors spoke to the Southport coroner, hinting that there might have been an overdose of morphine, and enquiries were begun.

The police discovered that the matron of the nursing home to which Mrs. Clements was admitted had remarked at the time about the patient's pin-point pupils. Dr. Clements was interviewed at his flat. He said simply that his wife died of mycloid leucaemia, which, he added, was incurable.

People who knew Dr. Clements and his wife remarked that Mrs. Clements had been subject to sudden bouts of unconsciousness; yet, strangely, her husband always seemed to know when these were likely to occur. Friends who had been in the habit of talking to Mrs. Clements on the telephone suddenly found themselves unable to do so – Dr. Clements had the instrument removed. This was surely a remarkable action for a doctor with a sick wife at home.

Heir to a fortune

Slowly, the story began to take shape. Mrs. Clements' health had deteriorated over a period of time – she was prone to vomiting, her complexion yellowed, and she was lethargic – all the signs of a morphine addict. Finally it was learned that Dr. Clements had prescribed large doses of morphine for a patient who never received them. The conclusion was obvious. A second post-mortem on Mrs. Clements was ordered.

The Home Office pathologist was surprised when he found that some of the body's internal organs were missing. He was told that after the first post-mortem Dr. Houston said they could be destroyed. Nevertheless, the result of the second examination showed clearly that Mrs. Clements had died from morphine poisoning.

● *Dr. Clements after their wedding*

Police officers called on Dr. Clements, only to find that he was dead. He had committed suicide by taking his favourite drug – morphine. No doubt he knew the game was up. He left a note: "To whom it may concern – I can no longer tolerate the diabolical insults to which I have recently been exposed." Dr. Houston was also found by the coroner to have died by his own hand. In his case, the fatal drug was cyanide. He, too, left a note in which he referred to mistakes he had made in his work.

Dr. Clements was found to be the murderer of his fourth wife by a coroner's court. Mrs. Clements was heir to a fortune which, in the event of her death, would have gone to her husband; all of Dr. Clements' marriages had been for money. He had a liking for the good life and had the knack of attracting rich women.

His record is quite remarkable. In 1912 he married his first wife; she died in 1920 from sleeping sickness; in 1921 he married again; his second wife died of endocarditis in 1925. He took his third wife in 1928, and she died of cancer in 1939: in each case, he signed the death certificate.

Some suspicion was voiced about the death of his third wife, but by the time this reached official quarters she had been cremated. Dr. Clements had cheated the gallows by taking his own life; it was not thought necessary to exhume the bodies of his first two wives.

e, his fourth wife ...on in 1940.

MEDICAL PRACTITIONERS have access to the deadly drug, morphine. Dr. Clements (above) and Dr. Buchanan (right) with the wives they murdered by this means.

Another celebrated case involving murder by morphine was that of Dr. Robert Buchanan in New York. Buchanan qualified at Edinburgh and in 1886 went to New York with his wife, where he set up in general practice. He was a successful practitioner, but he had an appetite for the seamier side of life; at night he forsook his respectable medical background and spent his time in clubs and brothels.

He became friendly with a woman called Anna Sutherland, a brothel madame, who was also one of his patients. In November 1890, Dr. Buchanan divorced his wife on the ground of her adultery. Shortly afterwards he persuaded Anna Sutherland to make a will leaving her money to her husband, or, if she died unmarried, to her trusted friend and physician Dr. Buchanan. Within weeks, the doctor married Anna Sutherland, who was twice his age, ensuring himself of inheriting her wealth.

The doctor continued to enhance his professional reputation, only to find that his wife's brothel madame's ways were a source of embarrassment; he was afraid of

losing patients, and his wife was fast becoming a liability. Early in 1892, Dr. Buchanan announced that he was travelling to Edinburgh for further study. It was his intention to leave his wife behind, but Mrs. Buchanan thought otherwise and declared that unless she accompanied her husband she would cut him out of her will altogether. Despite this threat, Dr. Buchanan bought a single ticket for a passage on April 25.

Four days before he was due to sail he cancelled his passage and told friends that Mrs. Buchanan had been taken seriously ill. A Dr. McIntyre was called in to attend her. She went into a coma and died within a matter of hours. Cause of death was certified as cerebral haemorrhage, and Dr. Buchanan, showing few signs of grief, inherited $50,000.

Disappointed suitor

The following month, a man who had been the late Mrs. Buchanan's partner and disappointed suitor visited the coroner. He declared that Dr. Buchanan had murdered his wife in order to secure her money. The coroner was disinclined to take any action, but the *New York World* got hold of the story and started to ask questions.

The interest of New Yorkers had been aroused in 1891 by a case of morphine poisoning in which a medical student called Carlyle Harris was convicted of murdering his wife with the drug. The poisoning was diagnosed by the victim's characteristic pin-point pupils.

Dr. McIntyre was interviewed by the newspaper about Mrs. Buchanan's death, but refused to consider the idea of morphine poisoning because the contraction of the pupils was entirely missing in this case. The newspaper persisted with its enquiries, and a reporter found out that Dr. Buchanan had lied about the date on which he cancelled his transatlantic passage. The ticket was turned in 10 days before his wife fell ill; not four days as he had said; but the real scoop was the discovery that 23 days after Mrs. Buchanan's death the doctor re-married his former wife.

It was not long before pressure was brought to bear on the coroner to set up an inquiry into Mrs. Buchanan's death. An exhumation order was granted. Postmortem examination showed no sign of cerebral haemorrhage, the certified cause of death, but Professor Witthaus, the eminent toxicologist, found 1/10th of a grain of morphine in the body which he estimated was the residue of a fatal dose of 5 or 6 grains. To the disappointment of the prosecutors, the universal indicator of morphine poisoning—pin-point pupils was absent.

Nevertheless there was sufficient evidence to arrest Dr. Buchanan. He was put

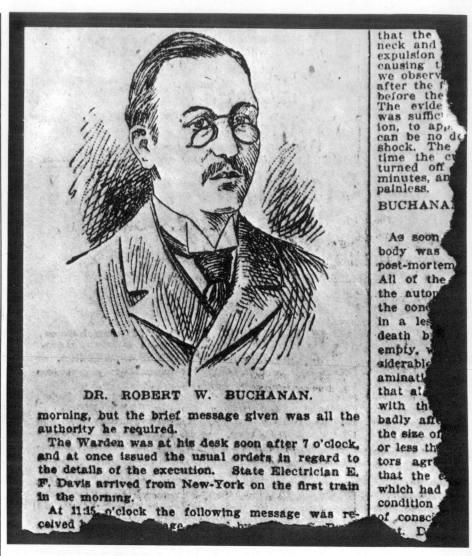

DR. ROBERT W. BUCHANAN.

morning, but the brief message given was all the authority he required.

The Warden was at his desk soon after 7 o'clock, and at once issued the usual orders in regard to the details of the execution. State Electrician E. F. Davis arrived from New-York on the first train in the morning.

At 11:15 o'clock the following message was received ...

PRESCRIPTION for murder: one overdose of morphine, add belladonna eye-drops to eliminate pin-point pupils . . . but make sure prosecution hasn't had same idea.

on trial in New York on March 20, 1893. Witnesses came forward for the prosecution who stated that at the time of the Harris case Dr. Buchanan had called the medical student a "stupid fool" and a "bungling amateur". He hinted that he knew how to disguise morphine poisoning with belladonna; the suggestion was that the doctor had put belladonna drops into his wife's eyes which counteracted the pin-pointing of the pupils, and the dead woman's nurse confirmed that Buchanan had put some drops into his wife's eyes for no apparent reason.

To make their case, the prosecution killed a cat in court with morphine and put belladonna drops into its eyes. The drops completely disguised the pin-pointing. There followed a battle of the experts. The defence showed that the colour reaction tests used to identify morphine in the organs of the dead woman were not infallible. Again with a dramatic

court-room demonstration it was shown that the test which produced a red colour in the presence of morphine was not specific. The same test resulted in a red colour when morphine was not present.

With the case swinging in his favour, Dr. Buchanan mistakenly insisted on going into the witness box, and the prosecution gave him a severe grilling. He failed to answer why he took such an unlikely person as his wife, and he could not convincingly explain away his lies nor his boast about knowing how to disguise morphine poisoning. Dr. Buchanan was found guilty of murder in the first degree. After two years in Sing Sing prison while various appeals were heard, he died in the electric chair on July 2, 1895.

Modern toxicological methods are fortunately more precise than those available to Dr. Buchanan's prosecutors. Drugs can be clearly identified by a variety of methods, and their presence determined down to amounts as small as 1/5000th of a grain. Methods commonly used by the forensic toxicologist include colour reactions, thin-layer chromatography and gas chromatography.

GAS

Accident, suicide . . . or murder? So stealthy is the slow, sleepy poison of gas that the victim rarely knows what hit him. Skin colour (below) is a clue to suffocation by carbon monoxide (which killed most of the family shown here). But where is the clue to trap a killer?

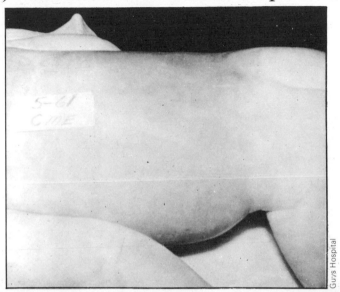

Guy's Hospital

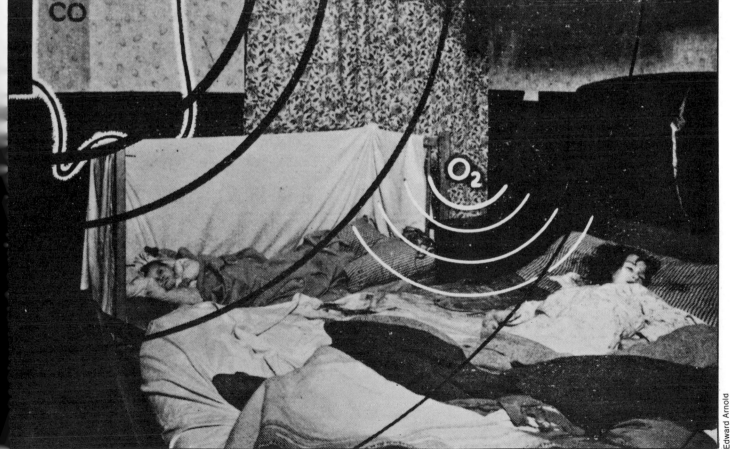

Edward Arnold

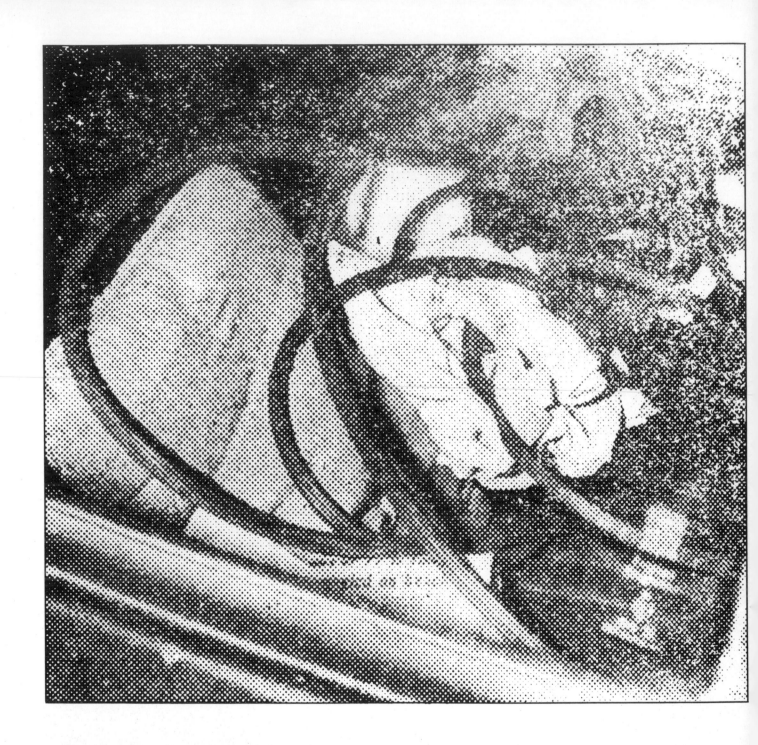

DOMESTIC GAS was used by John Christie in the bizarre murders he carried out at 10 Rillington Place, London. Sexually impotent in normal conditions, he rendered the women he lured to his house unconscious by feeding gas through a rubber pipe to a bowl of inhaling mixture (carbon monoxide was found in the blood of three victims); then he raped and strangled them. He probably killed seven or eight women in this way, and then buried their bodies under the floor boards or stacked them in a cupboard. Incredibly, a lodger in the house, Timothy Evans, had confessed to the murder of his wife in the same house and had been hanged before Christie's crimes were discovered. To this day, no one knows who killed Mrs. Evans.

THE everyday domestic coal-gas supply is, in fact, something of a menace; it accounts for large numbers of accidental deaths and suicides and for a smaller number of murders. Murder dressed up to look like suicide by gassing is one of the ruses that the forensic pathologist has to be aware of.

The killing component of coal-gas is carbon monoxide, and death from coal gas is really carbon-monoxide poisoning. The proportion of carbon monoxide in coal-gas varies according to the nature of the supply but is usually within the range of 5 to 10%. The introduction of natural gas, which contains little or no carbon monoxide, is a safeguard against suicide by this means; some years ago, a major British university converted its gas supply to "natural" and thus dramatically reduced suicide among its students.

Carbon monoxide is also produced by various forms of incomplete combustion; paraffin heaters in unventilated conditions, for instance, can be lethal, and smouldering upholstery and furnishings in burning buildings also produce the poisonous gas. Another major source of carbon monoxide is car-exhaust fumes, both accidental and suicidal deaths are common.

Readily absorbed

Carbon monoxide is odourless and non-irritant. For these reasons its action is often insidious; it is readily absorbed by the body and quickly accumulates, poisoning the bloodstream. Vital oxygen is normally carried to the body's tissues by haemoglobin in the blood; haemoglobin is the blood's colouring material, and oxygen, brought in through the lungs, combines with it to form oxyhaemoglobin. But oxyhaemoglobin is unstable, and its oxygen is easily displaced by carbon monoxide.

Consequently, carbon monoxide, which has 300 times more affinity for haemoglobin than oxygen, forms carboxyhaemoglobin, which is stable. The effect is that less and less oxygen reaches the body tissues, and death results from oxygen starvation. Since nerve cells, especially, cannot long survive lack of oxygen—those in the brain begin to die after about eight minutes—deterioration is rapid.

Symptoms of poisoning vary according to the amount of carbon monoxide accumulated in the blood. There are seldom any symptoms at all until saturation has reached 20% and then usually only when

DEATH BY GASSING can be detected by the pink colouring of the victim, and can be confirmed by the use of a Hartridge reversion spectroscope (right). In this a solution of blood is viewed through a prism, and its spectrum is analyzed to discover the proportion of oxygen to carbon in the blood.

the subject is engaged in physical acts of exertion. The first signs are dizziness and difficulty with breathing. The symptoms then move progressively to unconsciousness and death as the level of carbon monoxide builds up in the blood.

Saturation level	Symptoms
30%	Even when the subject is at rest there are feelings of dizziness and headaches.
40%	General lack of co-ordination, staggering, mental confusion and appearance of being drunk.
50%	Increased lack of co-ordination. Mental deterioration, slurred speech, vomiting, exhaustion and general weakness.
60%	
70%	Unconsciousness and death.

The onset of symptoms is insidious. Muzziness leads to a feeling of weariness and a disinclination to make any exertion, then unconsciousness intervenes and death ensues. Even where there is a willingness to make the effort to escape or to open a window, the limbs are often too weak to respond.

A level of 1% of carbon monoxide can cause unconsciousness in 15 to 20 minutes. Coal-gas containing between 5 and 10% carbon monoxide is likely to be lethal within two to five minutes. Exercise quickens the respiration and merely serves to speed up the poisoning process.

Even small proportions of carbon monoxide in inhaled air may prove fatal due to the steady accumulation of the gas in the blood. A person at rest inhaling 0·1% carbon monoxide from the atmosphere may have a blood saturation level of 50% in just over two hours. With exercise, this time would be halved. In general, conversion of more than 50% of the haemoglobin to carboxyhaemoglobin will cause death.

Post mortem appearances of carbon monoxide poisoning are distinctive. The blood, which often fails to clot, has a bright cherry-pink colour. It colours the organs and muscles so that the face usually has a high pink colour. Post mortem lividity—when the blood sinks by gravitation to the lowest parts of the body—is also bright pink. Similar colouring can occur in cyanide poisoning and in bodies exposed to cold conditions.

Diagnosis of carbon-monoxide poisoning therefore should not be made on the basis of colour alone but should be backed up with chemical and spectroscopic tests of the blood. The lungs are usually congested and often contain quantities of frothy fluid. Pin-point capillary haemorrhages (petechiae) are seen in the lungs, brain and conjunctiva of the eye.

Saturation level

Kunkel's tannic acid test is used to detect the presence of carbon monoxide in blood. A few drops of 3% tannic acid are added to a sample of blood that has been diluted 1 to 10. A precipitate forms which ranges in colour from pink to dark brown, according to the saturation level of carbon monoxide.

Confirmation of carbon-monoxide poisoning is made by a standard spectroscopic test. The various compounds of haemoglobin have a typical spectrum

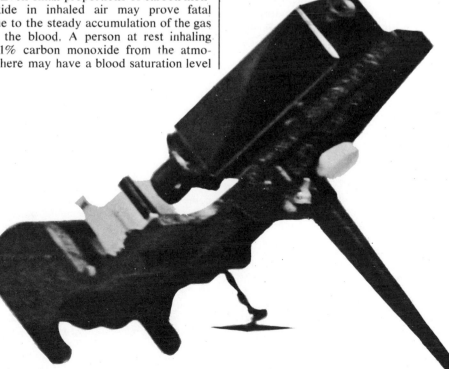

which can be identified on an instrument called a Hartridge reversion spectroscope.

Blood affected by carbon monoxide contains oxyhaemoglobin and carboxyhaemoglobin in varying amounts, and these show up as dark absorption bands in the spectrum formed when light is passed through a solution of blood and then a prism.

The spectrum is displayed on a scaled screen, and the various absorption bands are designated A, B, C, D, E, F and G, starting from the red end. Oxyhaemoglobin and carboxyhaemoglobin each have two absorption bands, D and E. The carboxyhaemoglobin bands lie a little closer to the violet end of the spectrum than those of oxyhaemoglobin. This difference or "shift" may be measured on the spectroscope and the saturation of carbon monoxide in the blood calculated. Values of 60% or more are taken as clear evidence of carbon-monoxide poisoning — 20 to 30% is considered sufficient in elderly persons.

Carbon-monoxide poisoning falls into the usual three categories of accident, suicide and murder, the domestic gas supply commonly being the source of death for many accidents and suicides. Leaks from supply pipes and appliances such as hot-water geysers, radiators and gas fires allied to inadequate ventilation have accounted for many deaths.

Weariness and lethargy

Special hazards trap the elderly who allow pots to boil over and put out the flame on a gas cooker which, unless re-ignited, fills the air with lethal fumes. Again, elderly persons, and sometimes drunks, turn on the gas and forget to light it. With an impaired sense of smell, or stupefied by alcohol, the gas is undetected and is allowed to pour out its deadly poison; the subtle nature of carbon monoxide produces weariness, and its victims sleep on till death.

Reduction of ventilation caused by blockage of air pipes with birds' nests has been known to cause accidental poisoning from hot-water geysers in bathrooms. Deliberate but foolish blocking of ventilation to conserve warmth in rooms and caravans heated with gas fires or paraffin heaters can also be lethal.

Accidental poisoning occasionally results from car-exhaust fumes which build up in a garage with doors and windows shut. In these circumstances the air is made lethal by exhaust from the car inside five minutes. Car exhaust contains between 1 and 7% carbon monoxide. The suicide usually sits in the car, having fixed a tube to the exhaust pipe to bring the poisonous fumes into the vehicle.

The classic suicide by gassing has unmistakable signs of preparation. The doors and windows of the room are sealed and

a note is left. A feature of self-destruction by this method is that the victim first makes himself comfortable. Cushions or pillows are placed so that he may conveniently put his head in or near the oven of a gas cooker. Some suicides prefer to die in bed, and connect a tube to the gas outlet which they lead under the bedclothes, thus forming a kind of gas chamber. Another method is to place a plastic bag, into which a gas tube is introduced, over the head.

Accident and suicide

The distinction between accident and suicide is sometimes complicated by other considerations. Such proved to be the case with Major James Dunning, a 59-year-old retired American army officer living in London. Dunning, who had financial interests in the City, lived in fine style in a house in Chelsea. He also had a farm in Sussex.

The Major owned a 1913 Rolls-Royce of which he was very proud; one of his pleasures was to carry out his own mechanical repairs on the vehicle. On February 17, 1931, he sent the car to a specialist garage for some major repairs that would take several days to complete, and on February 23 he set out by train for a business appointment in Birmingham. The next day he sent his wife a telegram saying that he would collect the car on his way home to London. He did not return to Chelsea where his wife was expecting him.

But he did collect the car; he drove it down to his farm in Sussex, and on arrival there he told the maid that he had run into some mechanical trouble and would be staying overnight. After dinner he told the servants that he was going to work on the car. This was about 10.35 p.m.

The maid and cook went to bed about 11.15 p.m. They heard the car engine running in the garage beneath their bedroom, and they smelled the fumes. They thought the engine stopped at 11.45 p.m.

Early the following morning, Major Dunning was found dead on the floor of the garage beside his car. Tools were scattered about, and the circumstances suggested that the dead man had been working on the car when he was overcome by exhaust fumes; the ignition was switched on, but the engine had stopped. The garage doors and windows were firmly shut, but the chauffeur explained that this was standard practice during cold weather, as the garage was draughty.

Post mortem examination showed that Major Dunning died of carbon-monoxide poisoning. The blood contained a high level of the gas. A verdict of death by misadventure was brought in. It appeared that the dead man's life had been heavily insured. The policy had amounted to £10,000. This was an accident policy

which excluded death resulting from suicide, and the company refused to admit liability.

The case eventually came before the courts. The insurance company contended that there were suspicious circumstances attending Major Dunning's death; apparently his financial position was in some jeopardy as a result of income tax difficulties, and this was suggested to be sufficient cause for suicide.

Medical experts, on the other hand, supported the original verdict of accidental death. It was calculated that the Rolls-Royce would emit about two cubic feet of carbon monoxide every minute. Taking into consideration the cubic capacity of the garage at the Sussex farm and the fact that the doors and windows were closed, 30 minutes' running of the car engine would result in a 2% level of carbon monoxide.

This was ample to cause death. The fact that the car engine seemed to have stopped of its own accord could be accounted for by the reduction of oxygen in the closed atmosphere of the garage. Arbitration was given in favour of Major Dunning's widow.

In the aftermath of killing, some murderers try to cover their tracks by "gassing": they arrange the body to simulate suicide. Evidence of a struggle and of injuries on the victim usually give the game away to the skilled forensic examiner. Gassing has featured in a number of murder cases, but, except in rare incidents, it is usually the killing stroke after the victim has been overpowered by physical violence or stupefied with drugs or alcohol. Blood samples taken from persons found dead in suspicious circumstances are always routinely checked for both drugs and alcohol.

The so-called Murder Trust Case in New York in 1932 was one in which the victim was first stupefied before being gassed. Michael Malloy, having survived various attempts on his life by a gang who wanted to secure the money for which he was insured, finally succumbed to coal-gas poisoning. Having been generously plied with alcohol, he had a rubber gas pipe held in his mouth until he stopped breathing and died.

Gassing was also part of John Christie's murder technique. Carbon monoxide was found in the blood of three of his victims, a phenomenon for which Christie provided an explanation at his trial. After he had got the women partially drunk, he persuaded them to sit in a deck chair of the type that had a sun canopy over the head. He then made them fully unconscious with coal-gas drawn from the domestic supply and brought to the lethal deck chair by a rubber pipe. In Christie's case this was a prelude to strangulation and rape.

KNIFING

A corpse is brought into the forensic laboratory bearing the marks of savage knife wounds. Was it suicide, or murder? How do the experts tell?

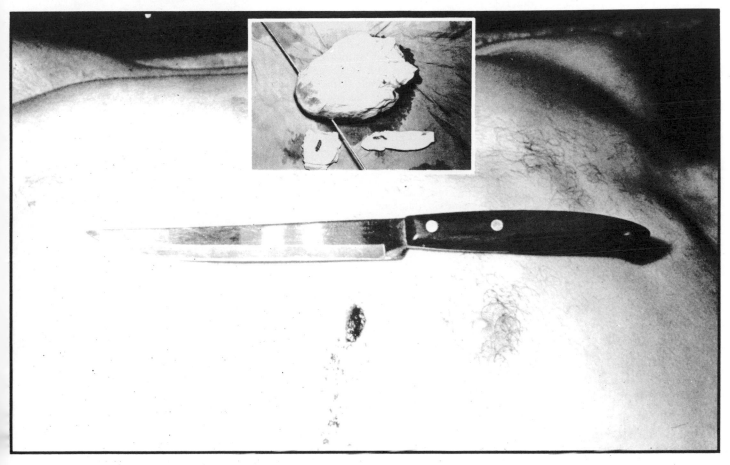

IN EVERY case where a dead body is found to have knife wounds, one of the first questions is: "Are the wounds suicidal or homicidal?" Injuries made with a knife fall into two basic classes—incised wounds or cuts and stab wounds. Because cuts are made with a sweeping movement they are usually found on unprotected parts of the body such as the hands and face. The injury most frequently requiring expert opinion—murderous attack or self-inflicted—is the throat wound.

In general, suicide throat-cutting has a clean and deliberate appearance, whereas the homicidal cut-throat is normally crude and suggests a death struggle. Since a suicide usually extends the head before making the cut, the line of the wound is frequently transverse. This stretching action causes the carotid arteries to slip back, thus escaping the knife and reducing the loss of blood.

A right-handed person cuts the throat from left to right. Considerable pressure

HUMAN HEARTS are intensely vulnerable to knifing attacks. The photographs (above) show knife and entry wound with the heart itself.

on the knife at the beginning of the cut makes the wound deep at first but this becomes shallow as the knife is drawn across the throat and slopes slightly up towards the chin. In addition, there may be a few tentative shallow cuts on the throat—sizing up the stroke before making the lethal incision. As many as twelve of these tentative cuts have been noted on a suicide victim.

In a murderous wounding of the throat, the injury lacks the precision of the suicide. There may be several cuts from different directions, depending on the positions of the victim and assailant. The wild struggle of the victim and the desperation of the attacker combine to make gross wounds, and a key factor is the presence of defensive injuries on the victim. Protecting hands trying to force

away the knife are usually heavily slashed across the palms or between the fingers. The classic "ear-to-ear" cut severs the neck muscles, blood vessels and windpipe down to the spine: the wounding may be eight inches long with a gape of three inches.

Neville Heath inflicted such a wound on Doreen Marshall, whose body was found in some bushes at Branksome Dene Chine, Bournemouth, on July 8, 1946. The particular savagery of this killing was indicated by signs of a violent struggle; these included severe cuts on the victim's hands where she had attempted to fend off the knife.

The Grand Master of the cut-throat murder was, of course, Jack the Ripper. The body of Mary Ann Nicholls, one of the six known victims of his knife, was found in the early hours of August 31, 1888, in Bucks Row in London's East End. Her injuries were reported in detail in the *Star* newspaper:

"The throat is cut in two gashes . . .

There is a gash under the left ear, reaching nearly to the centre of the throat. Along half its length, however, it is accompanied by another one which reaches around under the other ear, making a wide and horrible hole, and nearly severing the head from the body."

In some cases of cut-throat wounds the injured person does not fall at the place where the wound was inflicted, but collapses at some distance from it. Sir Bernard Spilsbury, the eminent pathologist, recorded an example of a suicide who not only replaced the knife in his jacket pocket but walked nearly a hundred yards before collapsing and dying.

Apart from observing that a sharp cutting knife has been used, there is not much that the forensic expert can deduce about the nature of a weapon used to cut a throat. His main objective is to note the direction and dimensions of the wound and to examine the victim's hands for blood stains, defensive injuries, hairs and pieces of torn clothing.

Main points of comparison between suicidal and homicidal cut-throats

SUICIDAL

Incised and careful

Hands uninjured (suicidal wrist slashes may be present)

Tentative cuts

Cut slopes upwards

HOMICIDAL

Slashed and gross

Severe defensive cuts on hands

No tentative cuts

Cut slopes downwards

Stab wounds are characterized by their penetration into the body. Their points of entry are usually fairly small slits which look relatively trivial, and frequently there is little external bleeding. For these reasons the seriousness of such wounds can be underestimated. In reality a single entry wound may be of great penetration causing internal haemorrhage and death.

The weapon used in stabbing is most commonly the knife but stab wounds are caused by all manner of pointed instruments including bayonets, scissors and even hat-pins; unlike cut-throats, examination of stab wounds can give an indication of the weapon used. Most stab entries are elliptical but the ends of the wound may suggest whether the knife was single- or double-edged.

Stab entry wounds

Double-edged knife:
wound is sharp at both ends.
Single-edged knife:
wound is rounded at
one end, sharp at the other.

In a case of multiple stabbing it is likely that some of the entries will be torn as the victim struggles under the assault or as the knife is twisted in the body. The least torn wound will be the best indicator of the type of weapon used, and because the knife may not have penetrated to its hilt, the deepest wound will only indicate the minimum length of the blade.

Suicide or homicide?

The length of the entry wound is a guide to the width of the knife but it is only an approximation, for allowance has to be made for the elasticity of the skin under the impact of the knife thrust. Roughening or bruising around the edge of the entry would indicate that a blunt instrument such as a poker or a pair of closed scissors was used. The sharper the weapon, the cleaner the wound will be.

Like cut throats, stab wounds may be either suicidal or homicidal, although self-inflicted stabbing is thought to be less common than throat cutting. Homicidal stabbing, on the other hand, is frequently encountered by the forensic expert, and such wounds are usually found in the neck, chest, abdomen and back. The chest is the area usually selected for murderous use of the knife, presumably because it contains the heart. Penetrating wounds of the chest frequently pierce the heart or large blood vessels and lead to serious internal bleeding; loss of blood varies widely but the effusion of as much as two or three pints in the chest cavity has been known. Wounds in the neck often damage the carotid and jugular blood vessels.

The distinction between suicide and homicide is fairly easy in the case of stab wounds. Persons bent on suicide select a "target area"—usually the region of the heart. Because suicides are deliberate, the "target area" is often narrowed even further to the epigastric region. It is here that the average person feels the heart beat most strongly and the area is also free of obstacles such as ribs. The clothing is sometimes lifted in order to make the knife thrust easier, and the wound is usually a single or, at the most, it may be a double thrust with no tentative or trial efforts.

Wounds outside the general target area of the heart are regarded with suspicion, especially if they have been made through the clothing. The suicidal wound naturally must be in an accessible part of the body —the stab in the back obviously being homicidal; a further distinguishing feature is the likelihood of finding defensive wounds on the hands of the victim of a murderous attack.

The angle of a knife wound in the body is also important in helping to establish whether or not a stabbing has been self-inflicted. Expert examination of this

POLICE tended to fantasize about capturing Jack the Ripper (above). But he evaded detectives with total success. Below: One of his victims, after death.

Main points of comparison between suicidal and homicidal stab wounds

SUICIDAL

Target area selected

Single (at most double) wound

No defensive cuts on hands

Wound site accessible to victim

Clean entry wound

Clothing often pulled back

"Target" area for suicidal stabbing: heart

HOMICIDAL

Random wounding

Multiple wounds

Defensive cuts on hands

Wound sites not accessible to victim

Torn wounds due to struggling

Wounds penetrate clothing

Common areas for homicidal stabbing: chest or stomach

aspect of knife wounds enabled Sir Bernard Spilsbury to advise the police about the death of Patrick Swift at Stockton-on-Tees; Swift was found dead in the kitchen of his house — the fatal wound was a single knife thrust. His wife told the police that he had stabbed himself following a drunken quarrel.

There were no witnesses, and although the police suspected Mrs. Swift they could

SUICIDE or murder? The evidence indicates (below) that the deceased was a murder victim. Defensive cuts would not appear on the hands of a suicide . . .

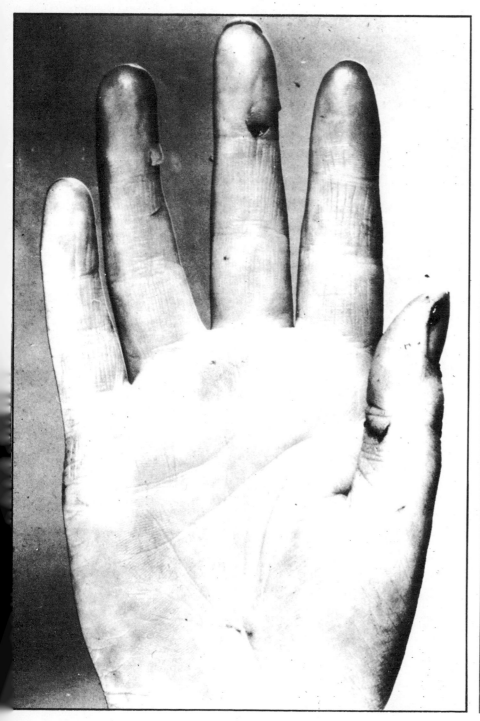

not disprove her story — not, at least, without Spilsbury's help. The pathologist demonstrated that the single downward thrust of the knife in the chest which killed Patrick Swift could not have been self-inflicted, for Swift was right-handed and the angle of the wound was such that he could not have stabbed himself with that hand, nor was it possible for him to have used his left hand to produce the fatal thrust. Therefore, it was a case of murder and not suicide.

The knife is not only an instrument of death. Its use in a number of celebrated dismembering cases testifies to other

needs. John White Webster, a 57-year-old professor at Massachusetts Medical College, was certainly adept with the knife. The first count of his indictment for the murder of Dr. George Parkman read that he ". . . feloniously, wilfully and of his malice aforethought did strike, cut and stab . . . giving . . . one mortal wound . . . of the depth of three inches".

This was Webster's way of settling his inability to repay money owed to his elderly colleague. But having killed Dr. Parkman he was faced with the problem of disposing of the body. In his own words, "The only instrument was the knife . . .". With a doctor's skill he dismembered the body and put it in the cellar beneath his laboratory. The Massachusetts Supreme Court repaid Webster by sentencing him to death. He was hanged in August, 1850.

Easy disposal

As dead bodies are difficult to transport, many murderers have sought to ease the problem by cutting them into smaller parts — five or six pieces being the general rule. The fragments may then be disposed of by burning, burying, treating with chemicals, or by a variety of other means. In 1949, Donald Hume, for example, stabbed Stanley Setty to death in London, England with a German SS dagger. Then he cut the body up and made it into three parcels which he dropped into the English Channel from an aircraft.

Dismembering a corpse is not an easy task and the results usually reflect the skill or otherwise of the perpetrator. Cartilage and bone are remarkably tough but yield easily to disarticulation with a sharp knife in the right hands; the unskilled and unknowing merely hack with brute force and desperation.

Charles Avinmain in Paris in 1867 deposited portions of his dismembered murder victims in the River Seine. Some of these were washed up and their most notable feature was that the severing cuts were clean and even. A surgeon advising the police suggested that the murderer was probably a man who had worked in a hospital and either watched or assisted with surgical operations. Avinmain had indeed worked in a hospital and had attended many post-mortems. When arrested he told the police, "I do not wish it to be said that I dismembered my victims . . . I dissected them in a decent and proper manner. I am not a bungler."

The same could not be said of Patrick Mahon, whose spectacular fragmentation of his victim horrified England in 1924. Mahon, a thirty-three-year-old salesman, was in the habit of leaving his wife at weekends. He failed to give very convincing reasons for these absences so Mrs. Mahon decided to find out for herself. Her first thought was to search through her husband's clothes. She turned up a railway left luggage ticket in the pocket of a suit, issued at Waterloo Station. She asked a friend to find out what had been deposited, and he exchanged the ticket for a Gladstone bag. Though locked, the bag was prised open sufficiently to reveal some bloodstained clothes and a knife, and the discovery was immediately reported to Scotland Yard.

Mahon was quickly apprehended. He said the bag had been used for carrying dog meat. The fact that the blood on the clothing in the bag was shown to be human left him with a good deal to explain. A tennis holdall with the initials E.B.K. was also found in the Gladstone bag. Mahon admitted that the initials stood for Emily Beilby Kaye, a young woman who was his mistress, and a sinister story began.

Mahon mentioned an old coastguard house on a lonely stretch of beach at the Crumbles, on the Sussex coast near Eastbourne. He had taken Emily Kaye there for the weekend on April 12. A quarrel had taken place and a struggle ensued during which he claimed that Emily fell and hit her head on the coal scuttle, fatally injuring herself.

Detective officers accompanied by Sir Bernard Spilsbury visited the house, and even the great pathologist was appalled by what he found there. Pieces of flesh and organs, many of which had been boiled, were discovered in a variety of containers — a hat box, a fibre trunk and a biscuit tin. A carpet was sodden with blood and blood-stained female clothing was strewn about. In the fireplace and elsewhere were ashes containing human bone splinters. In the kitchen there were saucepans and other receptacles containing unmistakable evidence of having been used for boiling human flesh. A rusty saw with bits of flesh on it also told its story.

The pathologist collected together the hundreds of human fragments and returned with them to St. Bartholomew's Hospital, London. In the post-mortem

BLOODSTAINED carpet from the Setty murder was cleaned at this cleaner's. Hume lived next door. Below: Exhibits are brought into the Old Bailey for the trial.

preparation room he began a painstaking reconstruction of the body to which they had once belonged. It was a feat of brilliance. He identified all the pieces as human and corresponding to a single adult female body. The head was never found. From bruises on a portion of one shoulder Spilsbury was able to show that a heavy blow had been struck before death.

"One of the foulest crimes"

He could not say exactly how Emily Kaye had died but knew enough to smash Mahon's lies. The cook's knife and saw were said by Mahon to have been bought after Emily Kaye was dead, but the proprietor of a Sussex ironmongery shop produced receipts showing that they had been bought on April 12 — the day Mahon travelled down to the bungalow. Mahon denied using the cook's knife to dismember the body, saying that instead he used an ordinary carving knife from the bungalow's kitchen. But Spilsbury unmasked this pretence, for the carving knife was not keen enough to cut through skin. The cook's knife, however, was designed to cut raw flesh.

Patrick Mahon was found guilty and hanged without lamentation on September 9, 1924. Spilsbury's remarkable care and skill in this case won wide admiration. The Director of Public Prosecutions referred to Mahon's killing of Emily Kaye and subsequent dismemberment of the body as ". . . one of the foulest crimes".

GUNSHOT

A criminal detective examining a fatal gunshot wound on a dead body may be able to determine from the entrance wound the type of weapon used and the range from which it was fired; the exit wound may indicate the direction of the shot.

FORENSIC ballistics is the study of guns and ammunition. It is a highly developed subject falling within the province of the firearms expert, though examination of gunshot wounds is part of the forensic pathologist's work. The starting point for an understanding of gunshot wounds is the weapons that cause them; firearms in crimes of violence can be divided into

PIONEER EXPERT on ballistics, Robert Churchill (below), pictured in 1927. His painstaking methods and encyclopaedic knowledge made him invaluable to police.

smooth-bore weapons and rifled weapons.

The smooth-bore class of weapon is characterized by the shot gun, the inside of the gun barrel being smooth throughout. Guns of this type are designed for sporting purposes and they fire a mass of tiny lead pellets or shot, accurate to a

Popperfoto/F. Watkinson

range of about 50 yards. Smooth-bore guns may have one or two long barrels which take hand-loaded cartridges, and the empty cases are retained in the gun after the shot has been fired.

The calibre of shot guns is usually expressed as the "bore"—the term "12-bore" is well known. This is the traditional method of expressing calibre and refers to the number of lead pellets exactly fitting the barrel which can be made from a pound of lead. It is common nowadays to give the calibre of all types of gun as the inside diameter of the barrel expressed either in decimals of an inch or in metric units; hence the 12-bore shot gun has a calibre of 0.729 inch.

Shot-gun cartridges consist of a cardboard cylinder about 2½ inches long with a rimmed brass base. In the centre of the base is a priming charge or detonator. At the top of the cartridge is a quantity of lead shot held in place with discs of cardboard. Separating the shot from the explosive powder at the bottom of the cartridge is a thick cardboard disc called the wad which drives the shot before it and

THE ONLY WAY to prove beyond doubt that a crime bullet was fired from a particular gun is to test fire the gun and compare the groove marks (right). Below: A Thompson sub-machine gun.

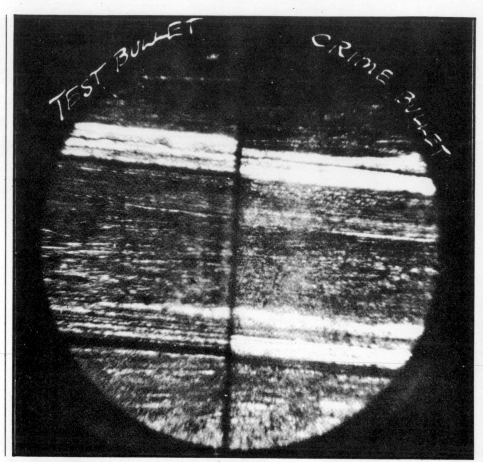

out of the gun's barrel when the weapon is fired. The principle of the firing action is the same for most guns. When the trigger is pulled a hammer snaps down on the detonator at the base of the cartridge; this in turn ignites the main explosive charge and expels the shot or bullet.

The shot leaves the gun as a solid mass at a velocity of about 1100 feet per second. Up to about 3 feet the effect is of a single shot, but beyond that the lead pellets spread out and the effect is of multiple shots. The cartridge wad leaves the gun with the lead pellets and is projected for several feet before falling to the ground. The end of the barrel is often restricted or "choked" in order to hold the shot together over longer distances.

Rifled weapons are distinguished by a

spiral grooving, or "rifling", on the inside of the barrel. This spins the bullet, making it more stable in flight and giving greater accuracy. Rifled weapons may be either long-barrelled rifles (2 to 3 feet), or short-barrelled pistols (1 to 12 inches). The long barrel of the rifle makes it accurate for ranges up to 3000 yards and the weapon has a high muzzle velocity of 1000 to 4000 feet per second; pistols with their short barrels and low muzzle velocity (600 to 1000 feet per second) are intended for shooting at close range and bullets carry only 400 to 600 yards.

Pistols form two classes—revolvers and automatics. The revolver is the classic six-shooter of cowboy fame. It has a revolving chamber which brings each cartridge into position after the previous

one has been fired. Spent cartridge cases remain in the chamber and usually have to be removed by hand; revolver chambers commonly hold five or six rounds of ammunition. The automatic is a self-loading pistol with ammunition stored in a magazine, usually in the butt. Each round is fed into the barrel by a spring mechanism and spent cartridges are ejected automatically from the weapon.

The calibre of rifled weapons is expressed as the internal diameter of the barrel in either inches or millimetres, the measurement being taken between the raised parts of the rifling which are known as "lands", and not between the grooves.

Ammunition for rifled weapons consists of a brass cartridge case filled with explosive powder and a solid metal bullet at its tip. Bullets are made of hardened lead or a lead core covered with cupro-nickel coated steel. The bullet is held in the end of the cartridge case by a grooved indentation known as a cannelure; the base of the cartridge has at its centre a detonator which ignites the explosive powder when the weapon is fired. All rifled weapon ammunition, except that for automatic pistols, has a rimmed base which retains the spent case in the firing chamber after the bullet has been fired. Spent rounds are then ejected manually. Automatic weapon ammunition is tapered at the base with a groove for the automatic ejector.

Bullets fired from rifled weapons spin at 2000 to 3000 revolutions a second, but over the first few yards of trajectory—distance varies with the weapon—their

ASTOUNDING in their variety, the very differences which exist in size and shape between types of bullet and shot have greatly assisted ballistics experts.

flight is slightly unstable; the end of the projectile wobbles before it picks up a smooth flight path. This phenomenon is known as "tailwag" and is of considerable importance in evaluating gunshot wounds. A bullet with "tailwag" does not strike its target cleanly.

There are three basic kinds of gunshot wounds distinguished by the proximity of the weapon causing them:

1. Contact (gun muzzle pressed against, or within an inch or two, of the body)
2. Close discharge (6 inches to 2 feet)
3. Distant discharge (over 2 or 3 feet).

Wounds are always considered from two points of view—the point of entry of the bullet and its exit. The entrance wound in particular may have special features which will assist the crime investigator in determining the range and type of weapon used; the exit wound examined in relation to the point of entry will also help to decide the direction of a shot. Differentiation between entry and exit wounds is

essential in judging between suicide and homicide.

Unlike bullet wounds inflicted by a rifled weapon, a shot gun discharge rarely produces an exit wound in the trunk of the body. Shot has little penetrating power and is easily arrested by tough tissue, especially bone, but contact wounds in the head or mouth, such as those met with in the suicidal use of a shot gun, result in massive destruction.

Where a shot gun is discharged in contact with the body (or within a few inches) the shot does not scatter but enters as a solid mass. The hot gases and flame emitted from the gun's muzzle will tear the tissues and there will be evidence of burning on the skin. Powder particles are likely to be forced into the skin giving rise to a tattoo effect; the wad may also be forced into the wound and if this is the case, its extraction may prove a useful guide to the type of cartridge used. A contact wound in the trunk will make a round hole with a

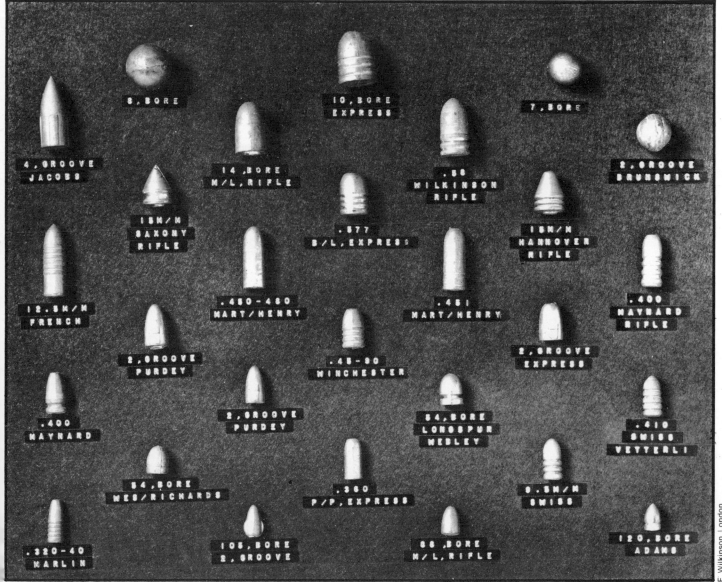

narrow rim of soot blackening. Bruising near the wound is often caused by the recoil of the gun.

At close range, from 1 to 3 feet, a more or less irregular wound about 1½ to 2 inches in diameter will be produced. There will be evidence of scorching and tattooing, also singeing of hair by flame, unless the weapon was fired through the clothing. Beyond a range of 3 feet, the shot begins to spread out and at 4 feet the wound will appear as a central hole with small perforations around it. There will be no powder deposits visible to the naked eye although a swab taken from around the wound may reveal traces. The wad is often found in such a wound.

At ranges over 4 feet the shot continues to spread out and produces a mass of small perforations with no central wound. An approximation of the range can be obtained by measuring in inches the diameter of the wound (including the outermost perforations), subtracting one, thus arriving at the range in yards. Thus a wound of 9 inches diameter indicates that it was inflicted by a weapon fired from about 8 yards: the exact range depends on the choke of the weapon and only test firing gives an accurate answer.

Bullet wounds are produced by projectiles fired from a rifled weapon and are the same for revolver and automatic. Entry wounds are generally clean, round holes slightly smaller than the bullets

which caused them; as the bullet travels through the body it produces a shock wave which damages the tissues around its path. This is known as "tissue quake". The bullet will be slowed by its passage through the body and its exit will leave an irregular hole. If the bullet exits nose-on, the wound will be smaller than the entry, but if it leaves the body at an irregular angle, or takes pieces of bone with it, the exit wound will be ragged. Should the bullet meet a bone and be deflected inside the body, its change of direction may cause considerable internal damage, and the bullet may even fragment, again causing severe injury.

Contact wounding with the muzzle pressed against the skin will produce not a round entry but a star-shaped hole with lacerated edges. If there is underlying bone—the skull for example—gases produced by the explosion of the cartridge may enter with the bullet and be forced back through the skin causing laceration. The tissue at the margin of the wound may contain soot and powder particles and show a degree of burning, and the skin will be tattooed. At close range, exit

THE ANSWER to many of crime's most important questions is to be found by patient research in the laboratory. The expert here is using a comparison microscope—an essential forensic tool used in matching and identifying bullets.

wounds are generally smaller than entries, but this is reversed at increased range.

At close range, between 6 inches and 2 feet, a different effect is noted. The wound is more or less circular and corresponds to the size of the bullet. Discharge gases do not enter the wound and tattooing may be absent. Injuries of this kind have been confused with penetrating stab wounds. If the bullet was "tailwagging", the entry would not be as clean as for a nose-on hit.

Guns fired at ranges over 2 feet are too distant to leave traces of the explosion at the wound site. The entry will conform to the size of the bullet, appearing as a round hole with an abraded margin. The edge of the wound will also exhibit a ring of grease wiped from the spinning surface of the bullet as it enters the body. The exit wound at distant ranges will be the same as the entry, and in some cases the only point of differentiation will be the grease or "soiling" ring around the entry wound. If the bullet has been deflected in the body, the point of exit may be lacerated, and may be misinterpreted as being caused by a blunt instrument.

The characteristics of entry remain virtually the same at distances over 2 feet, and it is therefore not possible to tell at what range a distant shot was fired. Evidence of direction may be obtained where a bullet has passed through bone, as the exit side is bevelled as a result of the destructive force of the impact.

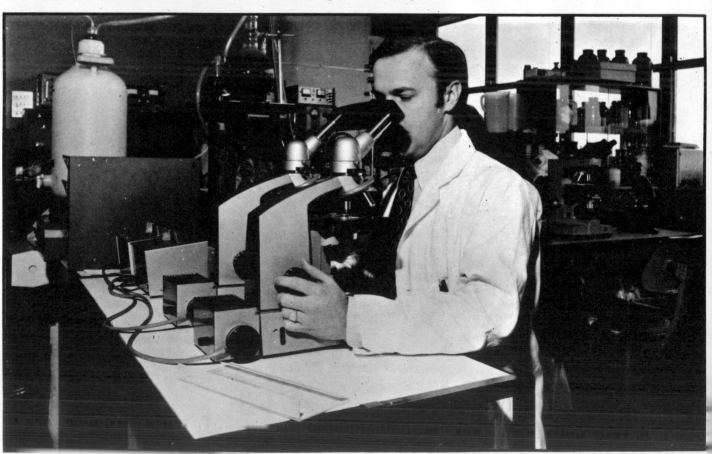

THE BEGINNINGS

A criminal may be caught red-handed, or simply give himself up. He may be ratted on by an informer, or spotted by a witness. Or he might be trapped by the resourcefulness of those whose mission is to beat crime. The battle against crime is as old as criminal activity . . . as old as man. But its weapons are ever-changing.

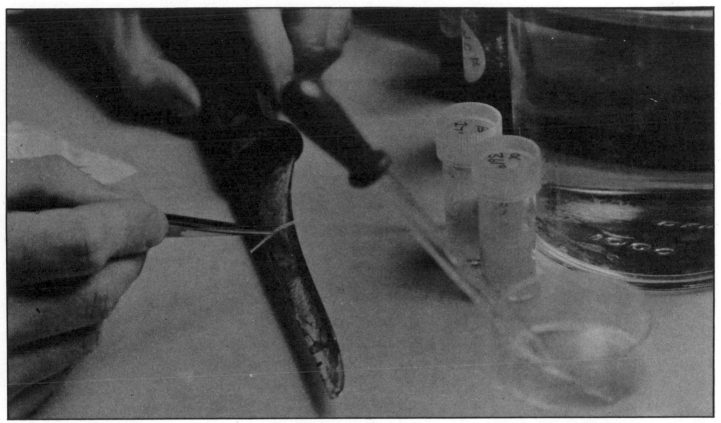

One of the most effective weapons in society's battle against crime is science. With the pace of advance in modern science, the battle becomes increasingly sophisticated, but the idea is hardly a new one. Indeed, it goes back to the days of the Old Testament. It was in 930 B.C., when Solomon, the third king of Israel, was confronted with the two women who had just had babies. One baby had died, its mother had secretly changed it for the live one (while the second mother slept), and Solomon had to decide which of the two shouting women was the live one's mother. "Bring me a sword!" he said. "Cut the living child in two; give half to one, half to the other." The women's demeanour instantly decided which was the true mother and the surviving baby was spared. There is reason to believe that the basis

BLOOD-TESTING is becoming an increasingly important area of forensic science. A key advance was the development of methods to test blood that has been dry for some time.

of the story is much older than Solomon or Israel, but it can be taken as marking the arrival in the courts, whenever it was, of forensic science in the form of experimental psychology. Today it would be called forensic psychiatry and it would all be done by doctors.

At a more practical level, the early development of forensic science was less dramatic. It was many centuries before this method of crime-fighting gained pace.

In 1786 a Scottish crofter and his wife came home to their cottage after a day in

the fields and found their teenage daughter murdered. Suspicion fell upon a young man named Richardson; but for some time there was no evidence on which he could be arrested. Even when there was judged to be enough, he promptly produced what seemed to be a perfect alibi. Then, rather belatedly it must seem today, the police took plaster-casts of some footprints near the cottage, and found that the pattern of the hobnails was exactly the same as that on Richardson's boots. Then further and similar "forensic" evidence began to accumulate. Stains on the stockings he had worn on the day of the murder were found to be bloodstains (though they could not, in those days, be identified as belonging to any particular blood-group). Mud and sand on the stockings *could*, however, be

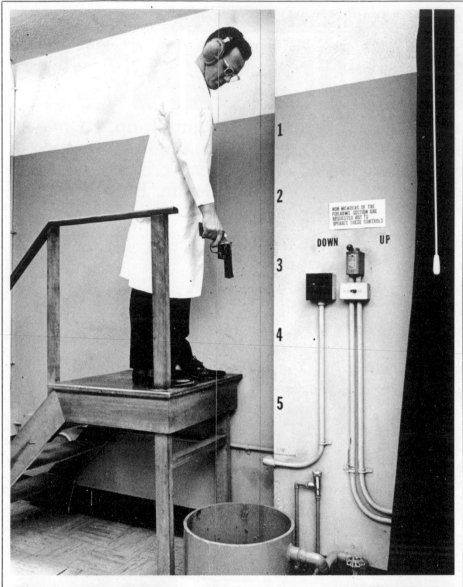

proved to be mud and sand from the cottage garden. It was largely on this evidence that Richardson was convicted at Dumfries in 1787.

The Richardson case thus offers all the classic features of a prosecution founded on forensic science: identification of the suspect (by footprints), identification of the clues (the blood and, more exactly, the sand and the mud), and association of all the clues with the man Richardson.

But that, in 1787, was about the extent of what could be called forensic science, and so it officially remained for the next 100 years—though outstanding members of the "Bow Street Runners" and the original "Peelers"—so called after Sir Robert Peel, the Home Secretary, who, in the 1820's, created the London police—who were given extraordinary personal licence and developed some ingenious stratagems of their own, were perhaps serving the interests of science without knowing it.

Man-measurement

In 1879 Alphonse Bertillon, of the French Department of Criminal Police, began to develop a system of classified "anthropometry"—which simply means man-measurement. It was not Bertillon's invention, but he was the first to persevere with it, in the face of universal ridicule, and finally gain reluctant official approval. No two people have the same measurements *in combination*: the circumference of the head and chest, the length of the ears, nose, fingers, arms, legs, feet and so on. List all these against one criminal's name, argued Bertillon, and you can always identify him whatever he does about his name, his beard, his hair, his walk, his clothing.

And Bertillon was right. His system was slow and laborious but it was just about infallible. If you recorded the measurements of 14 parts of a man's body, the odds against any other man's having the same combination of measurements were 286,435,456 to one. Nevertheless for six years he was derided as a crank (which in some ways he was), rebuked for wasting his time, and ordered by successive Prefects of Police under whom he served to stop romancing and get on with his clerical duties.

Meanwhile, however, the science of identification by fingerprinting—which was probably of great antiquity—had been revived, developed and applied to criminology by an official in the Indian Civil Service named William Herschel. Both in Bengal and in England he had to meet exactly the same kind of ridicule, fight the same kind of battles, as Bertillon was doing. It was soon established, of course, that the odds against two men having identical fingerprints ran into meaningless billions, that in fact, there

BALLISTICS is one of the most sophisticated areas of forensic science. "Whose gun fired the bullet?" may be solved by microscopically matching sections from a bullet found at the scene of the crime with a test fired specimen

existed no such possibility. But unlike Bertillon, Herschel allowed himself to be discouraged by official hostility or stupidity, and fell back on the use of fingerprints for his own administrative purposes—for example, getting the thumbprint "signatures" of Indian labourers unable to write when drawing their pay. He had been doing it for 20 years before he made his futile attempt to interest the authorities.

These two systems, anthropometry and fingerprinting, became almost battle slogans. Anthropometry had reached the United States, which had (and still has) about 40,000 separate police forces. Between them they spent so much money installing the measuring apparatus, the filing systems and the clerks that the usual "vested interest" barrier to further progress was quickly established. It is worth remembering that one of the most scornful critics of fingerprint identification was Bertillon himself; and that he allowed himself to believe, at the time of the Dreyfus case in France, that he was a handwriting expert as well as an anthropometrist. (He "identified" Dreyfus's handwriting, quite wrongly, and stuck to his confident and stupid opinion even when it was proved, five years later—while Dreyfus was on Devil's island—that he was wrong and Dreyfus innocent.) From 1880 onwards a Scottish medical missionary in Japan, Henry Faulds, was urging the infallibility of fingerprints for identifying the absent criminal who had left his prints at the scene of his crime. And Sir Francis Galton, the illustrious founder of the science of eugenics, or 'fine' breeding, began to urge upon the Home Office in 1894 that fingerprinting was an exact science of identification: even in 1892 he had calculated that the chances against error were 64,000,000,000 to one.

Sherlock Holmes

It was a Buenos Aires police officer, Juan Vucetich (born in what we now call Yugoslavia) who finally convinced world criminologists of every school—and they are a mutually critical lot—about the great superiority of fingerprints, in convenience and simplicity and above all in speed of operation. And it was Vucetich whose initiative and energy hastened the inevitable change, expensive as it was for everyone. Anthropometry had been used in England only from 1894 until 1900.

And it was in the 20th century that other forms of forensic science came into their own—encouraged, to an appreciable extent, by the ingenuity of the Sherlock Holmes stories and by Conan Doyle's friendly contacts with senior police officers. Not enough acknowledgment has ever been accorded to the effect of the imaginative detective fiction of that period on the climate of public opinion, and the

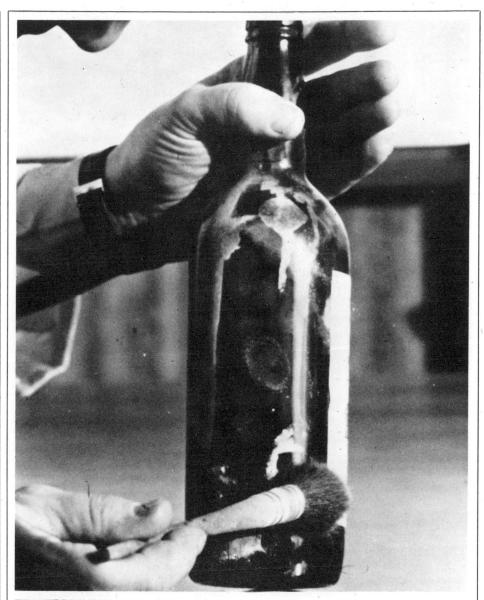

FINGERPRINTING was pioneered in the 19th century. A barely-visible print can be "developed" with the use of a powder, a brush and a trained hand (above). Just as no fingerprints are alike, so no two typewriters ever produce quite the same result when challenged by the microscope (right). When the written word has been obscured, defacing marks may sometimes be removed by infra-red photography (below).

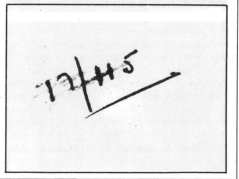

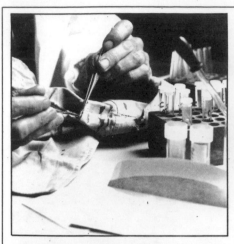

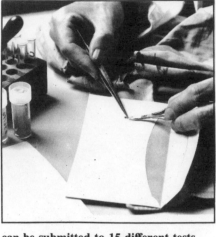

BLOOD-GROUPING techniques are becoming more and more sophisticated. Today the tiniest bloodstain can be virtually conclusive. Such a sample

can be submitted to 15 different tests. This way, the odds against an incorrect identification are reduced to one in a hundred, or even less.

THE TESTS all use varying systems by which blood can be grouped. Anyone's blood can be examined in this way, and rarely would the same combination of

results be produced. The tests are carried out by activating the blood with a re-agent substance. The reaction which takes place helps to establish its characteristics.

creation of an ideal sleuth beside whom the real-life policeman could be made to seem ineffectual—sometimes even in his own eyes. The Bordet blood test could already distinguish animal from human blood: today we can prove that human blood belongs to a group of individuals, though not (yet) that it is the blood of anyone in particular.

Spectacular advances

In America the famous Crime Detection Laboratory in the Northwestern University at Chicago has advanced the boundaries of forensic science at a speed that is almost spectacular. It is still the model for most police and university crime laboratories, and the man who put it on the map was Dr. Calvin H. Goddard, universally known for his work on the linking of firearms and bullets. But of almost equal importance in that story is the name of Charles E. Waite of the New York State Prosecutor's Office—a

man who "solved crimes as a hobby" and became involved, in 1916, in the investigation of a gun murder in Orleans County, New York. It was the case of Charles E. Stielow, a farm labourer accused of shooting the farmer and his housekeeper. It was one of those American cliff-hangers in which the convicted man is actually strapped in the electric chair when the reprieve comes through. Stielow's case is known to criminologists throughout the world as the one which established the new science of forensic ballistics, by which any bullet, so long as it is not seriously distorted by impact, can be proved to have come from a particular gun. Waite proved by microphotography that the murder bullets could never have been fired from Stielow's revolver. In doing so he established not only forensic ballistics but also the probability that many a man, in that gun-ridden land, had been executed for a crime he did not commit. It wasn't long before ballistic experts were able to

prove, not merely that a bullet could *not* have been fired from gun No. 1, but that a bullet could *only* have been fired from gun No. 2.

There are also peculiarities of individual typewriters—faults in spacing, type alignments, changes in type face through wear and tear. No two machines are alike. Similarly it has long been common knowledge and experience that no two people have identical *handwriting*. This leaves us a long way from being able to prove that one man must have written two separate documents or signatures; and yet this is what handwriting experts are sometimes expected (and will sometimes even profess) to be able to "prove". Handwriting experts, in their capacity to establish the falsity or even the genuineness of "questioned documents", are often witnesses of great value; but they have limitations which the genuine experts willingly recognise, while the quacks and charlatans (e.g. those who read "character" and fortunes) recognise none.

Contradictory evidence

The trouble about expert witnesses, even scientific ones, is that they have so often been able to discredit the name of "science" by giving evidence in total opposition to each other. This gave juries —and the general public—the feeling that the best forensic science was available to the highest bidder, whether prosecution or defence; and because the prosecutor is usually the State, it has the most money. The truth is that evidence which is genuinely scientific, *exactly* provable, cannot be refuted by science itself. In Britain, before the passing of the Road Safety Act 1967 and the introduction of breathalysers and blood-alcohol tests, eminent physicians often gave evidence flatly contradicting each other about a motorist's fitness to drive. Not any more. They can't argue with a blood-alcohol reading unless they can prove (or believe they can) that it was rigged.

Thus the many forms which murder takes, the many motives behind it, have generally nourished the development of forensic science: jealousy, greed, sexual excitement, fear, misery, compassion, superstition, political idealism, bravado. Each of them is likely to involve methods of aggression, and of concealment, which the scientific investigator is now more and more likely to discover or defeat. From 1910, when Hawley Harvey Crippen was arrested in mid-Atlantic as a result of a police radio message—the very first use of wireless telegraphy in a criminal case— until the modern use of microscopy, tape-recorded "voice-prints", the analysis of poisons, etc., the swift progress of modern technology has gone on increasing the greatest of all deterrents to murder: the growing certainty of detection.

BLOODSTAINS

When police have a strong suspect in a murder case, the temptation is to leave it at that, to close down the search for a killer. But a few blood samples submitted to tests in the forensic laboratory can change the entire case!

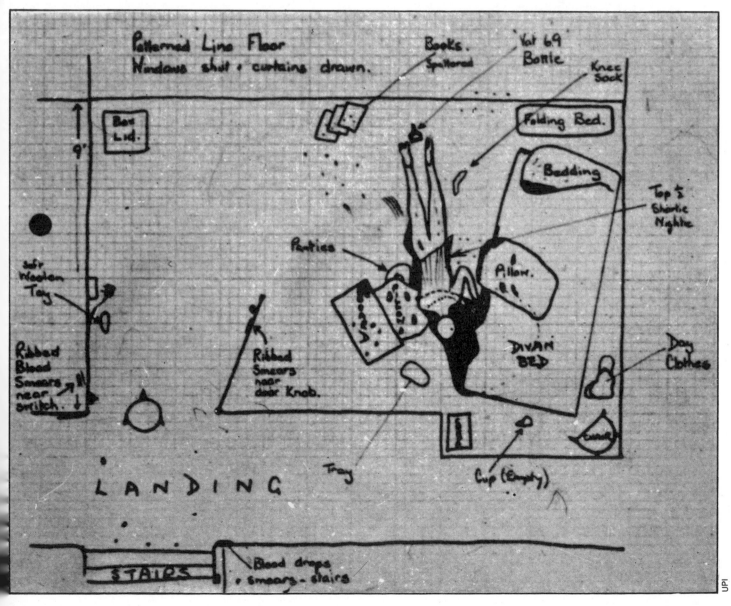

GOOD blood cannot lie, they say. Nor can bad. As the distinguished forensic expert Alistair R. Brownlie (Solicitor Supreme Courts, Edinburgh, Scotland) put it to Britain's Forensic Science Society: "Since Cain slew Abel, spilt blood has borne its mute testimony in crimes of violence. Stains of blood and body fluids still play an important part in crime *detection*, a lesser but increasing part in the proof of *guilt* . . ." And not only the nature and grouping of stains, but their position at the scene of the crime can be revealing and is now recognized as a vital piece of evidence in itself.

On June 15, 1965, a forensic episode in which a victim's good blood cleared a suspect occurred in a small Norwegian community in the village of East Hartland, in the Connecticut tobacco country, Litchfield County, U.S.A. On that day, book-keeper Arnfin Thompsen returned home to find his wife lying dead. "Her face and head were crushed, the jaw appeared to be broken, the left temple was smashed in. Her face was heavily caked with blood.

"It looked like she had been murdered in the kitchen and dragged through onto the porch. On the kitchen floor there was a big pool of blood, and then there was a single path of blood—maybe ten or twelve inches wide—like something had been dragged from the kitchen out . . . In a corner of the dining area the ironing board stood in the place where Dottie usually ironed; on it a partially-pressed white shirt, spattered with blood. The trail of blood angled past it to the sliding glass doors . . ."

Brown bloodstain

A bloody scene, indeed. The prime suspect was Dottie's mother-in-law who shared their white-board and grey-brick cottage—Agnes Thompsen, a religious fanatic with a failing mind, who had spent ten months in the Connecticut Valley Hospital for the mentally ill. Her opening words to the detectives were: "Is she dead yet?" Then police chief Captain O'Brien found a bloodstained dress in the clothes dryer in Dorothy Thompsen's kitchen.

"Teams of men combed the house," reported Mildred Savage in her classic book on the case. "They emptied the contents of wastebaskets and garbage pails into plastic bags. They probed into plumbing fixtures and took water from sink traps" (where blood had been detected) "and then took the traps themselves . . . Dr. Abraham Stolman, chief toxicologist for the state of Connecticut, arrived to do on-the-spot testing . . ."

During the probe, a brown bloodstain was found on a step landing up to Agnes Thompsen's apartment. Some attempt had been made to sand or scrub it clean. So

the whole stair was taken to the forensic laboratory. There, in an ordinary test by routine methods of serology, the prime suspect was eliminated. It was almost certainly her own blood and could not have been that of the murder victim since the two women had different blood groups. Later a neighbour of the Thompsens was sent to Connecticut State Jail for the crime and released after serving only eight months.

Petty theft

Blood is not the only body product which can be of use to the forensic blood grouper. The word serology comes from the ancient Sanskrit *sara*, meaning "to flow". Today it is known that every fluid which flows in the human body can be identified: sometimes to prove the guilt of a suspected person, but also very often to protect the innocent.

A different sort of innocent victim was discovered in the English Midlands, when a police officer reported the case of a young child thought to have been attacked and raped in bed. Specimens were rushed to the forensic laboratory—where a simple test startled the serologists. The "bloodstains" were those of a piece of plum tart the child had stolen from the kitchen. Her distress was due solely to the fear of the police officer calling and discovering her petty theft.

Bloodstains, types, and grades usually remain constant, but sometimes they do not. One problem concerning antigens —substances introduced into the blood to stimulate production of health-protecting antibodies, as in blood plasma— is that in recent years scientists have realized that the red cells can actually acquire an antigen of the B-type. This is caused by certain bacteria (proteus and clostridium are examples) which produce substances similar to A, B, and other blood-group substances, and thus may result in false grouping.

Leading in this research is the Department of Haematology and Forensic Medicine of Britain's London Hospital Medical College, with a team comprising G. C. Jenkins, J. Brown, P. J. Lincoln, and B. E. Dodd. They were inspired by the serologist Pierre Moureau who, in 1963, was called in to examine the body of a child which had been in water for some time.

The police had reason to suspect the mother. But tests showed that she had Group-O blood, while Moureau's absorption-inhibition tests at first showed the presence of A and B antigens in the dead child. An O-group mother, of course, cannot have an AB-group child.

Then Moureau repeated his tests. Gastric mucin at autopsy (active for Group-A only) and cultures of blood showing bacteria and a B-activity led to the dis-

covery that the B-antigen had been acquired . . . In layman's terms, the blood group had changed after death.

In their research in the 1970's, the London Hospital Medical College team was later asked to solve a query about the dismembered body of a woman found in the river Thames, London.

"The first part to be recovered," the team reported, "was the thoracic region, and from this it was possible to obtain a limited quantity of intact red cells, which were found to be Group-O Rh positive. From the pelvis, which remained in the water for a longer period, no red cells were recovered, but muscle tissue gave reactions of Group-B. The blood groups, therefore, did not support the conclusion that the (previously discovered) thorax and the (later found) pelvis were from one and the same individual.

Blood groups

"However, the shape of the cut surfaces proved beyond a shadow of doubt that the two parts belonged to each other, and this raised the suspicion that the B reaction might be of bacteriological origin. Further work confirmed this . . ."

Essentially, forensic serology is based upon facts known vaguely since the dawn of time, and with much more certainty since in 1628 the English physician William Harvey discovered the circulation of blood. Christopher Wren is said to have experimented with transfusion, and in his diary Samuel Pepys recorded that a donor was paid a sum of 20 shillings (about $500 in 1974 money), as well as speculating what would happen "were the blood of a Quaker to be let into an Archbishop". For centuries the English aristocracy were genuinely believed to be born with blue blood, and boasts such as "the blood of an Englishman" were taken seriously.

Then, in 1930, the Viennese doctor Karl Landsteiner received a Nobel Prize award for his research into serology. He had announced to the scientific world that all human blood can be grouped into four main types. His work stimulated other biologists. Today for convenience the groups are known as O, A, B, and AB.

Independent system

Landsteiner, in conjunction with Levine, was able to set up an entirely independent system of M and N groups. In 1940 he and his colleague Dr. Wiener experimented with animal blood, injecting into rabbits and guinea pigs the blood of an Indian rhesus monkey. A hitherto undetected antigen was discovered, and for convenience this was given the title Rhesus (Rh). It was observed that the animals produced an anti-Rhesus antibody which also agglutinated human cells and by which the human population could be

GROUPING SERA		
Anti – A	**Anti – B**	**Anti –AB**

	Anti – A	Anti – B	Anti –AB
Group O Cells	●	●	●
Group A Cells	✦	○	✦
Group B Cells	●	✦	✦
Group AB Cells	✦	✦	✦

divided into two phenotypes, Rh positive and Rh negative.

In criminology scientists do concern themselves with medical matters such as agglutination, but primarily the vital question involves whether or not a sample *is* blood. A minute sample in the laboratory is extracted from the stained material kept in a saline solution, and a tiny drop of the extract is mixed with a solution containing phenolphthalein and potassium hydroxide, powdered zinc and hydrogen peroxide. If this test is negative (no change), the sample cannot be blood. If the mixture shows a clear pink colour, it *is* blood.

Blood test

Biologists sometimes use a different test, in which glacial acid is added to a solution of hydrogen peroxide and benzidine—a drop of this being added to the test sample, which immediately turns a deep blue if there is blood present. The next step is to use an antiserum prepared in an animal which will react specifically with human blood, thus demonstrating whether the sample is of human origin.

"The blood of an Englishman" is not a subject over which forensic serologists wax racialist, because crime is international. The frequencies of the various genes within different blood group systems may, however, vary from race to race and could possibly provide important evidence. Blood group systems in general have acquired names such as Kidd, Duffy and Kell after the patients in whom the antibodies were first discovered, and all of them, of course, allow scientists to narrow down the field.

Summarizing all the international work of forensic serologists, the late Dr. F. I. N. Dunsford, Ph.D., of Britain's National Blood Transfusion Service,

BASIC to blood grouping are the four main types. The grid (above) shows in diagram form how scientists can test for any of these groups with full certainty.

stressed that, in crime detection, the "usefulness" of a blood group system is the measure of its efficiency in differentiating the red cells of one person from those of another.

From his tests, for example, it is known that the Rhesus antigen V is present in fewer than 0.5 per cent of white people, but present in 40 per cent of West African Negroes. The chromosomes (the rod-like structures which show as pairs in every developed cell) known as cDe are also more common among Negroes than whites.

The Duffy phenotype Fy is always completely absent from whites, but present in 90 per cent of West Africans. Kell antigen is virtually confined to white races, while Diego positives are virtually absent from whites, yet present in Caribe Indians, Japanese, and Chinese.

At the extreme of the blood groups is a certain LU (a−b−) factor, which many serologists believe to be so rare that an estimated total of only eight people among the world's 3200-million-plus can have it. One of the eight, a Sheffield (England) woman, had three pints of the rare blood flown to her in a British hospital from an American donor.

However, researchers may be only on the threshold of discoveries in investigation of body fluids. It is now nearly 75 years since serologists put blood samples under the microscope and found the elements which are freely suspended in the plasma—essentially the erythrocytes (red corpuscles), leucocytes (white corpuscles) and the blood platelets (egg-shaped and circular bodies suspended in

the straw-plasma more commonly known as the "serum").

But there is much more to serology than that: in many instances it is now possible to determine sex from examination of the leucocytes. This was demonstrated in Britain in a forensically interesting case of alleged sexual attack. The girl and the suspect volunteered for blood-group tests, when it was found that both people had the same blood group. A specimen for the test came from a mackintosh lining, on which it was alleged the man had wiped his bloodstained penis.

The serologist engaged in the examination knew that when the white cells of female blood are inspected under the microscope, they show minute, drum-stick-shaped marks.

Expert evidence

Although the girl's blood was the same group as that of the suspect, the stain from the mackintosh produced cells of feminine identification. Expert evidence on this was unsuccessfully challenged in court; it was obvious the male attacker had been in contact with female blood.

While it should be remembered that it is never possible to say "this bloodstain originated from this person", nevertheless it may be possible to conclude that "this bloodstain *cannot* have originated from that person". A defence case may depend on this crucial fact. One striking example came to light early in September 1961, when a 24-year-old army private at Aldershot was cleared of sexual attack on a 38-year-old mother walking on a local racecourse.

"I can't remember exactly what happened," the woman said to the police. "He jumped on me and got hold of my shoulders. I screamed as hard as I could . . . Then somehow I found I was at the bottom of a steep bank, and my little daughter was crying. The man had pulled off my blouse, but I gave up the struggle because he twice threatened to hurt my child . . ."

False identification

The doctor who examined the woman later confirmed there had been an attack. A soldier was picked out at an identification parade, and charged with rape. Bryan Culliford, from the New Scotland Yard Laboratory, demonstrated that tests proved the suspect was in Group-B, while the stains on the unfortunate woman were Group-A. "We find there is no case to answer," announced the chairman of the court.

In her distressed state, the woman had picked out the wrong man at the identification parade. But for serology and its forensic application an innocent man could have been sent to jail.

THE FATHER OF THE FINGERPRINT

Juan Vucetich, working in La Plata at the turn of the century, developed a fingerprint system which was used with success in his lifetime.

FINGERPRINTS meant nothing to John Vucetich when he was a young man, for though he was aware, like many literate Europeans, of Dr. Henry Faulds' famous letters to *Nature* in which he advocated the tracing of criminals through fingerprints, Vucetich, then, was only vaguely interested.

Vucetich was a Croat, born on an island off the coast of Dalmatia in 1858. The place was called Lesina, about 20 miles south of Spalato—now Split—which was then part of the Austro-Hungarian Empire, and because of its separation from the mainland a backwater largely untouched by the turmoil in the Balkans during Vucetich's youth.

His background was middle-class, his education sound. At an early age he

DEFEATED, embittered, banished . . . but he was wrong to fear that he would be forgotten. Criminologists the world over honour the name of Juan Vucetich.

learned to keep his head, for the Croats were—and are—an intensely proud and independent people, unwilling subjects of Austrian rule, a people dwelling uneasily in Dalmatian towns where Italian language and thought tended to be dominant, while under rigid Austrian control. Vucetich was a good scholar, with a knack for acquiring languages, and attended a university school in Spalato in his late teens.

Jack the Ripper

The police system in Lesina was modest

and not called upon to deal with more than the general run of rural sins; it jogged along without even the rudimentary knowledge of police science which then existed on the mainland of Europe, but Vucetich, who became a civil servant in police employ, acquired some knowledge of the profession that was to be his in the future. His job was not one for which he had any liking, but it was a living.

Like many of his fiercely nationalistic compatriots, Vucetich was not happy under the heavy-handed paternalism of Austrian rule, presided over by an emperor who was as stodgy and as conservatively reactionary in the eyes of the young people as was Victoria in Britain. John Vucetich found the weight of the ruling house, and the ideas which seeped

96

down from it, too much for him. In 1884 he emigrated to the Americas, but chose Argentina as more appealing to him than the United States. His final destination was La Plata, where he had a relative, and in his 26th year he joined the provincial police. He took to Argentinian life with all the great enthusiasm that was natural to him, even to changing his christian name to the Spanish "Juan".

With a natural bent for mathematics, a considerable knowledge of theoretic police work and forensic science such as it was, Juan Vucetich's progress was rapid; his Croat forthrightness, his hard-headed ability, and his enormous energy drove him rapidly ahead of his more casual Spanish-American colleagues.

By 1891 Vucetich was head of the Statistical Bureau of the police, where he worked quietly, reading of Britain's excitements of the "Jack the Ripper" case and the French jubilation about the work of the great Alphonse Bertillon. As a result of Bertillon's successes, Vucetich was ordered to set up an Identification Bureau on the Bertillon principle, which was, very broadly, a system of measurements of the adult human body by which identity could be proved. The Chief of La Plata's police, Nuñez, presented Vucetich with various publications intended to guide him in forming the new Bureau.

As an afterthought he added a French publication of that year, the *Revue Scienifique*, containing an article by a Henri de Varigny on the work of Francis Galton, the English scientist and criminologist, who, along with Sir Edward Henry, set up the "Galton-Henry" fingerprint system.

Vucetich, the shrewd mathematician, was not overwhelmed by *bertillonage*. He distrusted a system of measurements which, he was to argue, could depend to some extent on the abilities of the technician concerned. But he was under orders to create a system of anthropometry, as the Bertillon method was named, and he put it in hand. La Plata police headquarters acquired its own Bertillon department, headed by a chief who kept his views to himself.

State of hysteria

What actually set his imagination on fire was the fingerprint system or, as it was known, dactyloscopy. Vucetich realized the value of the system. He acquired such elementary material as was available; he studied the prints of the living and, in the local mortuary, of the dead. He recalled Faulds' communications to *Nature* and learned about Sir William Herschel, of the Indian Civil Service, who had taken his own hand impressions at intervals of 28 years, qualifying the permanence of the lines. By the next year, 1892, Vucetich had, in his own time and with his own money,

quietly worked out a fingerprint system which, though he did not know it, roughly followed the lines thought out by Galton.

Vucetich itemized four basic types of prints: 1, arches; 2, those with a triangle on the right side; 3, with a triangle on the left side and, 4, on both sides. He used the first four letters of the alphabet to qualify his four categories in referring to the thumbs, and numbers for the fingers. This enabled him to use a simple formula which might begin, for example, with a letter B for a thumb—triangle on the right—followed by numbers indicating the marks on four fingers such as 2—also triangle on the right—for the first finger with the next fingers listed accordingly.

An imaginary formula for both hands could be expressed thus: B2131/D2213, which permitted immediate classification. This was capable of enormous variations since there were four classifications for each finger which meant something like a good million possible combinations.

Exact classification was easy with a simple linked filing system which enabled new prints to be checked quickly with the files. Obviously sub-classifications would be needed with large expansion, but this Vucetich was to anticipate by counting so many papillary lines over an area of given measurement. This method foresaw something that, in later years, the great Dr. Edmond Locard of France was to use when he devised poroscopy, the system of counting the number of pore orifices, sweat gland mouths, over a given space in a fingerprint.

Juan Vucetich managed to interest one or two of his colleagues, among them Inspector Carlos Alvarez, of La Plata Headquarters. It was a form of bread upon the waters which was to return tenfold, for though Vucetich's superiors were quite unimpressed by his spare-time work on fingerprints he was suddenly and impressively vindicated.

In Necochea, a small seaside town some 200 miles south of La Plata, a tragedy happened. On a hot summer night an attractive 25-year-old woman, a casual worker named Francisca Rohas, summoned her nearest neighbour and, in a state of hysteria, explained that her two illegitimate children had been brutally murdered. They were found, a boy of five and a girl of four, in bed with their heads smashed in.

Rohas accused a man named Velasquez, a labourer on a nearby *estancia*, of the crime; he was known to be in love with her, but also known to be quite devoted to the children. Rohas stated she had seen him rushing from her hut when she came home, immediately before she found the children.

The police did not worry much about examining the scene of the crime, but cross-examined Rohas, who admitted that

Velasquez was madly in love with her but that she loved another man. On her evidence Velasquez, a pleasant, if somewhat simple, man, was arrested, and admitted his devotion to Rohas and the children. This the police would not accept, treating the unlucky suspect with great brutality, thrashing him to extract a confession and, when this failed, binding him to the bodies of the children to force the truth out of him. Other melodramatic methods were tried when he said nothing, and even Rohas was subjected to tricks in case she were the guilty one.

In the end help was sought from La Plata; Inspector Alvarez was sent and achieved results in record time. First, he found that Velasquez had an unbreakable and provable alibi for the whole period of the murders—he had not mentioned it "because nobody asked" him!—and then Alvarez did what nobody else had bothered to do; he examined the scene of the crime with care.

Shop-keeper murder

In his search he found a bloody thumb-print on the hut door. This he cut out and took with him to the local police station, had Rohas brought in and, with an ink pad, took impressions of both her thumbs. Even with his elementary knowledge, Alvarez was able to show clearly that the bloody print came from her right thumb.

Under questioning she confessed, admitting that her secret lover wanted her but not the children; she had battered them to death and put the blame on Velasquez. The case became a police and a press sensation; Vucetich's name, and his personal work on fingerprints, were quickly known all over South America. Then, soon after this, a man was accused of murdering a shop-keeper in La Plata itself, and the police proved his guilt when they found his prints on the shop counter.

Juan Vucetich and his system were on the way up. He paid for the printing of a book on his work, and wrote study after study for his superiors to show how fingerprints proved case after case with which he had worked, but that *bertillonage* was not nearly so successful. Despite this, Vucetich's progress was impeded by his superiors. Then in 1894, under Captain Lozano, a new and enlightened Chief of Police, the whole province of Buenos Aires adopted the Vucetich system.

Argentina thus became the first country in the world to adopt fingerprinting as a method of police identification. At a South American scientific congress Vucetich explained his methods and criticized the Bertillon system, for which Bertillon never forgave him.

As the years went by he was to see country after country in South America adopt his system; experts today suggest that if universal fingerprinting

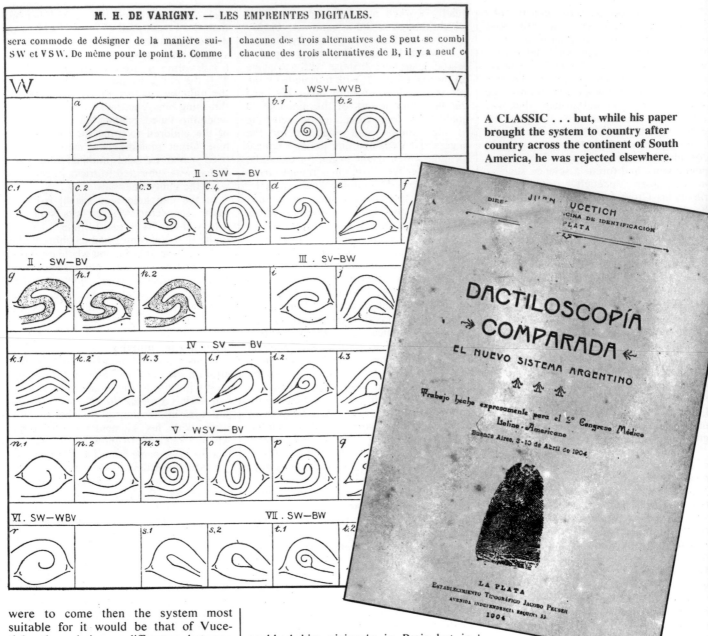

sera commode de désigner de la manière sui- | chacune des trois alternatives de S peut se combi
SW et VSW. De même pour le point B. Comme | chacune des trois alternatives de B, il y a neuf c

W   I . WSV—WVB   V

II . SW — BV

II . SW—BV   III . SV—BW

IV . SV — BV

V . WSV — BV

VI . SW—WBV   VII . SW—BW

A CLASSIC . . . but, while his paper brought the system to country after country across the continent of South America, he was rejected elsewhere.

were to come then the system most suitable for it would be that of Vucetich, there being a difference between the Henry (British) system and that of Vucetich, and the variations on both systems used in other lands.

But Juan Vucetich's fame was confined to his continent, for though western European ideas reached Argentina, that part of the world was quite uninterested in the Argentine, and Europeans tended to ignore the Vucetich system. His classic *Dactiliscopía Comparada*, published in La Plata in 1894, received no attention because it was in Spanish.

Viciously snubbed

Nevertheless, Vucetich's views on *bertillonage* had not gone unnoticed, and when he managed to convert his police pension into an immediate lump sum, he achieved a great ambition by setting out to travel the world, studying fingerprint systems, and meeting policemen. Bertillon

snubbed him viciously in Paris but in 1913 Vucetich discovered that his name had at last reached the outer world through the partisanship of far-seeing police officers in other lands. His name was honoured, he was given decorations, and he realized that the Vucetich system was widely appreciated.

However, the bureaucrats had not finished with him. Just as the Argentine government was poised to fingerprint the whole population—Vucetich's dream—the enemies of the idea intimated that people would not want to be fingerprinted like criminals. The Latin temperament took over from there. Riots broke out, there were arrests and the building intended for fingerprint registration records was badly damaged by the rioters.

In 1917 the whole project was cancelled, and Vucetich was banished to another city, his records and files seques-

tered, his work destroyed. Embittered and defeated, a mentally and physically sick man, Vucetich rested for a time with an English friend, Edward Lomax, who bred horses on an up-country *estancia*. There Vucetich told of his defeat and tragedy, but he also prophesied the future triumphs for the fingerprint system.

Vucetich was never a physically strong man, and in his last years was afflicted with both tuberculosis and cancer of the stomach. In 1925, the year of his death, he wrote to Edward Lomax: "I shall not see this year out, I fear. My work is destroyed and perhaps will be forgotten . . . nobody will ever remember me . . ."

He was wrong; today, the name of Juan Vucetich is honoured by criminologists throughout the world.

POLICE RECORDS

Detailed records of convicted criminals—their fingerprints and the way in which they work—are an essential to any police force, and more information is added every day.

EVEN FOR those detectives back in 1905, already hardened to criminal brutality, the sight of the elderly couple, Mr. and Mrs. Thomas Farrow, lying battered to death in their little shop in the South London borough of Deptford, was nauseating. It should have been obvious to anyone that the Farrows made only a meagre living from their business, and yet they had been mercilessly slain for the sake of a few pounds stolen from their tin cashbox. The only immediately visible clues were two stocking masks, thrown on to the shop floor as the killers made their escape.

But there was also the cashbox and this, as events turned out, was to assume its own very special place in the history of crime detection. The box, carefully wrapped, was sent to Scotland Yard's Fingerprint Department—then in its early years and still finding its way by tedious trial and error through the mysteries of the loops and whorls whose formation is unique to each individual person.

Inside the box, among fingerprints made by Mr. and Mrs. Farrow, the investigators found a separate and clearly marked impression left by a thumb. The person to whose hand the print belonged might well be able to "assist" the police — if he could be traced. Meanwhile, local detectives sought out all the known violent criminals in their "manor", and questioned them about their movements on the day of the murders. All seemed to have satisfactory answers except for a 22-year-old thug named Alfred Stratton. His fingerprints were taken and forwarded to the Yard.

When the prints were compared with the one found in the cashbox the evidence was beyond question. The cashbox impression perfectly matched the police print of Stratton's right thumb. On the basis of that and other evidence, Stratton and his 20-year-old brother, Albert, were put on trial at the Old Bailey—where, in

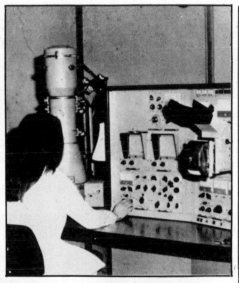

SOPHISTICATED EQUIPMENT is now needed even for routine investigations. The electron microscope (above) is one of the most important forensic tools.

order to understand the technicalities of fingerprinting, a juryman had one of his thumb-prints taken in court. For this was the first murder trial in Britain in which fingerprint evidence was presented, and it ended with the conviction of Alfred Stratton and his brother Albert, and their eventual execution.

Since then fingerprints have become a first line of investigation for Scotland Yard as for all other police forces. To-day at the Yard, scrutiny by eye and lens is still necessary for the final comparison of prints. But the initial sorting that once took hours, or even days, is increasingly being done by computers in minutes. Professional criminals have learned that gloves are an indispensable part of their equipment, and the mere thought of having their fingerprints taken is anathema to innocent members of the general public.

For that reason, when police have found it essential to fingerprint thousands of people in large-scale murder hunts, they have always taken elaborate and highly publicized measures to ensure that—once the murderer has been convicted—all other prints are immediately destroyed.

Prints of arrested persons are retained in what Scotland Yard calls its Main Fingerprint Collection—which serves to quickly identify incorrigible criminals returning time and again to their war with society. Equally, it serves to eliminate the many others who, having paid the penalty for past crimes, have set out to lead law-abiding lives.

Information, carefully recorded and stored, is the lifeblood of any police force, and every day more is pumped into Scotland Yard's Criminal Record Office, the national registry of crime. Within its three million neatly docketed files are the complete records of every person convicted of serious crime throughout Britain. Each file records the name, age, and personal description of the person, together with a photograph and list of convictions and prison sentences. Whenever a suspect is held, anywhere in the country, a message is sent to the Yard asking, in British law enforcement parlance, if "anything is known" about the man or woman.

As sub-divisions of the main collection there are further records showing details of the way in which known criminals work, their so-called *modus operandi*, and also an alphabetical index of the types of crime committed—running from Abduction, Arson and Burglary, down to Treason and Warehouse breaking.

Even the pseudo-respectable roles adopted by criminals are listed in A to Z files, from Actor and Architect to Wealthy Person (Posing As). Every type of detected fraud is meticulously noted so that the Yard has been able to pin-point the true identity of some con-men simply

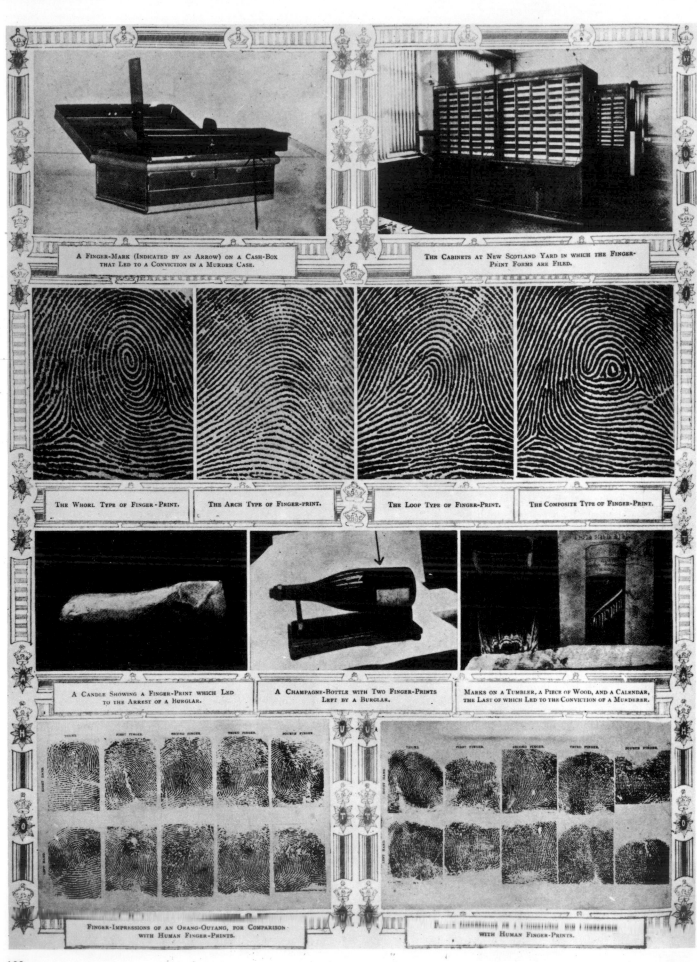

A FINGER-MARK (INDICATED BY AN ARROW) ON A CASH-BOX THAT LED TO A CONVICTION IN A MURDER CASE.

THE CABINETS AT NEW SCOTLAND YARD IN WHICH THE FINGER-PRINT FORMS ARE FILED.

THE WHORL TYPE OF FINGER-PRINT.

THE ARCH TYPE OF FINGER-PRINT.

THE LOOP TYPE OF FINGER-PRINT.

THE COMPOSITE TYPE OF FINGER-PRINT.

A CANDLE SHOWING A FINGER-PRINT WHICH LED TO THE ARREST OF A BURGLAR.

A CHAMPAGNE-BOTTLE WITH TWO FINGER-PRINTS LEFT BY A BURGLAR.

MARKS ON A TUMBLER, A PIECE OF WOOD, AND A CALENDAR, THE LAST OF WHICH LED TO THE CONVICTION OF A MURDERER.

FINGER-IMPRESSIONS OF AN ORANG-OUTANG, FOR COMPARISON WITH HUMAN FINGER-PRINTS.

WITH HUMAN FINGER-PRINTS.

from the literary style of letters written to potential victims.

One of the latest measures taken by the Yard to add to its storehouse of information is the development of a Criminal Intelligence branch, in which detectives keep close watch on full-time professional criminals in the London area and pool the results of their observations. Continually updated record cards present a detailed profile of the criminal—where he eats, the public houses he frequents, descriptions of his wife or girl friend, names and backgrounds of people with whom he associates. A sudden deviation from a man's regular routine, his mysterious absence from his usual haunts, can be an indication to the Yard men that a new "caper" is about to be launched.

Vital analysts

However, some Scotland Yard men and women, who play an important part in criminal detection, have never been to a scene of crime nor, sometimes, ever knowingly spoken to a criminal in their lives. They are, among others, chemists, physicists, toxicologists, biologists, handwriting and ballistics experts. They are the forensic scientists, many of them working in the Yard's own laboratory, seeking out half-hidden clues which help to bring the guilty to justice and punishment. The most minute scrap of evidence rarely escapes their expert analysis, and

it is true to say that, in the days when capital punishment applied in Britain, some murderers were hanged not only by a rope but by tiny scraps of cotton thread that connected them positively to their victims.

Daniel Raven, a young Londoner who, in 1949, beat his parents-in-law to death with the base of a television antenna, thought himself safe when he burned a heavily bloodstained suit in his kitchen boiler. But a tiny fragment of unburned cloth was retrieved by a quick-witted detective and sent to the Yard's laboratory. There the scientists found that the cloth bore minute blood spots and these,

FINGERPRINTS at the turn of the century (left) shown in an illustrated article. Below, part of the fingerprint room in the Yard's old headquarters, with, inset, a detective at work.

when analyzed, matched the blood group of the murdered couple.

Other traces of blood on Raven's shoes and in his car, which had survived despite frantic washing, also matched. All these pieces of evidence, painstakingly assembled in the laboratory, helped to send Raven to the gallows.

In recent years much of the laboratory's work has been concerned with tests on clothing and other articles for traces of narcotics. (Indeed, nearly 70% of the chemists' examinations arise from drugs, drink and sex crimes.) A notorious West End prostitute, suspected of trafficking in dangerous drugs, was several times searched by the police but always found to be "clean". Finally, her handbag was delivered to the laboratory and its contents scoured, down to the smallest piece of fluff, by a vacuum cleaner. When the little heap of debris was subjected to exhaustive tests it produced positive reactions for morphine and its derivatives.

It is now common knowledge that a fired bullet carries the imprint of gun-barrel markings that are almost as unique to any one gun as fingerprints are to each person's hands. But forensic ballistics is a comparatively modern science, and it was not until 1928 that evidence based upon it was first offered in a British criminal trial. It led to the conviction and execution of two men, Frederick Browne and William Kennedy, for the murder of

Police-Constable Gutteridge, attached to the Essex County Constabulary.

In 1946, a Miss Elizabeth McLindon, housekeeper in a Belgravia, London, mansion rented by the late King George of Greece, was found shot dead in her room. On the carpet was an empty .32 calibre shell case and a bullet of the same calibre was embedded in the wall. A man named Boyce, who was engaged to Miss McLindon, was traced to Brighton and found to possess a stolen .32 Browning automatic. A ballistics expert, who examined the spent shell case in the house-keeper's room and another found on Boyce, was able to prove conclusively from identical markings that Boyce's gun had fired the fatal shot. Boyce made the dreaded journey to the Old Bailey, and from there to a rope's end.

Establishing identity

At every scene-of-crime experienced police officers are careful to disturb nothing on the ground or the premises, since every mark, every particle of material, may hold vital clues waiting only for the specialist to unravel them. Even a quite small impression of a tyre tread may be enough for the expert to identify the make of the tyre, and—where there are indications of wear—to match it precisely to the actual tyre itself. From such a mark a skilled examiner can prove the direction in which the vehicle was moving.

Like motor tyres, scattered fragments of glass often have their own story to tell. In one typical case, the clothing of two men suspected of having broken into a London store by smashing the glass panel of a door was taken to the laboratory for close examination. Tiny shards of glass found on the clothes were compared with sweepings of the shattered door panel gathered by detectives. The scientists were able to show that both samples of glass exhibited exactly the same manufacturing characteristics. Each suspect had his own explanation for the glass on the clothing. One said the fragments had come from a public house beer glass which he had accidentally smashed, while the other claimed that he had been removing a broken window in his house.

Both incidents were found to be true, and the police obtained surviving pieces of the beer glass and the broken window. But they still did not prevent the conviction and jailing of the two men. The laboratory experts compared the glass fragments with the scatterings from the store, and proved the structure and peculiarities of the two groups to be different.

There are times when the Yard's forensic pathologists are asked to establish the identity of corpses, and even to piece together the outline of a once living body from a few, dismembered remains. This happened in 1948 when two small

TELL TALE bullets and shell cases. Pictured centre is Elizabeth MacLindon —shot to death with a .32.

boys, playing by a pond on the edge of a golf course at Potters Bar, 15 miles north of London, pulled a human hand and forearm out of the water.

The police drained the pond and brought in a mechanical excavator to scoop out the foul-smelling mud and slime into which stomach-heaving detectives delved and searched. Finally, they had gathered to-

gether many other portions of human remains which—when put together with the original hand and forearm—were re-assembled in the local mortuary and built up into the almost complete body of a man.

An initial examination showed that the man had been between 35 and 45 years of age, had been dead for between four and eight months, and that the body had been crudely dismembered, probably with an ordinary carpenter's saw. The front of the skull was broken and it was certain that the man had died from a violent head blow. The body's fingertips were so far advanced in decomposition that it was impossible to obtain fingerprints.

From their checks on men reported missing from the area the police found that all were accounted for except one— a 45-year-old railwayman named Albert William Welch who had disappeared from his Potters Bar home, not far from the golf course, on November 17, 1947. Detectives were almost certain that the remains were those of Welch, but they asked the Yard laboratory to make a positive identification.

The laboratory's forensic pathologists copied a photograph of Welch in the form of a transparency and superimposed it on a similar transparency, of exactly the same dimensions, of the skull found in the pond. The two fitted absolutely. From Welch's former workmates Superintendent Colin MacDougal, in charge of the investigations, learned that the dead man had complained of toothache shortly before his disappearance, and the laboratory found a jaw cavity which showed signs of having harboured a root abscess.

In the final and most important step of their investigation the laboratory men obtained from Welch's widow a pair of the dead man's boots. They then made a cast of the inside of each boot, using a mixture of plaster of Paris and gelatine. The casts, carrying clear impressions of Welch's feet, were photographed and scientifically matched with X-ray photographs of the feet taken from the pond. Once again, the match was perfect—even to the slightly enlarged big-toe joints. Despite all this patient effort, Welch's killer was never found. But by its work the laboratory was able to prove the victim's identity to the complete satisfaction of a coroner's jury.

Like so much of Scotland Yard's work, this science is continually developing, helped forward by new discoveries and new techniques coming both from within, and outside, the police service. Forensic science does not capture criminals, and may not by itself convict them. But it does, in increasing numbers of cases, supply the crucial supplementary evidence which makes it possible for detectives to secure the conviction of the guilty —and so maintain the high and well established standards of the Yard.

THE VOICE MACHINE

Edison (bottom) recorded sounds on wax cylinders. Modern forensic scientists can also produce "pictures" of sound (below). And these voice-prints can be as valuable as fingerprints in trapping crooks.

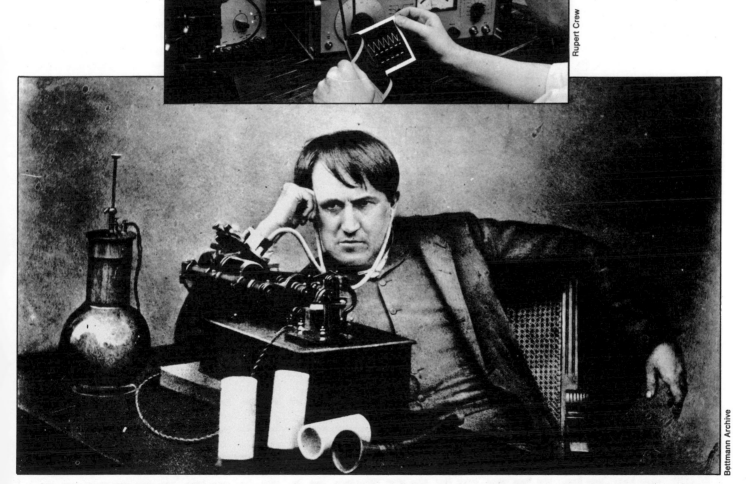

IN A small and cramped workshop near Detroit is one of the pioneer launch pads of that latest forensic tool, the voiceprint. It is not in the F.B.I. laboratory or any other forensic research centre as might be supposed, but in what is part of the Edison Institute complex at Henry Ford's fantastic Greenfield Village history-of-America centre.

When he had made his first million and was inspired by his American grass-roots origin, Ford began to gather around him all that he loved in the world: the Wright Brothers' cycle shop where the airplane was born; the Logan County Court where Abraham Lincoln practised law; the church where his mother worshipped; the house where he himself was born; the

103

little shop where Mr. Heinz prepared the first of the 57 varieties; the house where Webster compiled his dictionary . . .

Ford had them all transported to Dearborn, Michigan, and re-erected there. He even had the surrounding soil brought, to maintain a correct atmosphere. In all the 260 acres of this treasure-store of Americana, one of the outstanding buildings is the workshop from Menlo Park where Ford had worked once as a lad, assisting Edison in his inventions.

There, as a century ago, one can sit at the table where the first satisfactory electric-light bulb glowed through the night, and at the bench where Edison hand-turned his first drum-type phonograph.

In 1877, on this machine which still exists, Thomas Alva Edison produced the first voiceprint, traced by a stylus point on tinfoil wrapped around the cylinder — for it was left to others (notably Charles Tainter and Dr. Chichester Bell) to develop the wax cylinder that enabled a satisfactory *reproducing* phonograph to be manufactured.

Edison quickly patented his system in 1877 for *sound* reproduction, but one of the other early pioneers was Leo Scott, an inventor who in 1856 had devised a system of voiceprinting by a light stylus and membrane at the end of a trumpet. This drew a wavy pattern across a smoke-blackened cylinder.

Scott could not reproduce from this voiceprint, and in these early nineteenth-century years when battles were being waged between Edison and Alexander Graham Bell, Edison hastily patented his device with audio recording in mind. Neither he nor Bell foresaw voiceprint possibilities in other directions.

It was therefore a happy coincidence that some 90 years after the innovation of the Bell telephone, L. G. Kersta of the Bell Telephone Laboratories (where,

HOW IT WORKS . . . A voiceprint machine (below) and samples of the resulting "pictures" (bottom). But each person speaks slightly differently.

Bell Telephone Labs.

also, the transistor was born) proposed the voiceprint as a new forensic method of identification.

His system went much further than merely presenting a single audio waveform in physical means. He had solid-state amplifiers at his disposal, and the laboratory oscilloscope with its television-like cathode-ray tube to present a screen pattern of what he termed his spectrograms or "sonograms".

The essence of the system was to produce not merely an audio waveform (which today every television engineer does as a matter of routine when setting up his camera channels), but a pattern which is uniquely characteristic of the speaker. That there *is* such a characteristic was realized years before our present pitch of electronics.

"It was your voice that gave you away" is commonplace. So, too, the telephone booth trick so often used in motion picture and TV scenes, where the caller puts a handkerchief over the handpiece microphone to disguise his voice.

It must be said that Lawrence Kersta's work originally was not directed towards helping criminalistics, but as a general branch of the science of acoustics applied to aerodynamics and medicine.

Many voice-display systems were built — in the Bell Telephone Laboratories, at the R.C.A. Research Center and elsewhere — in connection with vibration and

SYLLABLE PICTURES

	p	b	t	d	k	g	s	z	f	v	th (THIN)	th (THAT)	sh	zh	ch	j	l	r	y	w	wh	h	m	n
e as in eve																								
i as in it																								
a as in ate																								
e as in bet																								
a as in at																								
a as in ask																								
a as in father																								
o as in not																								
a as in all																								
o as in old																								
oo as in foot																								
oo as in boot																								

Bell Telephone Labs.

shock waves of missiles, and uniquely in the analysis of throat sounds as an aid to diagnosis of lung and throat illnesses and defects.

What are known as the "articulators" — tongue, palate, teeth, and lips — are just one factor controlling the tonal quality of speech. Mouth, nose, and throat cavities also have a decisive effect. But the over-riding factor is the subconscious muscular control of all these, which produce speech patterns of varying frequencies and of characteristic timbre.

Women generally have a more limited and naturally higher vocal range than males. Because of resonant nasal cavities, actors, and others who have voice training, speak and sing with a noticeably different tone colour and resonance.

In developing voiceprint techniques, Lawrence Kersta, David Ellis and others realized that some of these factors were purely physical. For example, the characteristics are partly due to the two straplike membranes across the larynx, known as the vocal cords. The medial (central) part of the cords vibrates in the air stream produced by speaking. From the very first moment a baby cries, there is developed the subconscious control of these two membranes.

Pitch of the voice

Very shortly after birth the natural pitch of the voice is developed by individual control of the vocal cords; and, like everything else in audiophysics, the pitch is controlled by the frequency of vibration.

Women's cords are usually shorter than men's, although both men and women have a fairly limited control range so that for short intervals either can speak with an affected "deep" or "high" voice. This does not always affect the natural timbre (on which the success or failure of the voice-print depends), but is controlled also by the trachea, lungs, and diaphragm — all of which are usually also of different size in the female. Thus, the range of a soprano is approximately from top-treble A to the A below middle-C on the piano; the male bass range is from D above middle-C to the F an octave and a half below.

If forensic voiceprinting were concerned only with range, there would be little difficulty. The real breakthrough came with Lawrence Kersta's work when it was realized that an electronic sound analyzer could detect and record frequency characteristics and harmonics — all uniquely individual — due to fundamentals of the voice cavities, and the subconscious control in every individual of his own articulators.

Unhappily the first time a Bell Tele-

SOUND PICTURES ... the patterns made by common noises when they are recorded on a voiceprint machine.

phone voiceprinter was demonstrated in court, there was an inconclusive ending to the experiment. This was in the United States in April 1966. A subsequent use of the voiceprint technique (by a British team of physicists) in an English court in November 1967 was successful, and resulted in a conviction.

To Kersta's credit, he was not down-cast by the difficulties of the April 1966 case, and he decided to set up his own voiceprint company, manufacturing equipment for it and operating under licence from the Bell Telephone group, which still controls the patent rights.

This initial 1966 hurdle happened in the Westchester County court (at county court level) when a New Rochelle police officer was on trial for an unusual perjury. It was alleged that the police officer had warned a professional gambler of a planned police raid. The question of a tip-off had already been brought to official notice, so a phone-tap was arranged and Lawrence Kersta's staff were allowed to record voiceprints.

Later, with the suspect's permission, these prints were compared with open-microphone prints. In the opinion of Kersta and the D.A.'s office, these were identical.

Because of the novelty of the forensic evidence, Kersta was subjected to vigorous cross-examination. The defence chal-

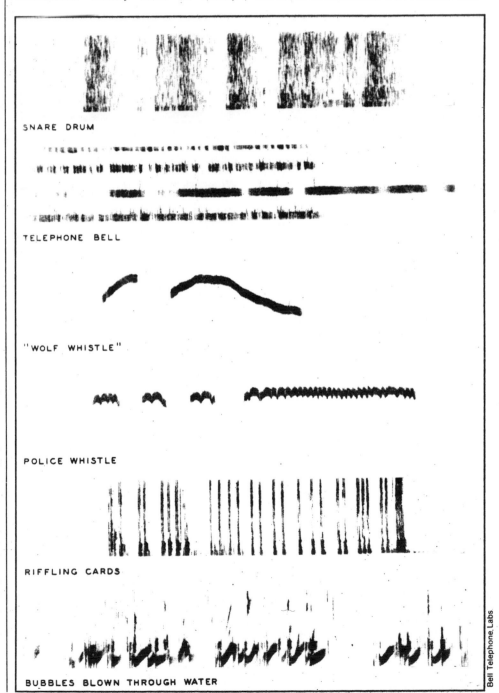

SNARE DRUM

TELEPHONE BELL

"WOLF WHISTLE"

POLICE WHISTLE

RIFFLING CARDS

BUBBLES BLOWN THROUGH WATER

Bell Telephone, Labs

lenged the legal (not, of course, the technical) competency of the witness, but the judge ruled that this was for the jury to decide. On the stand Lawrence Kersta showed how his recorder produced bar spectrographs, the amplitude information of a number of successive frequency bands being marked on sensitized paper. He gave details of some 50,000 preceding tests on other voices.

It is possible some members of the Westchester County jury did not understand this forensic milestone. They disagreed, and were discharged. A retrial was requested, but through the complex intricacies of the U.S. legal system, a case was stated to the United States Supreme Court who promptly ruled that the New York State law which allowed the phonetap (*not* the voiceprinting itself) was unconstitutional. Since this meant that none of the telephone evidence could be given at the re-trial, whether frequency-analyzed or not, the case against the police officer was dropped.

In Britain the technique was more successful at its introduction. At the Winchester petty-sessional court in November 1967 a man was charged with making malicious telephone calls. Here there was no shred of doubt about the legality of the police tapping and recording the conversations, so recordings were made on hi-band audio tape. These were frequency-analyzed at Leeds University. Spectro-analysis disclosed a number of distinct similarities which convinced the magistrates. The defendant was convicted and fined. Perhaps because of the novelty and uncertainty of it all, the case failed to make national headlines.

Seen by millions

Voiceprints made by Kersta from a TV news interview at the time of the Los Angeles Watts riot certainly hit the front pages. They put the technique right on the map so far as forensic science in the United States is concerned—indeed part of the proceedings were seen by many millions of television viewers overseas.

Bill Stout, a TV interviewer with the Columbia Broadcasting System, interviewed a group of coloured youths immediately after the Watts riots. One of them turned his face away from the camera while admitting that he had been involved in burning some shops in L.A. Stout's first duty was to his CBS-TV public, and only after the video-tape recording was it possible for the police to intervene. Without much difficulty they tracked down an 18-year-old Negro youth, Edward Lee King.

Everything depended on the weight of the forensic evidence, and whether the jury would accept voiceprint evidence from Kersta. As it turned out, they did. The arson trial took nearly seven weeks.

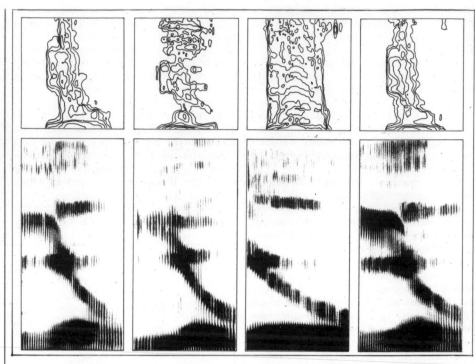

YOU . . . That's the word the subjects are saying in all the contour (top) and at (bottom) voiceprints. The prints extreme left and right are of the same person.

The police had been able to get a second set of voiceprints while King was in jail on a narcotics charge, and these were found to tally with those recorded at Watts. King was convicted and jailed.

In the United States two vital features now arose, since lawyers defending a suspect where voiceprint evidence might be given were concerned about self-incrimination, and also the rights of a defendant to refuse to make a print for comparison.

Both these questions were determined in the United States in 1967, and it is likely that the legal luminaries in other nations will follow this example.

State v. McKenna 226 A 2d 757 stands as the State of New Jersey Superior Court ruling that a defendant has no right to refuse taping or voiceprinting. And *U.S. v. Wade,* June 1967, is a U.S. Supreme Court ruling that the traditional American ruling (privilege against self-incrimination) does not apply to a defendant asked to record or voiceprint so that he may be identified.

While the first courtroom appearances of voiceprints were with audio-tape recordings made at $7\frac{1}{2}$ inches/sec., research is continuing at Polaroid Corporation (Cambridge, Mass.) and elsewhere on photorecording at different speeds, with other frequency ranges, and with systems of securing permanent photoprints off the television-like screens of dual trace oscilloscopes.

Photoprints now being researched by forensic workers using Polaroid Land PolaScope techniques are designed to show on the one print (for simple inspection by members of a jury) the specimen and control voiceprints.

Waveforms from the two separate audio tracks are fed to the two amplifiers of a dual-trace oscilloscope. Here on a 5-in. screen two separate timebases swing independent cathode-ray beams across the fluorescent tube screen. Any frequency differences or similarities between the voice of the defendant or suspect can be seen by comparison—then instantly photographed.

Ordinary amateur-camera film has an American Standards Association speed of around 25, and high-speed Kodak Ektachrome is 160 ASA. By contrast, the Polaroid Land stock used for oscilloscopes is 10,000 ASA-equivalent.

Separate research

It is therefore easily possible to photograph at a maximum trace writing-rate of 3500 centimetres per microsecond—fast enough to show up differences in an audio waveform.

All this research is entirely separate from the forensic work being done currently by the Kersta company, Voiceprint Laboratories.

But the strangest aspect of it all is that although Leo Scott produced his carbon-film voiceprints in 1856, and the Danish inventor Valdemar Poulson had his Telegraphone (the world's first magnetic-wire audio-recording system) working in Paris in 1900, it has taken society so long to realize that voices have fundamental differences. And that these can be recorded and *compared*—forensically.

THE LIE DETECTOR

Your heart pounds. Your throat constricts. Your eyes glaze, and you can feel the orbital muscles begin to twitch. No good trying to bluff: your every movement is recorded, and the mild-mannered questioner facing you is trained in every physical symptom of deceit. If you're lucky, like Dr. Alice Wynekoop, below, the truth will set you free. Otherwise . . . might as well confess.

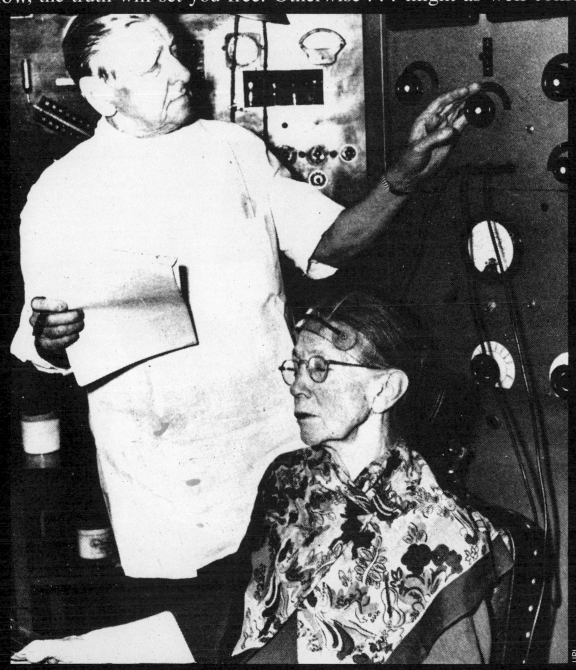

THE lie detector has a firm place in crime fiction writing as a magic machine which strikes fear into the hearts of hardened criminals. It is not quite like that, for although the lie detector is widely used in crime investigation in the U.S.A., information gained by its use is not generally accepted as direct evidence in the courts.

An English heart specialist, Sir James MacKenzie, invented the "ink polarograph" in 1908. This was a heart recorder and was the forerunner of the lie detector used in criminal detection. It has long been observed that persons telling lies are subject to involuntary physiological reactions. A pounding heart, an impulse to swallow and a twitching eye are all signs of deception. The principle of the lie detector is to record and interpret these reactions.

Early detectors recorded blood pressure, pulse and respiration changes — later developments added muscle movements and galvanic skin reaction. The modern lie detector is a mechanical device which uses well-tried instruments for recording individual reactions. For in-stance, blood pressure is measured with the pneumatic arm cuff apparatus common to the doctor's surgery.

Respiration is a most difficult activity to control consciously and tell-tale changes take place under the stress of telling lies; this is an important function to monitor. Fluctuations in respiration are measured by means of a flexible rubber tube fastened across the subject's chest; this expands and contracts with respiration and the movements are transferred to pen recorders.

In addition to changes in blood pressure and respiration, the act of deception leads to an increase in perspiration. This can be measured by electrodes attached to the palmar and dorsal surfaces of the hand which record changes in the activity of the sweat glands. This is the galvanic skin reaction (GSR) or electrodermal response. GSR, together with the other responses, are transferred by pen recorders to moving graph paper. A permanent record of an examination is thus obtained.

Agencies using lie detectors have developed their own codes of practice to make the testing procedure completely objective. The integrity of the examiner is highly stressed. Examination is carried out in a private room free from noise and interruption. The only persons present are the examiner and the test subject. Some agencies use a two-way mirror which allows another examiner to observe the test subject without being seen.

Detached and unemotional

The examiner is fully briefed about the events on which a subject is to be examined. He must have a full understanding in order to ask perceptive and unambiguous questions. It is essential that he remains detached and unemotional. Once the subject is hooked up to the lie detector, the examiner begins a sequence of questioning which is usually divided into four clear parts.

1. The examiner helps the subject to acquaint himself with the equipment. From general questioning the examiner seeks to form an opinion as to the character of the subject; a subject giving untruthful answers may be expected to delay his replies, to fidget in his chair and not to look the examiner straight in the

"MY GOD . . . I think they've killed Marilyn!" Sam Sheppard (right) faces a life sentence though lie tests "confirm" the confession of Donald Wedler (above).

eye. It is made clear that the lie detector is also a truth detector.

2. Questions relevant to the crime under investigation are asked. Replies are marked on the recording chart.

3. The card test. The subject is shown a series of cards placed face down on the table. He is told that each card bears a number and he is asked to select one and take note of the number. He is not to say what the number is. The examiner collects the cards, shuffles them and tells the subject to answer "No" to each question. In this way the subject tells a lie about the identity of the numbered card he has selected.

The card test is a kind of calibration. By looking at the recorded trace, the examiner will be able to tell the subject which card he selected. This is a convincing test of the lie detector's efficiency.

4. The subject is asked if he wishes to make any corrections or admissions regarding the truthfulness of the answers given in 2. If the answer is "No", the question routine is repeated. If "Yes", suitably modified questions are asked.

Where the results to this sequence of

Jack Pollard

questions are inconclusive, further tests are made; these involve changing the order and wording of the earlier questions.

Interpreting the recordings made of a subject's replies to a question sequence is a matter for the skilled and experienced examiner, but the visible evidence of a lie is often quite dramatic.

Three or four lie detector test records are usually considered sufficient for analysis. Evidence of deception must be recorded on at least two separate tests for it to carry weight. When properly used, the technique has a high degree of accuracy and is a widely used investigative aid.

Deep suspicion and fear

Since 1923, advocates of the lie detector have fought a long battle to have information obtained by the apparatus recognized by the courts. Many of the decisions refusing recognition have implied that the method has insufficient scientific validity. In some quarters there is deep suspicion, even fear, of the machine which, though it may trap the criminal, is thought capable of ensnaring the innocent too. Some States prohibit the use of the lie detector altogether. On the other hand, various Federal and local government agencies use the technique as a matter of course for screening job applicants. The appointment of police officers in some cities is also conditional on passing a lie detector examination.

Many police departments ask suspects voluntarily to submit to the lie detector and a convincing number of confessions has resulted. The mere threat of the lie test is often sufficient to make a criminal confess. Confessions obtained as a consequence of a voluntary lie test, but not as part of it, have been admitted in the courts. Apart from mistrust of justice dispensed with the aid of a machine, the main anxiety over the lie detector concerns the examiner. He must obviously be trained to a high standard and be answerable to professional discipline in the way that doctors are. Another factor which prevents ready acceptance of the lie detector is the possibility of disputes arising out of an individual's privilege against self-incrimination.

A celebrated case in which the lie detector featured at a late stage was the Sheppard murder. On July 10, 1954, Dr. Sam Sheppard was questioned by the Cuyahoga County Police about the murder of his wife six days previously. Sam, youngest of three doctor brothers, worked in the Cleveland osteopathic clinic run by the Sheppard family. When questioned by the police he had obvious facial injuries and his neck was in a medical collar; according to Sheppard he had been injured when grappling with an intruder at his house on the shore of Lake Erie.

Sheppard told the police that he and his wife had dinner at home with friends on the evening of July 3. The friends left after midnight. He was dozing on the couch in the living-room—his wife went upstairs to bed. His next recollection was of hearing his wife cry out. He ran upstairs. In the bedroom he grappled with an intruder who knocked him unconscious.

When he came to, Sheppard had a hazy memory of seeing his wife lying on the bed. He thought the intruder was still in the house. He went downstairs and chased a person out of the house, there was a struggle and again Sheppard was knocked out. Recovering consciousness for the second time, Sheppard found himself lying shirtless in shallow water at the lake's edge. He staggered to his feet and went into the house, immediately going up to the bedroom. In a dazed condition, he took his wife's pulse—he realized then that she was dead. He telephoned a neighbour. "My God, Spence, get over here quick. I think they've killed Marilyn."

The police were called to the scene and Dr. Sheppard's brothers also arrived at the house. His brothers were concerned at Sam's injuries—he had a fractured neck vertebra—and they took him off to hospital. It happened that the nearest hospital was also the family clinic. The family's action in taking Sheppard away from the house caused a great deal of subsequent controversy.

The main bedroom of the Sheppard house contained twin beds. On one of them, lying on her back, was Marilyn Sheppard. Her head had been terribly battered and the sheets were soaked in blood. Blood was spattered on all four walls, though not on the ceiling, and there were spots on Sam's bed which was undisturbed. There was no trace of the murder weapon.

A search of the grounds

Sam's study was in disarray. Desk drawers had been turned out and the contents of the doctor's medical bag lay strewn on the floor; a strange feature of the case was that the T-shirt worn by Sheppard on the night of the murder was missing. A search of the grounds around the house revealed a cloth bag belonging to Sheppard, which contained the doctor's wrist watch with the hands stopped at 4.15. Blood on the watch proved to be that of his wife.

The police concluded that Sheppard had killed his wife in a fit of anger and tried to cover it up by feigning a burglary; the missing T-shirt they presumed had been destroyed because it was bloodstained. Sam said that blood must have got on his wrist watch when he took his wife's pulse. The discovery that Sheppard had been having an adulterous affair with another woman did nothing to placate

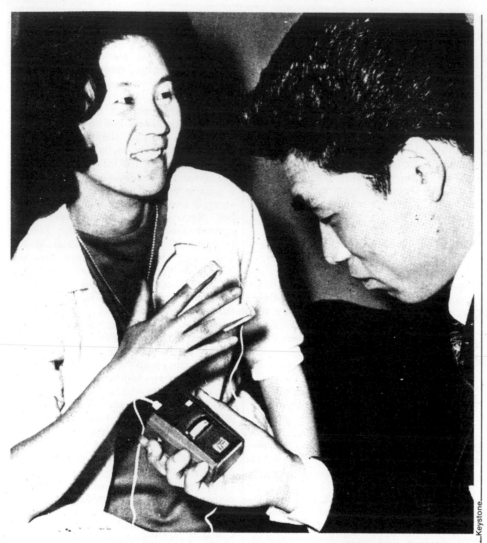

BLOOD PRESSURE changes betray any effort to deceive. This miniature lie detector from Japan records emotional disturbance through the fingertips.

public opinion. His guilt was widely assumed in the Cleveland area and rumours abounded of debauchery and a cover-up. When the inquest on Marilyn Sheppard's death opened on July 21, the public were openly hostile to Sam and on July 30 he was arrested.

The case of the State of Ohio versus Sam Sheppard opened on October 18. The prosecution made much of the lack of fingerprints in the Sheppard house—only one identifiable fingerprint was found. That was a print of Sam's thumb on the headboard of his wife's bed. This was thought to be odd, as a few hours before the murder there had been four adults and two children in the house. There was a strong suggestion that furniture had been wiped clean of fingerprints.

Blood on the pillow

The scientific evidence was confusing. There were arguments about blood spots found on the stairs and about a bloody imprint on a pillow.

The jury deliberated for three days. They found Sheppard guilty of second degree murder, and concluded that he had tried to fake a burglary, had in-

flicted injuries on himself and had hidden the murder weapon and his blood-stained T-shirt. They could find no evidence of premeditation. Sam Sheppard was sentenced to life imprisonment.

Sheppard's lawyers went through all the appeal procedures in an effort to introduce new evidence and get a retrial. Finally, in October 1956, the U.S. Supreme Court refused to set aside the conviction. But in July of the following year, a 26-year-old Florida convict named Wedler told prison authorities that he had murdered a woman in Cleveland in 1954; there had already been a number of confessions to the Sheppard murder but none worth considering seriously. However, Donald Wedler's story sparked off a concerted attempt to prove Sam Sheppard's innocence.

Wedler said that he had stolen a car in Cleveland and broken into a lake-side house intent on theft. His attempts at burglary awakened a woman whom

he silenced by beating with an iron pipe. He used the same weapon to knock out a man who tackled him on the stairs. Wedler did not mention the name but the similarities make it possible that it was Marilyn Sheppard he killed.

The Cleveland police were reluctant to take any action but interest was quickly roused when the story appeared in the press. Erle Stanley Gardner, a highly successful crime writer and also a practising lawyer, suggested that Wedler be given a lie test; Gardner wanted this carried out under the auspices of the Court of Last Resort, a non-profit-making organization which gave professional services in cases of injustice. The Sheppard family had already appealed.

Put through their paces

Sam Sheppard's brothers and their wives were the first to undergo lie tests. An impressive array of lie-detector experts was assembled and the Sheppards were put through their paces. On July 15 the news-stands sold copies of *Argosy* magazine carrying an article by Erle Stanley Gardner—its title was "Are the Sheppards telling the truth?" It was the view of the lie-detector experts that they were. The examiners were satisfied that the Sheppards were sincere in their view that Sam did not kill his wife and that the family were in no way connected in any attempt to conceal evidence.

Next, Wedler was subjected to the lie test. He spent three and a half hours hooked up to the detector. The examiners' conclusion was that he too was telling the truth or, as they modified their statement to the press, ". . . what he believes to be the truth". Wedler was subsequently interviewed by reporters who seemed satisfied with his story.

The Court of Last Resort now won approval from the Ohio State Governor to give a lie test to Sam Sheppard in the Ohio Penitentiary. Arrangements were made to carry out the test although critics were quick to point out that Sheppard's lawyers had earlier refused to let him submit to the lie detector. Opposition to the lie testing of the convicted man mounted and the trial judge objected to the Court of Last Resort setting itself above the United States Supreme Court.

The Ohio Governor's permission to allow the lie test to be given was withdrawn; it was a bitter disappointment to Gardner and to the advocates of lie detector examination, and it was a blow also to public interest in justice. The results of lie testing the Sheppard family and Donald Wedler seemed to merit the final step of examining Sam Sheppard himself. While the possible outcome of such a test can only be speculated upon, both Sam Sheppard and the lie detector were denied final vindication.

SCRAPS OF EVIDENCE

Police can examine a scrap of paper and detect vital evidence in the ink, the style of the handwriting or the typewriter letters.

TAINTED MONEY: Thefts have been taking place regularly, so banknotes are marked with a powder which is invisible until exposed to ultra-violet light.

IT WAS a saying of the French criminologist Professor Edmond Locard, one of the greatest forensic scientists of the twentieth century, that "Everything a man does leaves traces". But when a man tries to alter those traces deliberately, he is in trouble.

Documents are so much the basis of modern life that they are obviously often involved in crimes. Documentary evidence does not mean forgery alone; the document examiner covers, both figuratively and literally, a large amount of territory.

Paper, the root of most of his work, is, to be briefly technical, an aqueous deposit of any vegetable fibre in sheet form. The name, as most people know, comes from the Latin *papyrus,* which in the hands of the early Egyptians, its first known users, comprised the pith of a sedge-like plant which was sliced into layers and beaten or pressed into sheets.

But, as so often happens, the Chinese were ahead of everybody and nearly 2000 years ago were using paper made by hand, fashioned by processes used all over the world until not long ago—though paper, as such, did not appear in Europe until about the eleventh century. In Britain paper first came from a paper mill erected around 1490; its products in fact were used for an edition of Chaucer's *Canterbury Tales.*

The forger, in his efforts to defeat science, has tried his hand at artificially aging paper. For example, the general discoloration due to age is a process of oxidation, which is easily confirmed by the expert examiner. The faker tries to imitate this, using liquids like coffee or tea, woodfire smoke, extract of tobacco, and even permanganate of potash to achieve that vital faint brown effect.

Age is also attempted by pressing a false document into folds and rubbing these folds along a carpet or an old wall to simulate an ancient fold; the micro-

111

scope will pick out in seconds the rubbing or dirt grains along a bogus fold.

Watermarks, another weapon of forgers, began in Italy about the thirteenth century. They are made when paper is a wet pulp. A dandy roll, a woven wire gauze-covered skeleton roll, has the watermark device soldered on to it. The impression of the roll on the wet pulp causes a thinning of fibres which, when the paper is finished, is the familiar watermark.

A faker's trick is to process finished paper by imprinting with his own dandy roll, using some sort of oily substance as a watermark; this looks genuine to the casual eye. But test it with a damp cloth or a petrol soaked paintbrush and the watermark will vanish.

One of the problems which bedevil

document, brilliantly forged, as it turned out. It was supposed to be 400 years old. The false writing was almost foolproof; the forger had found some old paper of the right age; the ink used was genuine carbon ink which goes back, according to the great Egyptologist, Professor Flinders Petrie, to Egypt 5000 years ago.

The expert working on this document saw hours of investigation ahead to produce evidence that would stand up in court about something he only "felt" was wrong. Then, through his microscope ocular, he saw something incredible. Embedded in the ink of a letter was an almost invisible particle that looked metallic. Elaborate examination showed that there were minute particles embedded in that ink—aluminium.

This modern metal was the giveaway,

the examiner of documents is what experts call "sample". A document cannot always be cut, marked, or touched with reagents—chemicals which act in certain ways on materials. Suppose it is desired to find out if a paper contains linen and cotton, important in dating it. It can be touched with something called zinc-chlor-iodine. The marked spot will turn wine red, unthinkable on a perhaps valuable document.

Then the microscope steps in. Dates of paper origins are generally well authenticated and if an old type of paper is examined, say, one made from rags, the linen or cotton fibres in it show distinctive features which are absolutely different from modern wood pulp papers. But—and here is the exception—many high grade modern papers are still made from linen or cotton.

There was the case of a questioned

for the police were later able to show that the forger's brother, working in the same room during the actual writing, was filing an aluminium casing. Aluminium dust, floating invisible in air, settled in that carefully processed carbon ink writing until the microscope found the answer.

Inks, next to paper, are usually the expert's friend. When a letter is written in ordinary ink, and not blotted, it seems natural to the naked eye. A simple hand-lens, or magnifying glass, will reveal clues. The writer paused for a second to think of a word and then hyphenated it. The lens shows the faintest difference in ink shading, or perhaps the pen is lifted in the middle of a letter and then it carries on; the lens shows that, too.

Ink itself will "talk". One notable forensic chemist in the 1920's, claimed that ink in ancient times was made from soot taken from cooking vessels, which accounts for its almost indefinite life. Iron gall ink (a mixture of ferrous sulphate with an infusion of nuts, galls and gum) came in about the first century of the Christian era. The Romans generally used an iron compound ink, the one, for example, used in the *Codex Sinaiticus,* which dates from the fourth century A.D.

So the dating goes on—iron gall ink had logwood put into it in the middle of

A SCRAP OF EVIDENCE solved the murder of Vivian Messiter (left). He was killed in a garage (far left and above), and there seemed to be no clues until a sharp-eyed detective picked up a dirty scrap of paper (top). A "washing" in benzene removed the dirt, oil and tread-marks to reveal a name (ringed) which was to prove vital. This name also appeared in mail filed by the victim, and thus led police to suspect a man named Podmore (right). See pages 120-122 for details.

the eighteenth century to improve its colour. A hundred years later they were using logwood with potassium chromate, and no iron, for writing purposes. All this and more means reasonably accurate dating.

The first modern ink, aniline dye ink, came in a blue form in 1861, a fairly impermanent writing fluid. This was followed by a famous advertisement for blue-black ink which showed a large blot, dark in the centre and light at the edges. Indeed it was incorrect, for in practice the

reverse order would have been the case.

In current years that well-known enemy of all who love good handwriting, the ball point pen, contains a so-called "solid" ink which is, in fact, a thick suspension of dye in a drying oil. Its stable companion, the fibre-tipped pen is one that, unluckily, does present problems in forensic document examination.

Traces of metal, usually iron, can be found when ordinary pen marks have been erased or bleached out. Ultraviolet light will reveal these interferences. Pencils or ball point pens often leave no residue which can be picked up after erasure, but embossing occurs in the paper used; fibres are disturbed in the paper as well, and these will answer to the expert.

The fibre-tipped pen, as it is usually called, is so light in its effect that it leaves behind no clue after erasure—other than disturbed sizing on the paper. But where additions or amendments have been made on a fibre-pen written whole, then all is reasonably well—close examination soon reveals the differences in ink quality, shading and such.

The copying pencil, the one which leaves mauve marks on the tongue when it is accidentally licked, can be a godsend to the document examiner. In the Southampton garage murder in England in 1930 a man named Messiter was found killed; there were no apparent clues until a sharp-eyed detective picked up a dirty little scrap of paper. The back was a lodging house receipt, the front also seemed to bear words—but they were invisible under tread marks, dirt, and oil.

Words bleached out

A simple method worked this time. The paper was very delicately "washed" in benzene and there, under the dirt, was the name "F. Thomas" written in copying pencil. A letter was found in the victim's files bearing this name, later proved to be an alias of a man named Podmore. It was not long before evidence was found to support a charge of murder. Podmore was duly convicted, the scrap of paper becoming vital court evidence.

Erasures have been mentioned and these continually arise in document examination. Erasures are, simply, the removal of words, bleaching out before substitution; such partial interference with documents being a not uncommon crime.

A first test is to hold the suspect document on an angle before a good light. The eye, or a hand-lens, often reveals interference—chemical erasures tend to "stand out", particularly those on paper with a high finish.

Suppose a word has been bleached out and another put in its place. The original word can generally be read by using ultraviolet light with the correct

A BANK FIRE "destroyed" these cheques . . . but they were identifiable after being photographed by infra-red light on specially-sensitized film.

plate and filter. This method shows up the original disturbed fibres of the paper, assuming an ordinary pen has been used, and a "shadow" of the word is revealed.

One of the most delicate and adroit recovery methods is one used by the late Paul Kirk, a leading American documentary expert. To recover erasures, obliterations, or indented ("ghost") writing he used plastic casts, a process so exacting and so difficult that an ordinary man would not have patience to try it. Kirk, however, achieved some excellent results.

Burning a document is not always a successful evasion. One man in a crime burned a vital cheque in a grate, and broke up the ashes with a poker. Experts worked for hours, spraying the fragments with diluted lacquer until they were strong enough to be touched.

Then the bits—they were no more—were reassembled until they were almost complete. Strong oblique light showed up the inked writing, which had carbonized, and the case was solved. The point of these examples is that the expert is a trained man who never neglects anything, no matter how trivial or even silly it may seem, and who possesses

patience so limitless that it appears unearthly.

Another facet of document examination is graphology. This is a suspect word, for it suggests people who profess to read character from handwriting. To some extent this may be possible, but it is seldom taken seriously.

Once, at a court hearing, the writer of a letter was designated by a "graphologist" (*not* a handwriting expert) as "French, middle-class, and young". When the man in question was called as a witness he turned out to be the English son of an Armenian father, educated in the United States and well over 50 at the time of the hearing.

But handwriting can turn out to be dangerous when the expert deals with it. Writing, after all, is the conditioned reflex of a person using a writing instrument, and to disguise one's natural *self* in such circumstances is extremely difficult.

For example, in 1970 a great controversy raged when a British journal, *The Criminologist*, published an article which indicated that the Duke of Clarence, Queen Victoria's grandson and until his death, heir to the English throne, might have been "Jack the Ripper"—the sex murderer who terrorized London's East End in the autumn of 1888.

The journal itself later put an end to all this excitement by asking Professor

C. L. Wilson, an important document examiner in government service, to study the handwriting of the Duke and the handwritings ascribed to the "Ripper".

Professor Wilson wrote: "To sum up, on the basis of the handwriting, all the evidence is against identification of Jack the Ripper with the Duke of Clarence."

Nor is the typewriter proof against the expert. The wear, the defects, the individualities of each machine all "talk" to the expert, who, given a sample, can produce all sorts of vital facts. The hand-lens, the microscope, and measuring devices play their part in studying wear, defects, accidentals (dirt, damaged letters, and so on).

The slant of the characters, angles, alignment, and footing are important—footing being that a letter may strike heavier on its right, its left, or its bottom.

Every typewriter is peculiar to itself, after a little use. Similarity in all details in two machines may be ignored (the chance of complete similarity of two machines is estimated to be one in 3,000,000,000,000).

Last comes forgery, and in this field, free writing is one of the most skilful forms. It means the forger practises endlessly from the subject's handwritten models until it can be copied without an original. In time and place it can be successful, but it does not stand up when the expert examines the *corpus delicti* (which does not mean corpse but "the sum or aggregate of the ingredients which make a given fact a breach of given law").

Counterfeit chaos

Banknotes, postage stamps, and insurance stamps are fair game for forgers. But the false banknote is often marked by indifferent or incomplete work—these poor examples the forger usually passes in crowded shops or presses on busy, overworked cashiers.

Forgery on a massive scale is not always successful. During World War II the Hitler government produced numerous £5 banknotes as a weapon against Britain—intending that the counterfeit money would find its way to England and cause chaos in the businesses and banks.

The full technical resources of German experts were used, and with what result? Ultraviolet light showed that the ink was different. There was a fault visible to the naked eye just above the B in the *Bank of England* watermark; the watermark also had three lines too many on one sample, and two lines lacking in the second.

A forged note and a real one were given to an ordinary bank cashier, who was blindfolded. He indicated the forgery immediately—it did not "feel" right.

CRIME IN CARS

Forensic investigation of car crimes—rust and paint fragments, motor body fillers, pieces of glass, skid marks—has now become extremely sophisticated.

WITH A scream of tyres a hit-and-run driver swung across a boulevard in Berkeley, California, colliding with another automobile then careering off into the darkness. It seemed a grim eternity before the police came, and reports were being made under the staccato flashes of official cameras recording the scene for forensic examination . . . because, as is so frequently the case with hit-and-run, there were no effective witnesses.

Electron beams

Yet within hours the police came upon a suspect vehicle, and the incident at Berkeley made forensic history as the first occasion on which the SEM (scanning electron microscope) was used to nail down an offender—when every other crime-laboratory method had failed.

The experts concerned in the examination were J. I. Thornton and G. T. Mitosinka of the School of Criminology, and T. L. Hayes of the Donner Laboratory, all at the University of California, Berkeley, U.S.A.

It was in 1963 that the first scanning electron microscopes became available to forensic workers, and five years passed before they were demonstrated at a forensic symposium before the American Chemical Society at Atlantic City in 1968.

They were greatly needed—for even with the best glass lenses the limit of magnification of an optical microscope is 1300x (that is, 1300 times the size of the specimen), whereas by scanning the specimen with television-like electron beams—as in a TV picture-tube—workers can get magnifications in excess of 25,000x. And, what is just as important when studying small forensic samples, a depth of focus of about 100 microns. (One micron is a thousandth of a millimetre.)

From the case-history of Thornton,

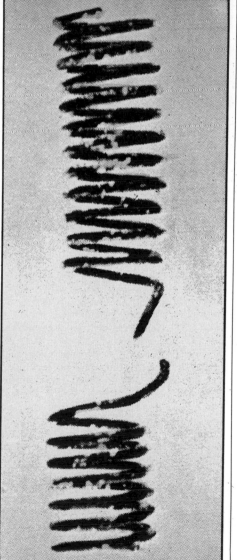

Mitosinka, and Hayes it was shown how effective this proved in the Berkeley hit-and-run offence.

Metal helix

"An alert police officer at the scene recovered, in addition to glass and paint evidence, an exceedingly minute metal helix, all that remained of an auto headlight filament. The piece was some 1-mm in length, and the problem was to match it with a portion of tungsten filament still attached to the filament-post of the suspect car."

An initial check was made with a stereoscopic binocular optical "comparison" microscope, which suggested the possibility of striae (minute lines of furrows and scratches, capable of being matched) along the tungsten wire surface. Filaments are made by drawing fine tungsten wire through steel dies, so the score-marks are similar along the entire length.

Same die

The Berkeley team, with the help of the Donner Laboratory and facilities of the United States Atomic Energy Commission, took but thirty minutes to photograph the two samples of hair-like filament in a scanning electron microscope. Taking picture after picture, they were able to keep the 200-micron-diameter wire fragments in focus.

"Examination of the filaments," the team reported, "indicated that the striae persisted throughout the length of the helix, indicating that the two fragments had been drawn through the same die."

FRAGMENT of filament found at crime scene (bottom) compared with fragment found attached to car filament post. The electron microscope (top) provided proof that the two had the same origin.

But presumably there could be other filaments with essentially identical draw marks . . ."

This is as far as the forensic scientist can go. It is then left to the police and the District Attorney to show that the possibility of the damaged automobile *not* being involved in the hit-and-run incident would be several millions to one?

While the SEM is among the latest sophisticated forensic tools, some years went by—and doubtless many criminals escaped identification—until a basically

dustrial Research, Lower Hutt, New Zealand, devised a new auxiliary wheel for the New Zealand Police Department. This clamps on with rubber pads to almost every style of wheel, and is currently becoming a universal piece of police forensic equipment.

Next, from a neighbouring crime laboratory, at Private Bay, Petone, New Zealand, came another forensic aid to auto investigation.

Almost every report of a car chase includes details not only of debris such as

Depending upon the resins in the car-body fillers (epoxy and polyester resins are mostly used in the auto body trade, internationally) Cleverley was able to identify fillers by spectra colours ranging from black through shades of brown, yellow and green, to silver and white.

A different application of spectrophotometry has enabled Britain's Dr. J. B. F. Lloyd, of the Home Office Forensic Science Laboratory, Birmingham, to give world forensic workers a precise new technique—characterization of mineral oil traces.

Oil drips

"The circumstances may be," says Dr. Lloyd, "that oil and grease may be found on pedestrians struck by motor vehicles, oil drips left where vehicles have been parked, or oil carried on stolen engine parts. Waste oil is a widely-distributed material likely to be transferred at scenes of crime . . ."

Back in 1951 a continental worker characterized petroleum products such as car oil by the fluorescence of a sample diffused on blotting paper, and in 1955 Dr. A. D. Baynes-Cope disclosed his technique for examination of pitch (as from car-battery cases), mineral oil, and grease.

A few years later, using a Baird Atomic SF 100E spectro-photofluorimeter at the Home Office Laboratory in Birmingham, England, Dr. Lloyd made use of a completely new technique known as synchronous excitation of fluorescence emission. The spectra of minute samples of car oils and fuels were examined, and the fluorescence noted while the samples were excited at varying wave lengths.

Crashing distance

In the crime laboratory graphs were plotted of the fluorescence spectra of hydrocarbons likely to be encountered in car-crime cases. Then it was the work of only a few minutes to check a new suspect sample against a known control.

In most accident and hit-and-run cases there are skid or brake marks left on the road, and forensic workers may have to interpret these. Few ordinary motorists even consider what enormous forces produce the familiar burn marks on the road. They are actually the result of the car's energy in being braked changed into heat and then burning the road.

Forensic workers need to determine stopping and "crashing" distances from these marks, and a cross-section of them were told by Mr. S. S. Oldham (a consultant engineer specializing in this aspect of car-crime research) at a Forensic Science Society meeting in Great Britain.

"The energy stored up in a moving vehicle varies as the square of its speed—in other words, if you double the speed

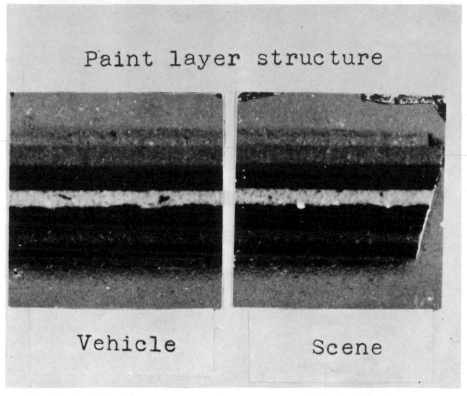

COMPARISON of paint fragments found at crime scene with suspect vehicle . . .

simple device was adopted by forensic workers. An auxiliary steering-wheel was introduced so that a suspect car could be driven by police to the crime laboratory without destroying finger-prints or other material evidence.

Not until 1954 when a detachable steering wheel was devised by Superintendent Fred Cherrill (then head of the New Scotland Yard Fingerprint Bureau, responsible for indexing the Yard's first ten-million dabs) was it possible to handle an abandoned or "crime" car without risk. Until then, all dabs had to be dusted or sprayed and photographed on the spot.

The Cherrill auxiliary wheel fitted the type of symmetrical-spoked steering wheel then in vogue, but it could not be bolted to the more modern American and European wheels.

Then, in 1968 Mr. D. D. F. Hardinge of the Department of Scientific and In-

rust and paint, but of motor body fillers. The complex body pressings of modern cars are given a crack-free and seam-free surface with plastic or other fillers—thus when there's an impact, identification of the filler may prove evidential.

In 1967 research on this was started by Mr. B. Cleverley of the D.S.I.R. Chemistry Division at Petone—who built up a file of infra-red spectra, so that a suspect filler sample could be matched against a known control. With a Perkin-Elmer model-21 spectro-photometer, he put pellet after pellet of filler into the optical system, and brought it to incandescence. The resultant light was viewed through a prism and lens system, splitting it up not only into the colours of the rainbow, but disclosing identifying dark bars or bands between the colours.

To get an absolute standard, pellets 13-mm in diameter were prepared in the laboratory, ground up with potassium bromide in a few drops of tetrachloroethane, blended and dried.

has four times the energy stored in it, so that in reducing the speed from 40 to 20 m.p.h. the brakes have to convert to heat three times the work they would have to do in completing the stop from 20 m.p.h.

"As an example, a fully-laden vehicle weighing six tons, travelling at 30 m.p.h., has stored up a kinetic energy of 404,000 foot-pounds. If the brakes can stop it with even a 50 per cent reading on an efficiency meter, the dissipation is equal to 267 horsepower, in less than three seconds!

"When the wheels are locked during brake application, the tyre slips over the road surface and the heat generated is concentrated in this area. It can, and does, melt the tar in the road surface, producing the characteristic black marks."

New techniques

For forensic tests after a running-down accident, the police usually drive the vehicle over the same road surface at the scene, producing identical burn marks. This enables forensic experts to testify that, to produce the marks found, the vehicle had to be driven at such-and-such a speed, and the brakes applied until the wheels locked—when the vehicle slid to a standstill in so many feet.

Not all car accidents and car-crimes are deliberate, and a good deal is due to "the nut at the wheel". As Mr. Oldham put it: "I am sure that the average car driver has no conception of the tremendous power and kinetic-energy-potential that he is in charge of, or how ill-fitted he is by nature to drive a motorcar at all—when one considers the very slow reaction-time possessed by humans.

"It is about three-fifths of a second which, at 30 m.p.h. or 44 feet-per-second, means that he will travel roughly 27 feet before he can react to anything!"

Escaping criminals, drunken drivers, and almost every category of motorist driving crazily, depend upon tyres. It is not surprising, therefore, that forensic and allied workers in many countries are still building up a fund of new techniques—not always in agreement. Among world leaders in this forensic sphere are Mr. R. J. Grogan of Fort Dunlop in association with Mr. T. R. Watson of the Birmingham Home Office Forensic Science Laboratory, in Britain.

The Grogan-Watson team have found new facets quite apart from the obvious "fingerprint" matching of tyres to tread-marks at a scene of crime. In most cases they can instantly identify patterns by tyre width and features such as knife-cuts (sipes), decorative trade pattern lines, and so on. Tyres such as Henley Super Miler, Avon Super Safety and Avon Turbospeed will give similar patterns, but it is often possible to identify a type of vehicle from its tyre mark.

"There is a very common tendency," explains Mr. Grogan, "to believe that criminals reverse into the gateways to fields before discarding their wares: but examination of tyre prints in relation to gateways usually shows that the vehicle has been driven in forwards, and has either been reversed when out of sight or, more commonly, been driven in a circle inside the field.

"Oil spots will usually indicate the position of the engine, and when taken into conjunction with tyre marks show whether a front- or a rear-engined car has been used."

NEAT FIT . . . Flakes of paint taken from hit-and-run vehicle match those picked up at scene.

Forensic investigation of car crime often produces startling results—but seldom more surprising than in the case of gang-leader Georgie Day who in 1957 was taken terribly injured to St. Leonard's Hospital, Hoxton, in East London.

"He's been the victim of a hit-and-run accident," said the two men who brought Day to the Casualty Ward. But even before Day died in hospital, detectives of the Criminal Investigation Department were certain they were on a murder hunt.

There were no blood marks in the street where the two men said Day had been hit by a car. Then, less than twenty-four hours later, an abandoned truck was found in a Peckham (South London) street, and was discovered to have the rear wheels stained with blood of Group-B—the group of the dead gangster. Fibres from his blue serge suit were discovered adhering to an oily rear spring. And on the hub-caps of the truck there were smears of red brick dust.

At once the C.I.D. team began a hunt for a wall, possibly one which had been knocked down and hurriedly rebuilt. Local police reported such a wall in Brockley, South-east London, and when the detectives dug the soil at the base of the brickwork they found more Group-B bloodstains. Meanwhile the post-mortem examination revealed that Day had been hit by something heavier than a hit-and-run car blow.

A crime pattern was built up, and on December 11th at the Old Bailey Mr. Justice Glyn-Jones sentenced the two men who had "rescued" Day to terms of imprisonment—one of four years, and one of three.

The truth was that Day had been involved in a big theft of lead, and the truck had crushed him against the wall while it was being unloaded.

Of his two confederates, the judge stated that they had acted "with selfish cruelty" in finishing their theft before taking him to hospital.

Using techniques now routine in all cases of car crime, the London C.I.D. and the Metropolitan Police Forensic Laboratory had been able to reach the truth of the matter—thus ensuring that justice was done, and was seen to be done.

CLUES FROM HAIR

Looking at a human hair under a microscope the forensic scientist can obtain information about the age, race and sex of its owner.

HAIR can provide crime investigators with important clues. Apart from burning, hair is virtually indestructible. It remains identifiable even on bodies in an advanced state of decomposition or attached to objects after a crime has been committed.

The forensic scientist using a micro-scope can make even a single head hair yield information about the race, sex and age of its owner, and while hair does not have the same individual character as a fingerprint, it can provide vital evidence.

For example, in August 1951, a woman's body was found in a rural spot near Nottingham. The victim, Mabel Tatter-shaw, a 48-year-old housewife, had been strangled. Minute inspection of her cloth-ing revealed some hairs which were im-mediately sent to the forensic labora-tory, where microscopic examination showed them to be identical with the head

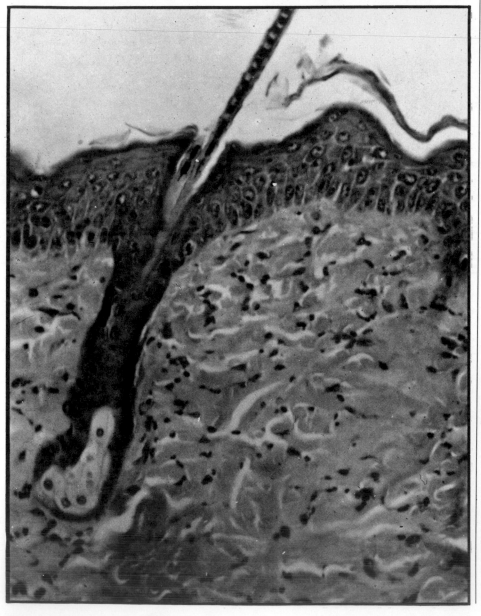

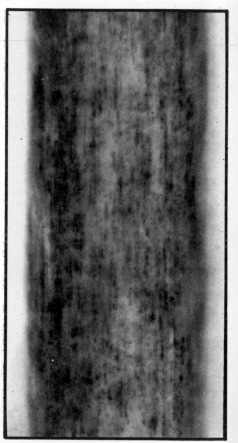

ANIMAL or human? The naked eye may not be able to discern the difference even between types of hair which are totally dissimilar. Under a microscope the distinctions become plain. On the facing page are three kinds of animal hair from (left to right) a dog, a cat and a horse. The picture (above) is of a human hair and (left) is a follicle. Com-pared with other branches of forensic science, the study of hair has a long way to go. But its value is undeniable.

hair of Leonard Mills, an 18-year-old clerk and the chief suspect. Together with other damning evidence, these hairs helped to take a murderer to the scaffold.

Chemical changes

Apart from the obvious characteristics of length, colour and texture, hair seen under a magnification of ×200 has an amazing variety of properties. An individual hair is a solid, roughly cylindrical structure. It consists of an inner core or medulla containing colouring pigment, a middle layer – the cortex – made of a dense, horny substance known as keratin, and an outer layer, the cuticle, composed of tiny overlapping scales.

The cuticular scales, which vary in shape between individuals, are of great value when matching hairs; most importantly, the scales enable human hair to be readily distinguished from that of animals. The differences between animal hairs are quite marked and any hair discovered is quite easily matched to a particular creature. Dog hairs, for example, found on a suspect's clothing can place him at the scene of a crime.

The part of the body from which a hair has come is also determined by its shape. Head hairs, for instance, are usually square at the ends while eyebrow hairs are finely tapered. Moustache hairs tend to be triangular in section.

Sex is not as easily determined from head hair except by the now vanishing differences in length. Hair that is treated; bleached, dyed, lacquered, singed or curled may give additional help in sexing hair, but there are differences in the pubic hairs, which appear rather longer in men and somewhat coarser in women.

Male pubic hairs are always looked for on alleged victims of rape.

It is possible to tell the age of hair, but only within fairly wide limits. Chemical changes occur with age, and laboratory tests can distinguish between hair from a child and an adult; hair also thickens slightly with age and this thickening can be measured.

Cross-section

When it is sent for examination to the Forensic Science Laboratory hair is normally dry mounted on a glass slide for viewing under a comparison microscope. To examine it in cross-section, the specimen is mounted in a wax block from which wafer-thin slices are cut and mounted on glass slides. The cross-sectional shape and appearance of the medulla is then viewed microscopically.

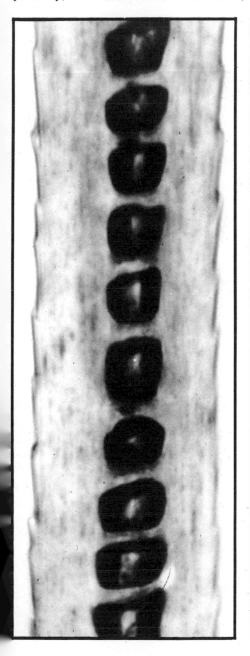 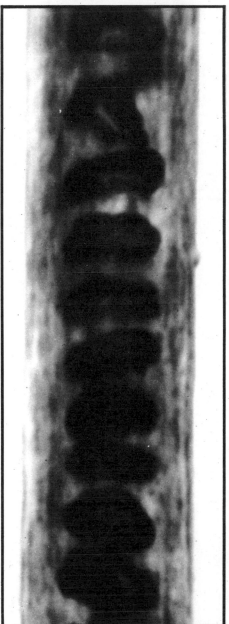 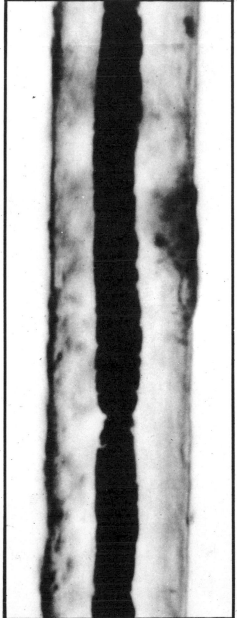

Ken Moreman

119

Impressions of the cuticular scales are sometimes made on cellulose acetate for detailed study; the forensic scientist also has a variety of tests available for dealing with dyed hair and examining for age.

The brilliance of the forensic laboratory cannot shine, however, without the most thorough and painstaking work of investigating officers at the scene of the crime; fortunately, in regard to hair, nature is on the side of the crime investigator. The hair of every part of the body has a definite period of growth and is continuously lost and replaced; minute examination of clothing and other articles can therefore pay dividends.

Decomposed remains

Evidence provided by hair has played an important part in a number of murder investigations. In October 1942, the badly decomposed remains of a woman's body were found buried on a heath near Godalming, Surrey. It was estimated that the body had been lying in the heather for about five weeks. This was the so-called 'Wigwam' murder, in which the victim, who had been stabbed and beaten about the head, lived in a crude shelter made of branches and heather.

Police searching the heathland made several discoveries which enabled them to confirm the victim's identity as Joan Pearle Wolfe. They also found a heavy birch branch with hair adhering to it lying in long grass about 400 yards from the body. Laboratory examination identified this as the weapon responsible for the head injuries; nine head hairs sticking to the heavy end of the branch proved to be identical with the head hair of the victim. August Sangret, a French-Canadian soldier from a nearby camp, had been living with the girl in the 'Wigwam' for several months. He was tried for murder, found guilty and executed at Wandsworth.

Scraps of paper

Probably the most famous murder featuring hair evidence was the Podmore Case. On January 10, 1929, a man's body was found behind some boxes in a locked garage at Southampton. The victim, Vivian Messiter, an oil company agent, had been dead for some time, and rats had attacked the body. A puncture wound over the left eye at first led the local police to think that the man had been shot, but the real cause of death was multiple fractures to the skull—Messiter had been battered to death with a heavy, blunt instrument.

Sir Bernard Spilsbury, the famous forensic expert, examined the body and described the terribly battered head as "being fractured everywhere except on top". Boxes near the body had been spattered with blood to a height of several feet. The pathologist concluded that a large hammer, wielded with great violence, would account for the injuries.

The dead man had been on the missing persons list for nine weeks and police had checked at the garage, but finding it locked, did not pursue the enquiry; it was only when another oil company representative came to take over the agency that the garage door was forced open and Messiter's body was discovered. Among papers found in the dead man's lodgings was a reply to an advertisement for local agents signed, "William F. Thomas". The police quickly got onto the trail of W. F. Thomas and discovered that a man of that name had worked for a Wiltshire building contractor. A large sum of money in wage packets had disappeared, and after being interviewed by the county police, Thomas had vanished.

The Press Association

TRAPPED by hair evidence were Leonard Mills, who strangled Mabel Tattershaw (left), and Auguste Sangret, who brutally slayed Joan Wolfe (right).

Thomas's departure had been so hurried that he foolishly neglected to tidy up his lodgings thoroughly. There, detectives subsequently found some scraps of paper bearing the words, "Podmore" and "Manchester". It did not take long to establish that a man called Podmore, a motor mechanic working in Manchester, had left that city three days before W. F. Thomas took lodgings in Southampton. Meanwhile, Scotland Yard turned up its files and the record of William Henry Podmore, a man who had been in the hands of the police several times, was brought to light; as a result of this careful routine police work Podmore was found and taken in for questioning. He had, it appeared, been Messiter's assistant, but his story about his movements and use of false names and addresses was very involved. The police did not have enough to make a murder charge stick, but Podmore got six months' imprisonment for a fraud committed in Manchester.

The detectives investigating Messiter's murder were convinced Podmore was their man. A bloodstained hammer had been found close to the murder scene—it was a heavy tool and one end of the head was sharply pointed. An engineer from another garage nearby told the police that he had lent the hammer to a stranger at the end of October. Podmore was included in an identity parade but the engineer failed to pick him out.

The breakthrough in the investigation came with a detailed examination of a receipt book for oil sale commissions. It was discovered that indentations between the lines of a genuine receipt had been made by pencilled writing on the sheet above, which had been torn out. The indentations when specially photographed revealed a fictitious receipt for commission made out by "W. F. Thomas".

Police theorized that Messiter had discovered that he was being swindled and tackled Podmore about it. Knowing that the Manchester police wanted him for fraud, Podmore lost his nerve and attacked his accuser with the hammer. Podmore was completely without sympathy at his trial, for it was obvious that as Messiter lay unconscious on the floor of the garage, his head had been smashed with blow after blow from the hammer.

The hammer was unquestionably the murder weapon. Spilsbury found on it a hair which corresponded with the eyebrow hair of the dead man. Podmore was tried at Winchester Assizes in March 1930—it had taken the police over a year to accumulate sufficient evidence. But the prosecution was successful and Podmore was convicted and hanged. Public opinion was against Podmore and a great play was made on the hair found on the murder weapon; one newspaper carried a headline, "Two hairs hanged this man!" and followed up with a sensational piece about "the revealing lens" and "the most vital clue of all".

The hair evidence in the Podmore case was only part of a painstaking police investigation. It undeniably identified the murder weapon and while it helped, it did not of itself hang Podmore. This underlines the judgment which forensic scientists bring to their job. They know how much reliance to place on evidence and, in the case of hair, realize that its incriminating value has to be carefully evaluated.

It is not yet possible to identify individuals by hair with the same exactitude as by fingerprints, but new techniques such as neutron activation analysis are constantly being developed to aid forensic investigation. In activation analysis, hair is irradiated in a nuclear reactor and the subsequent rate of decay is calculated electronically. This increases the individuality of hair and is one means by which the gaps in forensic knowledge are bridged in this important and ever-widening sphere of criminal investigation.

WHEN MESSITER (below right) was killed his hair was left on a hammer in the garage (below). A year later painstaking police investigations pinned the guilt on Podmore (below left).

POST MORTEM

Legal or "forensic" medicine plays an increasingly important part in the battle against the murderer, rapist, and violent criminal. Since the days of Hogarth (below) the medical profession has studied violent death with growing care. Today, the police photographer (bottom) is followed to the scene of the crime by the police pathologist, who begins his grim work on the spot.

Aldus Books/Ronan Picture Library

LEGAL MEDICINE is an American term for something which, in Britain, is called medical jurisprudence by some and forensic medicine by others (the latter is the more usual term, but the differences are, largely, a matter of interpretation). Newspapers frequently refer to a "medico-legal expert". Most European countries follow, in their own languages, the French *médecine légale*.

In the United States legal medicine belongs, broadly, to the nineteenth and twentieth centuries; the former saw the official beginning, apart from isolated earlier instances which were largely indirect legal medicine. A Dr. J. S. Stringham, an M.D. from Edinburgh, more or less initiated matters when he lectured on legal medicine in 1804; he was followed by a Dr. Benjamin Rush in 1811 who was the author of a book which contained a chapter on the "Study of Medical Jurisprudence"—he was also a stern opponent of capital punishment.

Two years later a Dr. Caldwell gave a course of lectures on legal medicine at the University of Pennsylvania (Britain had founded the first chair of forensic medicine in 1807 at the University of Edinburgh). The next important milestone was when a pupil of Dr. Stringham, T. R. Beck, was appointed professor of physiology and lecturer in medical jurisprudence in the College of Physicians and Surgeons, New York state; his classic *Elements of Medical Jurisprudence* was published in 1823, and appeared in several European countries.

Office of coroner

After this, various works of importance followed, but though many notable American books were published on the subject, progress was slow. Even doctors and lawyers were not generally impressed with the infant group of sciences which, collectively, did not impress the country at large. Legal medicine over the early years suffered from incompetents and self-elected "experts" who tried to get on the band-waggon, tending to create prejudice. The medical examiner system—the basis of legal medicine in some ways—was introduced in Boston in 1877 (the state of Massachusetts followed later); New York abolished the coroner in 1918 in favour of the medical examiner system.

The first step in early legal medicine, was the coroner, an Office which went to the States with the first wave of settlers, though the coroner today does not have the same powers as his counterpart in England. Indeed, he could even be open to actions by irate relatives because a post-mortem on a dead body had taken place, or parts of it removed for laboratory examination—while medical examiners have powers over the dead body almost as great as their counterparts in England.

To get this quite clear it is as well to look at both offices as often in the United States—and certainly in other English-speaking countries—they can be genuine puzzles to laymen.

As stated, the first settlers brought English law with them and the official known as the coroner first sat at an inquest in the Colony of New Plymouth, 1635, when a dead body was "searched" and it was found that the death was from natural causes. Today the coroner should be seen as an elective office, meaning that, usually, a country official gains the position by popular vote for a term of two or four years. Qualifications for the office are not usually required, but in England a lawyer or a doctor (generally the former) is coroner.

Unnatural death

It is a fact that in America anyone can be elected as coroner—undertakers, grocers, bowling-alley operators have been given the position in the past. On one occasion, in Indiana, it proved impossible to find the right man in a small locality and the pool-room inmates, sitting on the question, appointed the village idiot to the post.

The coroner, once elected, in a fairly large state could well have one or more

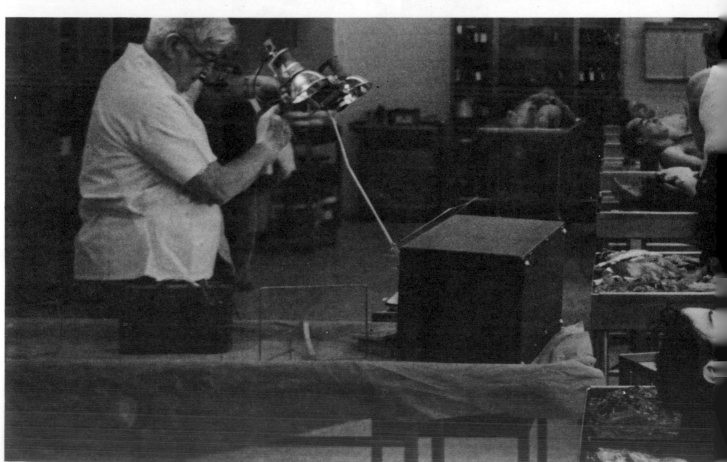

physicians on his pay-roll, together with a forensic pathologist. Depending on the amount of "business", they could also appoint deputies or assistants.

In the case of an apparently unnatural death, it is reported to the coroner by the police. The Coroner's Physician will view the body at a funeral parlour, or in a morgue. Usually a corpse that has suffered violent death is not always seen by the coroner or his assistants, but by a pathologist *after* it has been examined by the police and removed to a place of temporary rest. The pathologist is not always a man experienced in the forensic field, but may be a hospital pathologist or a physician, who would hold the part time appointment or office.

End corruption

On the other hand the medical examiner system was introduced by law in its first state, Massachusetts, in 1887, a post concerned "with dead bodies of such persons *only* as are supposed to have come to their deaths by violence". The basic idea was to end corruption among coroners in that state, but not until after World War II did the system really become nationwide practise.

The medical examiner, unlike the coroner, is a trained man in legal medicine, appointed by the state and on a par with the permanent state officials. He is pro-

NEW YORK'S Dr. Milton Helpern has conducted 60,000 autopsies (above). Work in police mortuaries is a grisly but vital part of criminology.

vided with a proper laboratory organization and staff, and he examines a dead body as a pathologist, but he is not concerned with the legal angles of the case.

The office by appointment varies from state to state. For example, in New York the choice is made by the Mayor, but the selected man must be taken from classified lists compiled by the Municipal Civil Service (New York possesses one of the most famous of all medical examiners in Dr. Milton Helpern, a "grand old man" of legal medicine—he has performed or supervised some 60,000 autopsies).

In another state, Maryland, the procedure is more cumbersome but equally efficient. The selected man is chosen by a board consisting of the Professors of Pathology at two universities, the Commissioner of Health in the chief city, the State Director of Health, and the Superintendent of State Police.

Progress required

There is one thing in common in every state—the medical examiner must be medically qualified. The nearest thing in England would be the police surgeon (who is first on the scene on police notification —when he and the pathologist are integral members of a team, the head of which is the investigating officer).

The medical examiner system is preferred by many to the coroner system

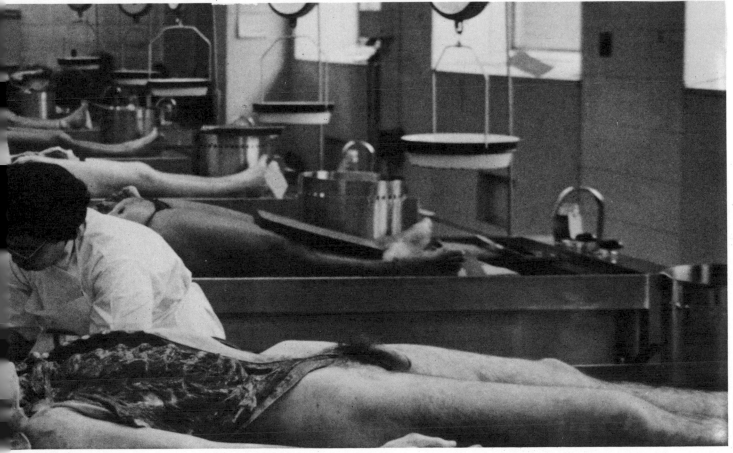

since it means that sudden or unnatural deaths are dealt with from the moment of official discovery by a man fully trained in legal medicine. Lack of money, or money insufficiently provided, tends to slow up the system in certain places — though, even when it exists, some homicide investigators have yet to see the importance of letting the pathologist view the body where it is found and before anyone, including the undertaker, has touched it.

Generally, after the two specifics of coroner and medical examiner, legal medicine in the States tends to follow broadly the rules in England, allowing for local and legal differences.

Progress, however, is more widely required; ". . . law schools and medical schools in the United States have fallen far short of their expected task in the education of law and medical students insofar as legal medicine is concerned" is the view of the Editor of the *Legal Medicine Annual* (Appleton-Century-Crofts, N.Y.C., 1969). And while there has been progress since this statement, it is still to be improved.

Legal medicine, however much or little of it there may be, is generally of a high standard, and its practitioners are able men, thrusting hard in search of new and useful discoveries, working under difficulties, but admirable at their tasks.

In rape, for instance, nothing can present the medico-legal examiner, or the physician, with quite so many imponderables. Forcible rape in the United States in 1971 reached an estimated total of 41,890 cases — a figure which has increased by 55% since 1966, and 10% since 1970. It is regarded by the F.B.I. as one of the most under-reported crimes because of fear or embarrassment on the part of the victims.

There is always modesty or shock on the victim's part which makes for difficulties, or a family "closing ranks" to protect the female concerned, and false accusations are nearly as hard to sort out as the real thing.

Abortion laws

The medical-examiner has, of course, numerous weapons on his side, once he can actually examine the victim. Blood grouping, which can be applied to semen, makes it possible at times to accuse or excuse the person named by the victim, or a person caught or found by the police. But, too often, the victim is in a state where the medical man must be his own detective, father confessor, microscope eye and combined psychologist and psychiatrist. He has to use physical conditions (or guidance from them), as well as a lot of sheer instinct to help him reach a prognosis or decision of sorts.

However, the case might result in pregnancy and, unlike England, the United States has a welter of complicated abortion laws. Unless it is manifestly therapeutic, abortion is against the law in various states. Abortions *can* be performed within the letter of the law (but the factor of protection of the mother has to be a very strong one indeed, her health, her sanity and so on). There is no federal law on the subject, but state criminal codes tend to be similar in their requirements in induced abortion. The primary term, therapeutic abortion, is generally covered by the fact "to preserve the life of the mother".

In England, before World War II and its present broader abortion laws, a surgeon aborted a girl who had been raped by four men; the abortion was deliberate to test, and to draw attention to, the injustice of the law. The surgeon was severely dealt with, but there is no doubt the present relaxation of abortion laws was sparked by his action.

In the United States Massachusetts, which so boldly pioneered the medical examiner system, is an example of general state laws when it lays down that an induced abortion, if the patient dies, can bring its operator from 5 to 20 years in the state prison. Or, if the patient does not die, anything up to 7 years imprisonment and a fine of not more than $2,000. The state of Pennsylvania, however, is implacable. For, depending on the case, the fine can be up to $6,000, or imprisonment not exceeding 10 years in separate or solitary confinement, *or both*.

Effective weapon

In America legal medicine accepts certain strictly defined rules of criminal responsibility of the mentally ill. But in order to modify the undoubted harshness of the rules the doctrine of the "irresistable impulse test" is accepted by some states. Federal and military penal laws acknowledge this supplementary view in the form of "if the defendant did know the nature and quality of his act . . . was he unable, because of mental disease or defect, to adhere to the right?"

As far back as 1869, however, New Hampshire rejected the prescribed rules. But no other state followed this trailblazing point of view until 1954, when the U.S. Court of Appeals for the District of Columbia handed down the Durham decision which accepted the New Hampshire attitude of 1869. This was welcomed by medico-legal psychiatrists with a feeling that progress was on the move — although many states have so far rejected the improvement.

Forensic psychiatry tended to be something of a Cinderella before the Durham decision, but it is now a far more effective weapon in the armoury of legal medicine in its work for the law. Every day brings some new force into play which will eventually result in legal medicine and its many ancillary sciences and disciplines proving to be invaluable in the increasing fight against crime.

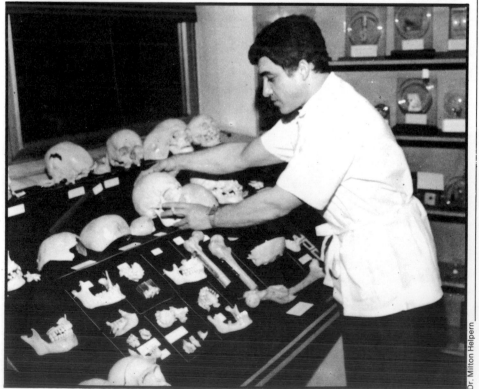

Dr. Milton Helpern

VIOLENCE has left its brutal mark on these relics, part of a New York forensic medicine collection.

GUNS

1 The wheel-lock pistol. "Evil disposed persons," said England's Henry VIII, "have done detestable murders with little short guns." This sixteenth-century weapon unleashed a crime wave which has never ceased. Good King Henry launched a campaign against them—but in vain. No self-respecting highwayman would have dreamed of robbing without one.

2 Peacemaker Colt ·45—one of the great guns that won the West. It also helped to turn Boot Hill into a mountain. Favoured by criminals and lawmen alike, the Colt ·45 is said to have been the most successful murder weapon of all time. Especially useful for lone duels at sun-up.

3 Remington "Elliot" Derringer. The small pistol that fired the big ·50 bullet, it was designed for only one purpose: to kill with the first shot. For the "dude" of the old West—the flashy businessman—it was the perfect instrument for disposing of unwanted rivals . . . and colleagues.

4 The Mauser 7·63 mm. semi-automatic. Powerful and deadly. Definitely not recommended for subtle murders, but excellent for felling police officers and persuading undesirables to keep their distance. More than 200 lawmen and troops were held at bay with two Mausers during London's siege of Sidney Street in 1911. Even the army had no answer.

5 Machine gun. Any make will do. It is quick and efficient—especially for mass murders—but requires a certain Al Capone-style panache. Pictured here is a handy 9 mm. Sten sub-machine gun. Light-weight and convenient for gang warfare, the gun's great advantage is its wastage allowance. At 600 rounds per minute you can afford to miss a few times

6 FN Browning 7·65 mm. model. Compact and decorated with a mother-of-pearl handle, it fits neatly into a lady's handbag or muff—and is at its best in the company of evening dress and a little perfume. Ideal for slaying an unwanted husband or lover—or dealing with mother-in-law

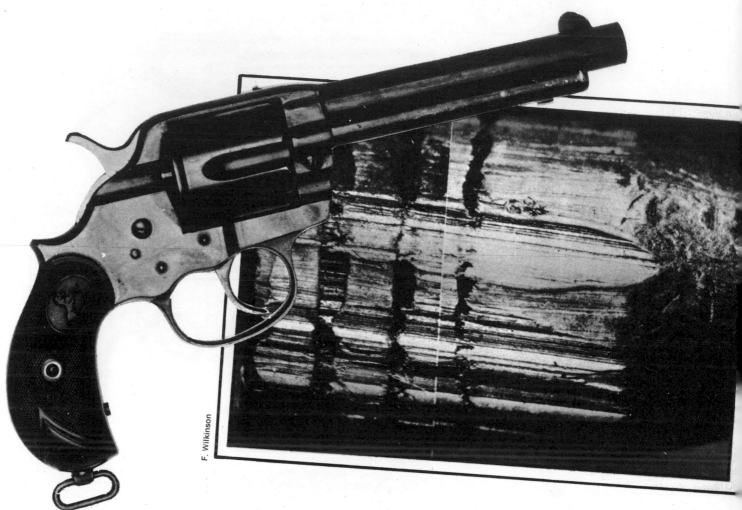

F. Wilkinson

RIFLE wounds are distinguished by the high velocity of the weapon—a bullet from 3000 yards away may still be travelling at 300 feet per second—on impact. Bullets frequently pass through the body and if no resistance is met, entry and exit will be almost identical; the only slight difference being that the former is inverted at the edge and the latter everted. Internal damage will be present as a result of "tissue quake" and extensive damage will be caused if the bullet is diverted within the body.

Although it ignites instantaneously, the explosive charge of a cartridge is still burning when the bullet leaves the muzzle of the gun; consequently, hot gases, flame, smoke and particles of unburnt powder are discharged with the bullet and their effects may be found around the wound.

Powder particles embedded or tattooed in the skin may indicate the range at which a weapon was fired, although this only applies to a maximum of three feet.

UNDER the microscope . . . By close examination an expert can tell not only the make and calibre of a bullet but also the weapon from which it was fired.

Traditional gunpowder is black and is composed of potassium nitrate, sulphur and charcoal, but is not used a great deal today except in the manufacture of shotgun cartridges. Most modern powders are smokeless and grey in colour, consisting of flakes of nitro-glycerine or nitro-cellulose which will be readily recognized by the expert. Smokeless powders are explosively more efficient and leave fewer traces of burning and tattooing even at close range. Infra-red photography is used to determine whether marks on clothing are due to powder. The resulting graphic representation of powder residues gives a clear indication of the range at which a weapon was fired.

Estimations of range at which rifle weapons have been fired can be made by

examining the lead deposits around entry wounds. Saturated aqueous solution of sodium rhodizonate sprayed on the previously acidified wound area gives a blue reaction if lead is present. Distinction between the lead patterns thus revealed can be related to the distance at which the weapon was fired.

One of the first questions to be asked at the scene of a fatal wounding involving firearms is, "Was the shooting homicide, suicide or an accident?" The answer given must take into consideration the probable type of weapon which caused the wound, the range and direction of the discharge and the site of the injury.

In a suspected suicide, the wound must be in an accessible place, that is, within the subject's arm's reach. The classic sites selected for suicide are the temple (right side for the right-handed person), forehead, mouth and the area of the heart. The range is necessarily close unless some device such as a piece of string or a

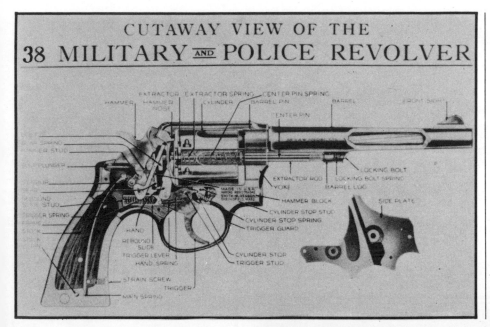

CUTAWAY VIEW OF THE
38 MILITARY AND POLICE REVOLVER

HOW IT WORKS . . . This Smith and Wesson .38 is one of the all-time great revolvers. There is probably very little room for further improvement of this gun.

length of wood has been used to pull the trigger. This is often the case where a rifle is the elected weapon.

Self-inflicted wounds are almost inevitably contact injuries with signs of burning and tattooing. Entry wounds not situated at the classic sites are always subject to suspicion and wounds inflicted outside of normal arm's reach are almost certainly not suicidal; it is rare for a suicide to fire twice in any one of the classic sites, and two or more wounds are therefore almost certainly homicidal.

The question of accessibility arose in a shooting incident at an army camp near Warminster in 1918. Corporal Dunkin was found dead on his bed; on the floor nearby lay a .303 Lee Enfield rifle. Dunkin had been shot through the temple. One round had been fired from the rifle. The bullet had passed through his head, entering in front of the left ear and exiting behind the right ear.

The police were undecided whether it was a case of suicide or murder. Sir Bernard Spilsbury examined the wound and estimated that it had been caused by a shot fired at a distance of 5 inches or more. The dead man's arms were exceptionally short for a man of his height and this proved to be a deciding factor. Spilsbury showed that the corporal lying full-length on his bed could only have reached the rifle's trigger by pressing the muzzle firmly against his cheek. Clearly, then, suicide was out of the question and the police set about a murder investigation. Eventually, another soldier at the camp was convicted of murdering

Dunkin as he lay asleep.

There are no distinctive features governing accidental shooting. The accidental discharge of a firearm may result from an action of the victim or by another person; the circumstances must be carefully considered and suicide and homicide specifically ruled out. Examination of the victim and the scene of death is important. Body wounds are inspected to determine the direction of the bullet — especially important is the track within the body linking entry and exit wounds.

Any weapon found at the scene must be carefully handled. Contrary to the practice of detectives in popular fiction, it is not correct procedure to lift up a pistol by inserting a pencil down the barrel — this may preserve any fingerprints but it is likely to damage important evidence in the gun's barrel. Any spent cartridges or wads should also be treated with care. If the bullet is still inside the body it should be removed with extreme

HOME-MADE . . . The impression of the firing-pin on the cartridge (left) is compared with a standard one for the same gun. The killer had made his own . . .

care; forceps are padded with gauze or rubber in order to preserve any marks on the bullet which may help identify the weapon which fired it. The clothing of the victim is also examined for traces of powder and other explosion products.

Where suicide is suspected the victim's hands are swabbed for powder traces. This is the "dermal nitrate test" which analyses for the presence of nitrate residues blown back onto the firing hand. The test is not conclusive as nitrates from other sources, such as cigarette smoking, may give a false picture; however, together with tests for lead, it may give useful confirmatory evidence of suicide.

The basis for identifying firearms lies with the bullets and cartridges they fire. When a bullet is fired from a rifled weapon it is impressed with marks made by the lands and grooves of the barrel. The lands leave a series of slanting, parallel scratches which vary in number

and width according to the manufacture of the weapon. Grooves also leave marks, for although calibre is measured between lands, the bullet is slightly larger and when fired expands to make contact with both lands and grooves.

Fired cartridge cases are also impressed with identifying marks. The firing pin makes an indentation in the base of the cartridge and scratches are left by the action of the ejector mechanism. The explosion which fires the bullet from a gun barrel also forces the cartridge case back against the breech block with terrific pressure — some twenty tons in a rifle. The cartridge case is thereby imprinted with any defects of machining marks on the metal surface of the breech.

Because the metal of every gun barrel

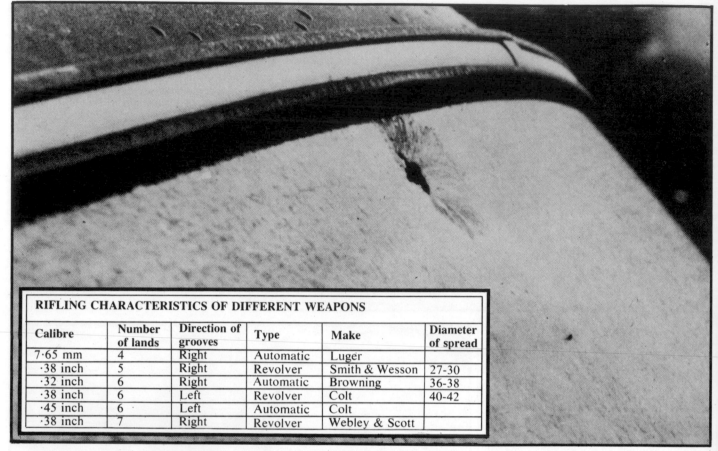

RIFLING CHARACTERISTICS OF DIFFERENT WEAPONS

Calibre	Number of lands	Direction of grooves	Type	Make	Diameter of spread
7·65 mm	4	Right	Automatic	Luger	
·38 inch	5	Right	Revolver	Smith & Wesson	27-30
·32 inch	6	Right	Automatic	Browning	36-38
·38 inch	6	Left	Revolver	Colt	40-42
·45 inch	6	Left	Automatic	Colt	
·38 inch	7	Right	Revolver	Webley & Scott	

and breech has individual irregularities and characteristics of wear, each cartridge and bullet fired from it will be "personalized", and the firearms expert, by examining the marks made on a bullet, will be able to identify the kind of weapon which fired it. The number, width, depth, angle and direction of grooves will speak to him as if they were a fingerprint. The tell-tale marks on cartridge cases also speak for the weapon that fired them.

In a murder case, test rounds fired from the suspected weapon are compared microscopically with the crime bullet. If the marks on the test rounds match those on the crime bullet, the suspected weapon without doubt fired the killing shot. This work is the realm of the firearms expert working with analytical precision, for a man's freedom may depend on his findings.

Test rounds are fired into containers of cotton wool to ensure that the only marks on the bullets are those made by the weapon. Test and crime bullets are examined side-by-side on a comparison microscope. This is essentially a pair of matched microscopes with a common eye-piece enabling two objects to be compared in the same field of view. A camera attached to the eye-piece of the microscope is used to make photo-enlargements which constitute important evidence in criminal proceedings.

On the night of October 10, 1927,

NEAT AND DEADLY . . . The small hole in the windscreen of the car (above) was made by a .22 calibre bullet fired by a gunman standing in front of the vehicle.

Enoch Dix, a 35-year-old labourer, was poaching in Whistling Copse, near Bath in Somerset. It was nearly midnight when he entered the wood with his single-barrelled .410 shot gun; his intention was to pick off a few roosting pheasants, rightfully belonging to Lord Temple, with the aid of a moonlit sky.

Dix's first shots were heard about a mile away by his Lordship's gamekeepers. Head keeper William Walker, and under keeper George Rawlings loaded their 12 bores and headed for Whistling Copse. They found Dix and challenged him. Dix's shot gun went off and Walker fell dying from a wound in the throat. Rawlings fired twice at the poacher.

There was no difficulty in identifying Dix as the poacher. Rawlings told the police that Dix had shot Walker at point-blank range. Dix at first denied any knowledge of the affair but the police found the gun at his cottage. He was asked to strip so that he could be examined for shot wounds as Rawlings was sure that he had hit him. Incredibly, his back, neck and thighs were covered with shot holes. His wife had dressed the wounds and he carried on the pretence of not being hit. It was useless for him to

deny that he had been in the copse but he said simply that his own gun discharged with the shock of his being hit by the blast.

There was no question as to who held the gun which fired the lethal charge—it was a matter of deciding who fired first and at what range. At this point the firearms expert was called in to assist the police. Robert Churchill, the famous gunmaker and ballistics expert, set about calculating the firing distance. He fired at a series of white-washed metal plates, using the under keeper's gun and identical cartridges, and varying the range. The weapon fired consistently, which was important.

After considering these test patterns, together with the wounds in Dix's back, Churchill concluded that the shot which hit the poacher was fired at not less than 15 yards—luckily for Dix, most of the keeper's blast was stopped by a tree.

If Dix's gun had discharged accidentally when he was hit, it must have gone off at a distance of 15 yards from the two keepers. At that range, tests showed Dix's shot gun to have a spread of 27 to 30 inches. But the wound in the dead keeper's throat was only five inches in diameter. To produce such a wound the poacher's gun must have been fired at less than five yards—at point blank range. The jury at Bristol Assizes returned a verdict of manslaughter against Dix and he was sentenced to fifteen years.

RECONSTRUCTIONS AND PROCEDURES

A woman's body plunges from the apartment building and crashes onto the street below. "It was an accident", says the husband. Or was it murder . . .

IRIS NINA SEAGAR plunged to her death 200 feet from a Baltimore penthouse. In the early newspaper editions it was headlined as the tragic suicide of a 48-year-old blonde whom all the neighbours in the apartment block liked about as much as they privately disliked her heavy-drinking, younger husband. Nearby neighbours, who continually overheard the couple fighting, had the deepest sympathy with the unfortunate Mrs. Seagar, saying that, of course, the conduct of a man like that would drive any decent woman to suicide.

It soon became horribly clear that Iris Seagar had not jumped from her balcony in a suicide's despair, but had been thrown out by her husband who was the $100,000 beneficiary of her insurance policy. Naturally, there was a suicide clause in the policy. But the husband's explanation was that she was meddling with a faulty window-fitted air conditioner and accidentally tipped over the guardrail.

Iris Seagar's was not the first "Did she fall or was she pushed?" tragedy to occupy the attention of the police, the insurance investigators and forensic workers, and the psychiatric reports and social reports on the couple led to the strong conclusion of murder rather than suicide or accident. But the course of factual events—after Iris Seagar hit the sidewalk 200 feet below in a mass of pulp, blood, and distorted bone—is illuminating to those who wrongly imagine that most forensic work is concerned only with tissues and test-tubes, fingerprints, and fibres.

This aspect of the final solution to the Seagar case involved, in addition to the Homicide Squad, a meteorologist, architectural photographers, and a physicist. Repeated tests were made with lifelike dummies built to simulate Iris Seagar's 5 ft. 3 in. 127 pounds, and a television production company assisted with a video tape recorder coupled to an RCA closed-circuit electronic camera with a zoom lens. This VTR recording of the test falls enabled the forensic team to get a visual record instantly, without delay of processing 16-mm film. The tapes were played over and over again on RCA monitors so that the various trajectories of the falling dummies could be studied.

The body fell 200 feet, landing 16 feet 8 inches from the building, and this was the first fact which caused suspicion. A body falling from such a height falls outwards for a second or two, and the curve for this part of the trajectory can be plotted from many tests. Then the body plummets straight down.

With the various architectural features of the building, it was demonstrated after repeated drop-tests with the video-recorded dummies that the body could have landed no further from the sidewalk edge of the building than $10\frac{1}{2}$ feet.

In free air a person cannot jump farther than on the ground. Weak, middle-aged Iris Seagar could not possibly jump a distance of 16 feet 8 inches in life. She certainly did not do so when plunging to her death.

The tragedy emphasizes the many details which must be observed in every death investigation, but naturally the forensic procedures are not universally accepted.

In the United States the chief medical investigator is required to be a pathologist, and to have a background in forensic pathology. He arranges the autopsies, which are done by him and ordered by the county medical investigator or the county district attorney.

The investigator and the police team then follow certain procedures which always concern forensic workers and (be it noted) the authors of detective fiction and motion picture and television scripts.

Examples? Time and place of notification of death (if an informant calls from some distant place as related to the body, this may arouse suspicion). Exact location of body (Did she fall or was she pushed?). Exact time of arrival of interested parties at the death scene. Identification of the victim . . . retain all possible witnesses, and record or audiotape even statements by bystanders . . . Find why the victim was at the scene (If not found lying peacefully in his own bed, the place of death may be an important clue). What was the conduct of the victim immediately prior to death? Who found the victim? Who last saw the victim alive?

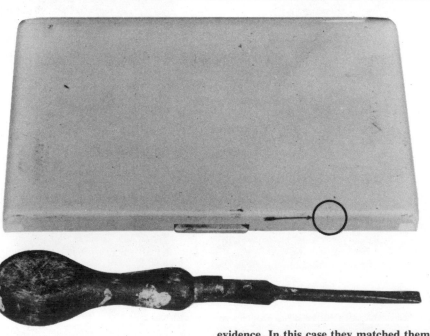

TELL-TALE marks . . . To a layman the minute scratches on the telephone coin box (arrowed above) would mean nothing. To police, however, they could signify vital evidence. In this case they matched them against samples from screwdriver (below) found in possession of the suspect. Photographs (right) showed that the so-called striations were sufficiently alike for the police to obtain a conviction.

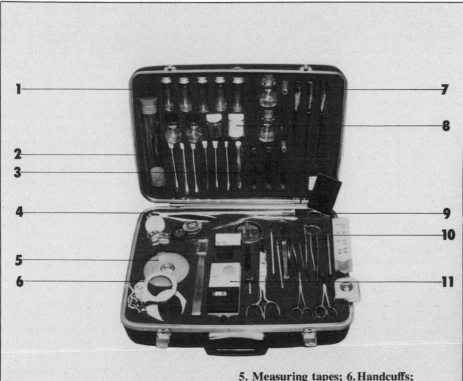

DEATH KIT for the forensic pathologist
1. Sample bottles; 2. Swabs for
blood and semen; 3. Pencil torch;
4. Pliers for extracting teeth;
5. Measuring tapes; 6. Handcuffs;
7 and 8. Fingerprint brushes and
powder; 9. Anal thermometer; 10.
Tweezers; 11. Taperecorder which the
pathologist uses for taking quick notes.

ON GUARD . . . Two plain clothes
detectives watch over the body of a
murder victim which has been carefully
roped off (below) to protect it from
possible interference. It has now become
standard practice to await the arrival
of a forensic pathologist before trying
to move the body. The most seemingly
unimportant details may provide the clue
which will lead police to the criminal.

What tools does the forensic pathologist need, as a preparation for autopsies
in homicide cases and as a bulwark
against totally-unexpected fall-or-push
questions? Dr. D. E. Price, M.B., B.S., a
distinguished pathologist attached to the
Harrogate and Nottingham (England)
Home Office forensic laboratories—and
at the time Consultant Pathologist to the
University of Sheffield (England) Department of Pathology—made no secret of
the equipment for autopsies (post-mortems) to fellow members of the Forensic
Science Society.

"I do not believe," he said, "in undue
disturbance of the body at the scene. I
prefer removal on a sheet of non-contact-
trace-producing substance such as rubber
or plastic; but any loose objects at the
scene are placed in labelled containers . . .
I carry in the back of my car a bag
containing the hundred and one things
one has learned from experience may
be needed . . .

"Adhesive tape for picking up microscopic fibres, measures, labels, pipettes,
syringes, needles, scalpels, scissors,
swabs, and so forth. A box of chemically-
clean bottles, varying in size from one
ounce to seven pounds for the larger
specimens and organs, is needed as well
as a full set of instruments, and protective
clothing . . .

"I carry enough for two or three post-
mortems, as one never knows the magni-

tude of the incident or the distance from one's base. Distance enters a lot into the problem, for the greater the interval of time, the greater the mileage that a suspect can cover and shed his contact traces . . ."

While the forensic worker may decide "she was pushed", a jury is free to come to the decision that "she fell". It was Dr. Price who drew attention to the strange death of a 60-year-old woman, a manic-depressive with a 41-year history of mental illness. At her sudden, tragic death, the usual insurance question arose. The correct decision was of great financial importance to the heirs.

Suicide by drowning had been attempted at least twice in the preceding three years (said Dr. Price). An adequate description was available, including that of an abdominal scar and foot deformities. Thirteen days after she absconded from the mental hospital the first portion of a dismembered body was recovered from a nearby canal in which there was heavy barge traffic.

"During the next fortnight other portions of the same body were recovered. Dismemberment was due to barge propellers. Organs were not found; and facial identity, direct or by superimposition photography, was not possible.

Exact results

"Evidence of stature, scars, hair comparison, foot/shoe deformity's agreement and fingerprint comparison failed to convince a jury, in spite of H.M. Coroner's summing-up.

"Subsequently the High Court (Probate Division) gave letters of administration to the relatives, to whom the estate represented definite financial advantage. It is pleasing to record that the police authorities took the initiative and advised the relatives, who were disconsolate, to seek legal advice with a view to having the verdict set aside."

Edmond Locard of the University of Lyons (a lawyer, not a forensic scientist) first put into words the guiding principle of so much successful forensic investigation. "Every contact leaves a trace," he said. A great deal of laboratory work is therefore concerned with contact traces, with taking moulds and impressions of marks in the hope of being able to fit a tool or a weapon to them, and thus linking the criminal with the crime. This might seem to be science applied to the handling of physical evidence. Yet it is dangerous to disregard the mathematical consequences.

If the tool is a perfect (hundred-per-cent) fit to the mark, it is of course better than a fifty-fifty chance that the suspect was at the scene of the crime. If, however, he has a perfect (hundred-per-cent) alibi, then the forensic worker must wonder what is the use of mathematics?

The matching of marks, etc., is a revolutionary branch of criminalistics which has caused many to investigate, from Burd and Kirk (1942) to Hatcher, Jury, and Weller (1967), leading on to the work of the Californian toxicologist J. W. Bracket, Jr. – Instructor in Physical Evidence in the City College of San Francisco.

Bracket concentrated on the fact that striated tool marks, such as those made by a slipping tool on a cash register, or by a gun barrel on a bullet, could be very important as identification evidence in justifying the conclusion that the two marks (that is, specimen on site, and a controlled mark) were generated by the same tool or instrument.

Occasionally, however, comparison of two sets of tool marks by different criminalists elicits varying opinions as to degrees of similarity, and indeed even different conclusions as to identity or non-identity of evidence. Bracket decided to investigate this problem mathematically.

The first step was to reduce the tool or weapon mark to the ideal state. Models were made in wax, plastic, and other materials, so that the striae could be seen. Each striation was considered to be an element of a set of striae, representing only a position in two-dimensional space between neighbouring elements. The position was then quantized; that is to say, a whole number of unit distances away from each neighbour.

Geometric, number-based and what he termed "outcome" models were then produced, complex graphs showing the "match" and "non-match" characteristics. Presently the mathematics of these tests are being computerized, so that juries (and others) will have a more precise ratio of forensic probabilities to consider, instead of – for example – the baffling proposition: "It's one hundred per cent certain she fell, and a fifty-fifty chance she was pushed."

While the forensic worker does not have to concern himself with whether a jury accepts or rejects his evidence, but only if it was 100 per cent true, he would be less than human were he not to be interested in the outcome. This may depend partly upon psychological techniques (in which the United States is greatly advanced), and also upon the application of law. As has been pointed out in the courts, the German Civil Code and the Code Napoléon "both engender a different psychological approach to questions of guilt and innocence". L. R. C. Haward of the Graylingwell Hospital, Chichester, Sussex, England, reported an interesting example for forensic psychologists to highlight sources of data and error.

The unpleasant case concerned a certain English town where the police had reports that a public toilet was being used for indecent purposes. To abate the nuisance, police officers were concealed in a shallow cupboard for several hours each day, their vision partly obscured by a piece of sacking screen and by iron bars.

Nevertheless, they reported observing two men committing an act of gross indecency. One man after using the urinal turned round and was handled by a second man. Immediately the two police officers sprang out of the cupboard and charged both men with committing an offence, which they denied.

Psychical factors

There was no scientific evidence – no tests for semen, no fingerprint checks, no photographic evidence. The case rested on probabilities. Fifty-fifty? One man was already under suspicion, and of dubious character. The other had previously been charged, but not convicted, with a similar offence. In any layman's terms that brings the probability of conviction to better than fifty-fifty.

A psychologist was appointed to assess the reliability of the police evidence. It was outside his terms to investigate the reliability of the defendants' evidence. But, as in English law the onus is on the prosecution to prove the guilt of the accused, it was therefore fitting that the prosecution evidence only should be submitted to psychological scrutiny.

This investigation ranged from sources of error (in memory and in perception), from psychical factors such as available light (photometer tests were made), the duration of time of the alleged indecency after urination, to the positions of the two men.

The passive participant gave as his explanation that the tail end of his pink silk scarf tended to stick out when his coat was undone. A large blow-up coloured photograph was therefore taken of the man wearing these same clothes, and line and wash pictures were also produced in court, based on plans obtained from the Borough Engineer.

Statistical experience disclosed that there is a probability exceeding 0.25 – that is, greater than one in four – that a mistake in perception will occur. What was the truth? Did they, or didn't they? Was there more a forensic worker could have done, for prosecution or for defence?

"We can never know in this case," says Haward, "for the quantitative evidence was not presented. Rather than confound the jury with expert opinion, counsel wisely introduced the main possible sources of perceptual and recall error in his own cross-examination and address, and succeeded in raising sufficient doubt about the reliability of the police evidence to secure a verdict of Not Guilty."

DETECTING SEXUAL CRIMES

Rape, incest, sexual assault: the crimes police regard with the most revulsion and contempt. But men like Rochester police chief William Lombard (below right) are fighting sex offenders with modern scientific aids. The men in the world's morals squads are now winning their tough battle.

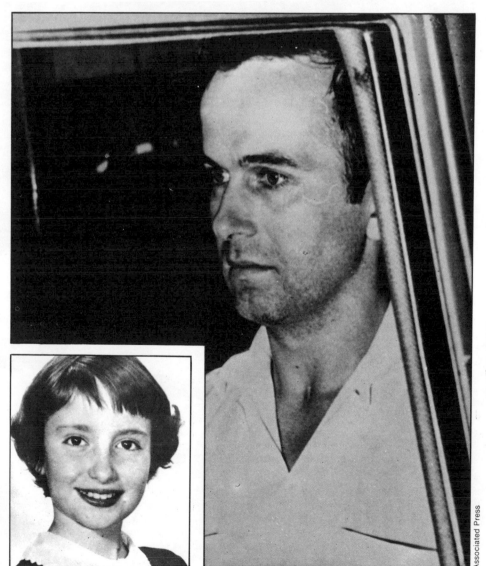

CAUGHT . . . Sex killer James Moore (left) ravished and murdered 13-year-old Pamela Moss (inset) and left her body in a gravel pit. Moore was the first man to be arrested by Rochester's Morals Squad.

Associated Press

135

"FEW criminals are regarded with greater fear and contempt, or dealt with more harshly, than sex offenders," says the Hon. John Rossetti, Judge, Stark County Common Pleas Court, Canton, Ohio, and former Assistant Attorney-General of Ohio. "Yet they are a part of our criminal population, and the public has every right to expect that proper measures are taken to provide a maximum of protection for potential victims."

Judge Rossetti worked to reduce sex crimes in Ohio for many years. Finally, after an eleven-year legal battle when he appeared six times before the Ohio Legislature, a bill requiring the registration of convicted sex offenders was enacted into law. This is the Habitual Sex Offenders Law; it became effective on October· 4, 1963, and since then has set the pattern all over the United States. It has reduced the grim total of sex offences, and decreased the work-load of the police and of forensic scientists in this sordid branch of crime.

For the benefit of U.S. criminalists it must be explained that the revised Code (2950.01 to 2950.08) demands that no habitual sex offender shall be or remain in any county for more than 30 days without registering either with the

CRIME BUSTERS . . . Joan Mathers (below) devised the Rochester system of classifying sex offenders. Her system — and the Photo-FIT technique (right) have helped police throughout the world solve sex cases.

Chief of Police of the city, or the Sheriff of the county.

Who are these habitual sex offenders? In brief, any person convicted two or more times in separate criminal actions of any of the following:

Assault with intent to commit rape (2901.24)
Abducting for immoral purposes (2901.31)
Assault upon a child under 16 years (2903.01)
Rape (2905.01)
Rape of daughter, sister, or any female under 12 (2905.02)
Carnal knowledge of female under 16 years (2905.03)
Rape of person under 14 years (2905.031)
Attempt to have carnal knowledge (2905.04)
Attempted rape; person under 14 years (2905.041)
Carnal knowledge of insane woman (2905.06)
Incest (2905.07)
Sexual intercourse with a female pupil (2905.13)
Indecent exposure: solicitation of an unnatural act (2905.30)
Sodomy (2905.44)

This was a great forward step, for a person so convicted, and who travels for business or pleasure, might well be under pressure so that he abandons his criminal sexual activity.

Then, in another area of the United States, progress was made to control and contain sexual crime by setting up what William L. Lombard, Chief of Police of Rochester, N.Y., dubbed the "Morals Squad". This was born after a cold morning in September, 1962, when Rochester police started investigation

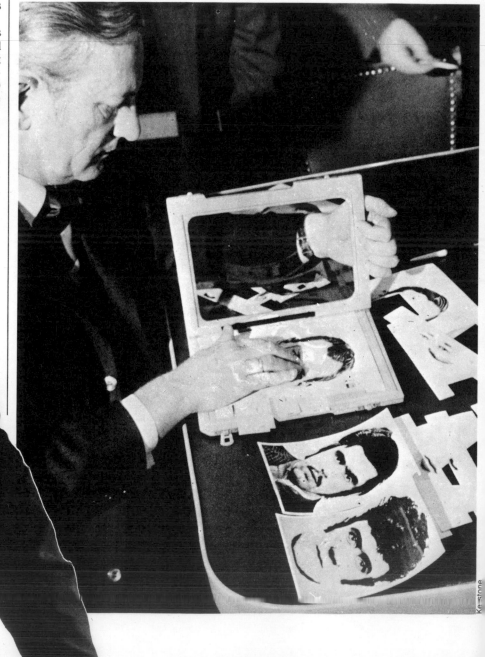

Keystone

into the brutal murder of a 13-year-old girl whose ravished body was found in a gravel pit.

With the aid of investigators of the New York State Police the murderer was apprehended within 10 days; but this case headlined the need for a different registration of sex offenders.

Special Agent (F.B.I.) Walter V. McLaughlin was called in to instruct a group of police bureau men and women in the F.B.I. Sex Crimes Investigation Course. The probe began to log all persons arrested on charges of rape, carnal abuse, sodomy, indecent exposure, and endangering the morals of minors.

A six-digit code for sex offenders is used including (first digit) (1) white, (2) negro, (3) other, and after four more digits relating to age, height, build and hair description, a code digit as follows: (1) limp or gait, (2) eye-glasses, (3) visible scars, crooked, deformed or missing limbs, (4) tattoos, (5) speech, (6) moustache or beard, (7) retarded, (8) ears, hearing defects, (9) teeth, mouth, (10) complexion, moles, and (11) left-handed.

Without delay, all past and current prowler files, carnal-abuse and car files were vetted and translated into a digital code. Then when a new sex crime is reported, all possible suspects can be checked.

Repeating crimes

Just by teletype digits a typical police bureau report on an alleged sex attack can be transmitted, an example of which reads: *"R (recidivist), 1965 in park, whistled at children, dropped trousers below knees. 1972, in High School zone, sitting in car, no trousers, pulled across intersection blocking path of teenaged girls. Drives 69 yellow T-bird. Licence No. 3X 412. Blonde straight, glasses."*

Even to save minutes in this way helps the Morals Squad to apprehend sex criminals and recidivists – those who keep on repeating their crimes. For example, from the Rochester case-histories there was grave concern when over an eight-week period a young man molested girls after presenting himself as a police officer.

An Identi-Kit composite was built up from the children's reports, but this did not result in positive identification. Then from a community 70 miles south of Rochester, N.Y., a young man was arrested on a sex charge. The Morals Squad checked the details of his offence with their digital system and computer-like file cards showing sexual modus operandi. Over the wire-service went photos from the agency which had arrested the man, and immediately the young children in Rochester were able to identify their assailant – who was sentenced on the felony charge of carnal abuse.

Forensic workers who regard sex crime as being bounded by the extremes of rape, buggery, indecent assault, exposure and carnal knowledge, are surprised at the wide range the Morals Squad has to cover.

These include incest, homosexuality, sodomy, boy molesters, rape, teenage molesters, child and adult molesters, theatre, park and bus molesters, school-area and playground molesters, downtown molesters (ramp garages, midtown plaza, department stores and parking lots), girls' dormitory molesters (university areas, nurses' homes and girls' boarding houses), home break-ins with sexual molesting, exposers and car exposers, transvestites, impersonating to commit a sexual offence (police, doctor, minister), enticers and annoyers, sexual involvement with animals (bestiality and cruelty to animals), frotteurs (strokers and hair offences), ladies' underwear involvement (stealing and wearing), procurers, setting fires in course of a sexual act, obscene pictures (distributing, processing, posing), obscene phone-calls, obscene letters and all written obscenities, abortionists, peeping-toms, prowlers, sadists and masochists, and various perversions.

At one stage the Morals Squad records relating to Rochester, N.Y. contained a total of more than 2000 known or suspected sex offenders. Of these 1932 were males, 87 females. Molesters made up the greatest number of offenders with a total of 731 males. There were 372 male exposers, and 271 offending homosexuals. The fact-finding branch of this particular Morals Squad knew that only 82 of the total were incarcerated in local or State institutions; conversely, there were approximately 2000 people with sex-crime potential at large in the area.

American characteristics

While basically sex – and therefore sexual crime – is universal, there are differences between nations when it comes to identification of sex offenders. Thus, prior to the introduction of the Identi-Kit system in the 1950s, there was no swift and reliable way in which the police investigating a sex crime (or even in routine duties with a Morals Squad) could get a "mug-print", or wire it to other police regions. And when eventually the Identi-Kit technique was developed by the Santa Ana, California company, the Townsend Company Inc., it was held by some British and Continental European police executives to deal chiefly with facial types of potential offender with notable "American" characteristics.

By 1970, forensic expert Jacques Penry had developed in the United Kingdom a system which became known as the "Penry Facial Identification Technique", abbreviated from its initials to the more convenient label "Photo-FIT". This was

built up from a representation of white male faces normally encountered in the British and European zones. Subsequently this was extended by John Waddington Ltd. (who handle Photo-FIT in these areas) to incorporate Afro-Asian and Caucasian basic facial types.

This is all of great forensic importance in sex cases, where victims and other witnesses need the most rapid means of creating a portrait of an offender. While some villains are international, sex criminals are generally "local". For urgent identification of alleged sex offenders, the police use a system which deals with full-face and profile (162 pairs of eyes, 151 noses, 159 mouths, and so on), in 12,000 million possible combinations.

Picture technique

Dr. H. J. Walls, when Director of the Metropolitan Police Laboratory, New Scotland Yard, clarified in 1963 a special monochrome photographic technique which helped in identification of alleged sexual crimes, by superimposition of transparencies.

For example, in a particular case of sexual attack, when a girl was strangled, it was helpful if the forensic workers could state if the victim was strangled on the floor, or on a couch believed to carry sexual stains. Under close examination the couch was found to have saliva stains at the top, mixed seminal and urine stains in the centre, and small tears at the lower edge, which could have been caused by heels of a woman's shoe.

A woman police officer of the same height as the victim was photographed on her back, and this transparency was superimposed on that of the couch with the stains and cuts marked in white. A combined print was then taken, which clearly supported the theory of strangulation on the couch.

Measurements of this sort can be important in sex cases. This was high-lighted in a sex murder at Morecambe, Lancashire, in the late 1940s, when Dr. F. B. Smith assisted at the post-mortem of 28-year-old Elizabeth Smith found drowned in a small stream.

There were curious facets of this murder, for when Dr. J. B. Firth, C.B.E. (then Director of the North Western Forensic Science Laboratory, Home Office) was called in to investigate he found no signs of a struggle. Yet the victim's underclothing was soiled and soaked, indicating a long immersion, and not such as might have happened had she accidentally slipped into the water.

Dr. Smith took specimens from the lungs, and prepared microscope slides. These disclosed the presence of very small single-cell water plants known as diatoms. This proved that water had been drawn into the victim's lungs, and that she had attempted to breathe while her mouth and nose were under water.

Police enquiries led to a Royal Air Force man David Williams being interrogated, and this action was so prompt that in fact he was discovered trying to dry out his clothes worn on the night of the murder. Dr. Firth found that the man's jacket was wet chiefly in triangular patches across the lower corners of the pockets, as if he had been bending down in water. The bottoms of the trousers were wet for about eighteen inches, and there were also blood and seminal staining.

"I reported," said Dr. Firth afterwards in his William Kimber case-history, "that the results of my examination indicated that the unconscious girl was removed from the stream, certain articles of clothing removed, and that then the prisoner attempted a serious assault. Williams was tried at Liverpool Assizes for murder, and sentenced to death . . ."

Morals Squads, murder squads and indeed all those likely to be given a heavy work-load as the result of misdirected sexual impulses of others, would be less busy if it were possible effectively and legally to decrease sexual desires.

One drug has been administered in Britain's gaols to volunteers, but has been no more successful than similar attempts in the U.S. prison system. As is well known, a British slang term for being in gaol is "doing porridge", and this comes from the diet of porridge and other plain food intended to diminish virility.

Now, however, as the result of the use of a new drug Anquil in West Germany and Denmark, tests have been conducted in London's Wormwood Scrubs Prison by a team led by Dr. Leopold Field. Fourteen "control" prisoners at the Scrubs and 14 other sex offenders were volunteers, and first results showed that over-sexuality could be controlled—although it might be necessary to take the drug three times a day. Janssen Pharmaceutical,

makers of Anquil, said: "It is something which we think will help in personal tragedies."

Personal tragedies can arise if unqualified people attempt to form their own Morals Squads, and this was emphasised in the tragic death of a retired shop-keeper in Flint, North Wales, in August, 1973.

Two eight-year-old girls had been molested in the neighbourhood, and when the elderly shopkeeper was seen giving sweets to other little girls, a local vigilante squad made the grave error of thinking he was responsible for the sex attacks.

A kind, lonely man

They beat him up, and next day he was found dead in bed. Yet he was absolutely innocent of any sexual offence. The police were already interviewing another man in connection with the attacks on the little girls. "He was a kind but lonely man," an observer said. "He was always glad to give sweets to the children." That kindness cost him his life.

Acid-phosphatase tests can detect the presence of seminal fluid, and serology can help to identify body fluids other than

blood. But forensic scientists have not yet reached a stage when the age of the secreter can be proved. Yet the "dirty old man" complex is hard to eradicate from the minds of some investigators, no matter how untrue it may be.

This was shown by the Rochester-N.Y. Morals Squad when, in one three-month period, it received from one district in the city 12 complaints of molesting. Four incidents were rape, and residents in the district were in a state of hysteria. Victims were females, aged 14-21.

Special assignments were given to investigators, thousands of man-hours were consumed, and eventually a male was apprehended and identified by three of the victims.

"He was reluctant to admit his involvement," said Police Chief William M. Lombard, "but through the factual information obtained from the reports and records of the Morals Squad, he was identified in each of the twelve unsolved complaints. "Since his arrest and commitment, there have been no similar crimes in the area . . ."

The attacker was not a "dirty old man", but a youth of fourteen.

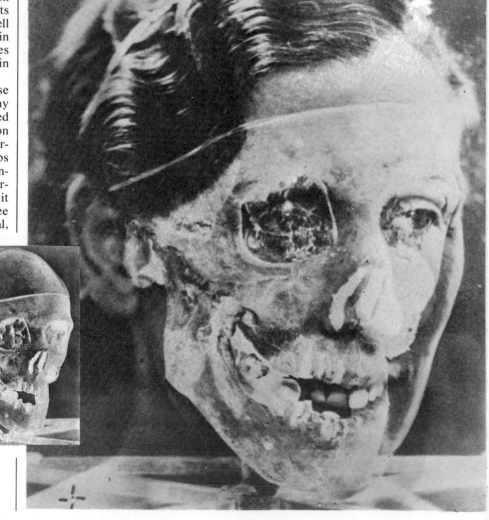

WHO'S WHO? Pictures of an unidentified skull can be superimposed on pictures of missing people to help identification.

PROOF OF RAPE

A judge's daughter is found brutally murdered. She has been stabbed 37 times and dumped near her home at the spot arrowed below. But had Patricia Curran been sexually assaulted too? And how do scientists solve rape cases?

Belfast Telegraph

RAPE is rape, nearly all the world over, bringing a moment of unimaginable terror to the poor victim and sometimes destroying her mind.

Only in the United States is rape split into two different categories by lawyers, police and criminalists: *forcible* rape is the carnal knowledge of a female through the use or threat of force, while *statutory* rape is usually in a lesser category, implying unlawful sexual intercourse with a female without her consent, but with ravishment which does not involve excessive force or violence.

The difference is one which involves the courts in lengthy, costly, hair-splitting forensic debates, because almost all sexual intercourse involves force on the part of one or other of the parties. Very often it has to be left to the forensic pathologist to produce the evidence on which will hang the verdict:

Did she want it, or didn't she? Did she struggle violently or was she attacked? Was she the completely uncooperating and unwilling victim of forcible raping, or after a show of force did she acquiesce in an act described in the current permissive cynicism: "When rape is inevitable, relax and enjoy it"?

One of the last official duties of L. Patrick Gray before he was politically ousted from his post as Acting Director of the FBI, was to give his Bureau's view on certain aspects of forcible rape —which caused forensic science laboratories in most countries to be extremely busy in close association with psychiatric investigators.

In Mr. Gray's final year (1971) 72 per cent of all offences reported in this crime class were actual rapes by force, while the remainder were attempts or assaults to commit forcible rape.

"This offence," he pointed out, "is a violent crime against the person, and of all Crime Index offences, law-enforcement administrators recognize this is probably one of the most under-reported crimes—due primarily to fear and/or embarrassment on the part of the victims.

"As a national average" (this, in the United States), "18 per cent of all forcible rapes reported to the police were determined by investigation to be unfounded. This is caused primarily due to the question of the use of force or the threat of force frequently complicated by a prior relationship between victim and offender ..."

Human passion

On the other hand the British forensic student might feel the position is legally less complex in the United Kingdom, where the law (the Sexual Offences Act, 1956) is stated bluntly: *"It is felony for a man to rape a woman."*

This goes back to the Offences Against the Person Act, 1861, and might seem to stop any hair-splitting between statutory rape and forcible rape. But as every lawyer knows, there are dozens of additions and sub-sections: and human passions being what they are, there are many shades of rape—from violation of a girl by her half-brother, to rape of a wife by her husband when they are living apart under a legal separation order!

The "forcible" part of the act is usually covered in English law by some allied act of "GBH" (grievous bodily harm), and punishment for this may be additional to the imprisonment for life for the rape itself, or seven years for an attempt.

Keith Simpson, MA, MD, FRCP, perhaps the senior professor of forensic medicine in Great Britain, once put it bluntly that: "The police surgeon at the scene should keep his eyes open, his hands in his pockets and his mouth shut." This is true, but when directing the production of evidence which may show if a rape is forcible, statutory or imaginary, the criminalist may have to be even more realistic. He may have to try putting himself in the place of the attacker, and frankly ask himself such questions as:

TROOPS with mine detectors (below) help police hunting for clues to the killer of Patricia Curran. Pathologist George Wells (right) also helped detectives.

"If *I* had wanted to try raping that girl in these surroundings, would I have pleaded and argued first, would I have had my trousers undone, and would I have tried to get her tights down or her panties off before knifing her?"

Such brutal questions must have been in the mind of the forensic investigator Dr. J. B. Firth, CBE, FRIC, when he was Director of the North Western Forensic Science Laboratory of the Home Office, and when the murder was first reported in Co. Antrim (Northern Ireland) of young Patricia, daughter of Lord Justice Curran.

This case, which opened in 1952, be-

Belfast Telegraph

came a *cause célèbre* lasting for ten years, involving a long campaign by a Sunday newspaper and political appeals to the then Northern Ireland Minister of Home Affairs.

Patricia's body was found in the grounds of her home at Whiteabbey, with 37 stab wounds including superficial face and neck injuries. There were deep cuts penetrating to the liver, but the limited amount of blood on the leaves of bushes suggested that the body had been dragged to the spot after the attack, and perhaps after the cuts on the face. The positions of her handbag, books and shoes also led the forensic investigator to believe they had deliberately been put there near the body, and not discarded in a struggle.

The post-mortem was conducted by Dr. A. M. Wells of Queen's University, Belfast, and Alan Thompson, a senior member of the North Western forensic laboratory staff started the examination until Dr. Firth could be flown across from Glasgow. It was decided that the attack was made with a narrow-bladed knife, and that face and neck injuries were received while the girl was standing up.

Tuft of fibres

In his subsequent report, made in conjunction with T. Alstead Cooper and his colleague Arthur Brooks, Dr. Firth talked of the girl's yellow wool cap.

"I removed a small tuft of fibres from the top of the outside of this . . . I found that it included a number of bright red fibres which, when put under the microscope, appeared to be composed of acetate rayon.

"Entwined in the red fibres were three wool fibres which were dyed an olive-green shade. There were a few wool fibres dyed bright yellow, which showed close agreement with the wool fibres of the cap, but the red and green fibres were not represented in the material of any garments worn by the girl . . ."

This kind of routine evidence, coupled with work by the Royal Air Force Special Investigation Branch, eventually led to the arrest, trial and conviction of Leading Aircraftsman Ian Hay Gordon. It took the jury only two hours to consider their verdict, and they found Gordon guilty but insane.

If there had been a sexual attack, what was the gravity of it? In his report Dr. Firth stated:

"I made copious notes on the condition of each garment, but the only facts of any significance concerned the girl's panties. I found recent tears all along the outer seam of the right leg, including the frilly edging in the region of the crutch. The back seam of the right leg was also torn for a distance of $4\frac{1}{2}$ inches, beginning an inch below the waistband.

"There were heavy bloodstains on the lower portion of the panties, mainly at the back of the crutch. The dispersal of blood indicated that the seams were torn *before* any blood reached the blood-stained zone—in other words, the results were consistent with the panties having been torn before the bodily injuries were inflicted, or at least very shortly afterwards.

"The elastic waistband was intact. It could be deduced from these facts that a determined effort had been made to remove the panties, and that it had not been successful, partly because the elastic waistband had remained intact, assisted no doubt by the additional protection of the girl's underslip and outer garments. . . ."

Under English law, penetration of the vagina by the penis has to be established, not necessarily the emission of semen. It was, of course, not necessary to establish this with Gordon, who was being tried for murder. The psychiatrist Dr. Rossiter Lewis said that in his opinion Gordon had been suffering from schizophrenia and hypoglycemia on the night the girl was killed, and that he did not have the full sexual inclination—"as we know it".

R. Heber (American Association on Mental Deficiency), W. C. Sullivan (*Crime in Relation to Congenital Mental Deficiency*) and Britain's D. J. Power have all researched into aspects of subnormality and crime, with relation to epilepsy and aggravated subnormality of the mind, incidentally probing the mental pressures which result in rape, grievous bodily harm, forcible rape and even sexual murder.

This is why males accused of, say, forcible rape, are not only invited to have their clothing and their person examined for seminal testing and blood grouping, but may be asked to take the "WAIS" (Wechsler Adult Intelligence Scale) tests —a battery of ten tests, in fact, comprising arithmetical reasoning, digit symbol tests, perceptual ability and memory-span.

Mental illness

It may affect a subsequent verdict of Diminished Responsibility on the grounds of subnormality and/or mental illness in the form of reactive depression, and is not so isolated from forcible rape as it may seem.

While the layman might take it for granted that an essential element of forcible rape is the male attacker's overwhelming desire for an orgasm, this is not always the case. Indeed, it might be said to be one essential forensic difference between statutory and forcible rape.

The male's natural desire for intercourse is kept normally within bounds by self-pride, affection and our many social disciplines; only where extreme temptations and circumstances allow does an irresistible erection and desire for orgasm take place.

Forcible rape by subnormals presents far more complex problems, and there may even be schizoid elements in the attacker's personality urging him to derive a perverted satisfaction from the knowledge that he has a new *power*—the power that he alone can decide how much the victim is to suffer in injury, or even in death, quite apart from the sexual assault.

Grave injuries may be inflicted before penetration, and the struggles may actually prevent emission and complete orgasm, because most women struggle frenziedly.

Whichever way it goes, the forensic worker is likely to be faced with identifying seminal stains; and one assumes it is now almost common knowledge that in the majority of cases such stains are as identifiable as blood groups.

Laboratory methods

As the stains dry out on a victim's clothing they tend to desiccate, and it becomes harder to find intact sperms. With current laboratory methods this is not always important, and we have certainly advanced since the early work of Alfred Swaine Taylor, one of the fathers of forensic research.

Citing a case of forcible rape tried at Edinburgh, Scotland, on November 27, 1843, Dr. Taylor recorded: "A man labouring at that time under gonorrhoea was charged with a criminal assault on a child. The shift worn by the prosecutrix, with other articles belonging to the prisoner, were submitted for examination. Some of the stains on the linen were of a yellow colour, and were believed to be those of gonorrhoea; others, characterized by a faint colour and a peculiar odour, were considered to be stains caused by the spermatic secretion.

"Digested in water, they yielded a turbid solution of a peculiar odour, and when submitted to a powerful microscope, spermatozoa were detected.

The stains were similar on the linen of the prisoner and the prosecutrix. I believe this to be a solitary instance of the use of the microscope for such a purpose in this country. . . ."

Some 75 years after Taylor, forensic laboratories all the way from those of the FBI and the British Home Office were making an initial quick check—as one must in cases of alleged forcible rape—by taking garments of both parties and fluorescing them under filtered UV (ultraviolet) light. Speed is essential, for stains tend to dry out and it becomes increasingly difficult to separate vaginal discharge, semen, urine, soil staining, and grass (chlorophyll) likely to be found

UNDER ARREST . . . Ian Hay Gordon, the man who murdered Patricia Curran. Doctors were called before the court to say if he raped her as well . . .

when a victim alleges forcible rape in the open.

Fortunately the AP reaction can now be used as a routine in semen tests. Chemists discovered in the 1950's, that in certain substances acid-phosphatase occurs.

The acid-phosphatase found in the human body is an acid medium, and in forensic tests for semen a complex substance is broken down into parts and a test solution produced which, if semen is present, exhibits a bright purple colour.

The stain itself is not destroyed, and as several tests may need to be made by interested legal parties in cases of alleged forcible rape, this is most helpful.

The clinical work in the forensic laboratory is, of course, almost at the end of the evidence-getting story. But the criminalist would not be human if he were not moved to pity by the sight he sometimes faces at the start of a rape case.

AN ANCIENT CRIME RECONSTRUCTED

A thousand-year-old pile of bones huddled at the bottom of a lead casket was all that remained of Saint Edward the Martyr. Until his death at eighteen he had been England's King Edward. The legends told of treachery, assassination in ambush. Then the scientists got to work.

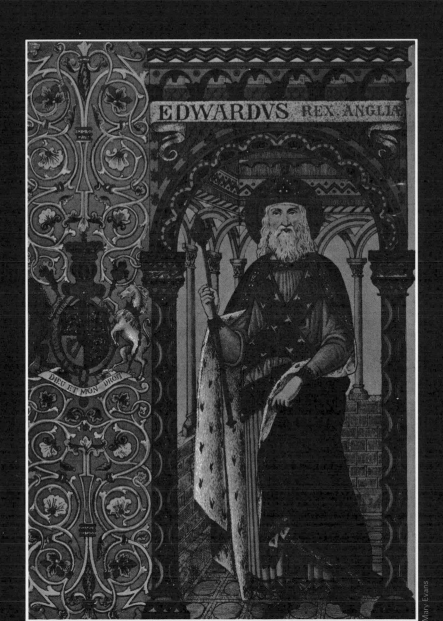

EDWARDVS REX ANGLIA

DIEU ET MON DROIT

Mary Evans

HIS BONES confirm the ancient stories of the young King's death in agony and betrayal. After reburial at Shaftesbury (above) the casket was lost until 1931.

THE considerable advances made by forensic medicine in the past half-century have led to the solving of literally thousands of violent crimes. Given a body—however badly disfigured or fragmented—medical detectives can build up a highly accurate picture of the victim and the manner of his death.

One of the most spectacular examples of this kind of forensic work occurred in Britain during the 1930's, when a pathologist working from a little pile of bones confirmed the details of a Saxon King's murder—a thousand years after the murder occurred.

During the reign of King Edgar—A.D. 959 to A.D. 975—in England, the established Church was split into two factions. On the one hand were the monks of the great abbeys and religious houses, dedicated to improving the quality of life; on the other were the "secular" clergy, bishops and priests who made fortunes from the administration of their parishes and spent their time drinking, feasting and womanizing. Many of the nobles supported the latter faction for their own ends, though at least two—the Northern King Oswald and Bishop Dunstan, later to become saints—fought for the reformation and unification of the Church.

Profligate life-style

King Edgar himself, despite his own profligate life-style, supported the monks and built forty great monasteries during his reign; when he died his fifteen-year-old son Edward took up the cause, aided by Oswald and Dunstan. But Edward was to reign for only four years. In his eighteenth summer, while on a visit to his young brother Aethelred—later dubbed "The Unready"—Edward was ambushed and murdered.

An account of the killing is given in the *Life of St. Oswald,* written about the year A.D. 1000 by a monk who was in Edward's entourage at the time of the attack: "Soldiers were therefore holding him, one drew him (the King) to the right towards himself as though to give him a kiss (of welcome), another seized his left hand violently and wounded him, but he cried as loud as he could, 'What are you doing, breaking my right arm?' and he fell from his horse and died."

Piecing the details together from the rather complicated report—it was, of course, written in Latin—a fairly clear picture emerges. Two soldiers approached the King, one on his left, the other on his right. The latter, while pretending to give him a kiss of peace, grasped Edward's left shoulder with his own right arm, at the same time getting a grip on the King's right forearm—the sword arm—with his left hand.

While Edward was pinioned in this fashion, the man on the left grasped his left arm and stabbed him with a knife. The king's horse, frightened, reared up and forced its royal rider back onto the high cantle of the saddle; with the soldier on the right still gripping the King, Edward's thigh was pressed across the cantle with enormous force.

Caught in the stirrup

The horse then bolted, Edward fell from the saddle and was dragged along the ground by his left foot, which was caught in the stirrup. The breakages thus incurred, coupled with the stab wound, finished the King off; within a few days his younger brother Aethelred, who appears to have instigated the ambush, had begun his own disastrous reign.

Some years went by, and the unfortunate young King was canonized as "Saint Edward the Martyr"; his shrine at Shaftesbury in the south of England was a place of pilgrimage up until the early sixteenth century, when King Henry VIII finally dissolved the monastic system.

After the dissolution of the monasteries, Edward's relics, like those of many another early English saint, appeared to be lost for ever. But on January 2, 1931, an archaeologist named J. Wilson Claridge discovered a lead casket containing bones on the site of the Abbey Church at Shaftesbury.

The casket was 21 inches long, 11 inches wide, and about 9 inches deep; the bones had been neatly arranged, the small ones at the bottom, long ones at one side, and part of a skull on top. Certain clues, coupled with legends of the place, indicated to Claridge that the remains might be those of Edward the Martyr.

It was, said the scholastic world, a "tremendous discovery"—if, that is, the identity of the bones could be proved.

And at this point forensic science stepped in, in the person of Thomas E. A. Stowell, M.D., a Fellow of the Royal

INSPIRATION of pilgrims and a favourite subject for religious artists, Edward the Martyr broods eternally over the site of his death in A.D. 978.

College of Surgeons and a distinguished pathologist. Stowell met Claridge, heard of his discovery, and asked to see the bones; after the first brief examination he announced that they were those of a young man who had sustained a remarkable number of "greenstick fractures" — fractures which occur in the pliable bones of the young. But he would need considerably more time to reach a complete conclusion. The British Museum Department of Anthropology saturated the remains with synthetic resin to strengthen them, and then handed the bones over to Stowell for his 1,000-year-late post mortem.

Stowell began by establishing the height of the dead man; by measuring the long bones of his arms and legs, making obvious allowances for scalp and heel pad thickness, and estimating various other factors from the other bones available, he was able to say that the deceased had been between five feet six and five feet eight inches in height.

"Sexing" the skeleton

He had already guessed that the bones were those of a male, and he now set out to prove it. There are several methods of "sexing" a skeleton. The pelvis is generally most informative, but the sacrum — the wedge-shaped bone at the bottom of the spine — or the femur or thigh bone are also informative. The skull too can be used as a guide and there are what might be called "mathematical" methods for sexing a skeleton by measuring the "heads" of the humerus — upper arm bone — or femur.

Having established the height and sex of the remains, Stowell now began to investigate his age. An American report, *Skeletal Changes in the Young,* sets out various guidelines, and from these Stowell deduced that the dead man was between 17 and 21 years of age; he plumped for the lower age because of the characteristic greenstick fractures.

Stowell then set out to establish the race of the deceased. The skull, he decided, was *dolichocephalic,* or long-headed. The Saxons were typically long-headed, whereas the "ancient" Britons and the Celts, the two predominant races in the England of King Edward, were among the "round-headed" races. So almost certainly the remains were those of a Saxon.

After examining the sutures, or bone-joins of the skull vault, Stowell went on to the vertebrae of the spine — the small bones which carry the spinal cord from the skull to the pelvis. In the neck there are normally seven of these bones, but the "Edward" casket contained only portions of the first, second, and seventh; the missing third, fourth, fifth and sixth cervical, or neck, vertebrae may have

Ken Moreman

DRAGGED by his terrified steed, the royal thighbone splits like a green stick — and the crime busters relive Edward's last moments . . . a millennium later.

disintegrated, and by following up further clues Stowell concluded that the four missing bones tallied with the dead person having suffered a severely broken neck.

An investigation of the thoracic verte-

brae — which run down the middle of the back — showed that the "laminal spurs" or projections from the main bone were very small. These laminal spurs grow with age, and through them Stowell was able accurately to pinpoint the age of the dead man: he had died in his eighteenth year.

An examination of the lumbar vertebrae, or lower backbone, clinched this finding.

Assault victims

Stowell then came to the forearm bones. The left radius, which along with the ulna supports the arm from elbow to wrist, had been broken in at least four places, while the ulna itself showed the beginning of a transverse fracture. Going by the *Life of St. Oswald* and these bones, Stowell was satisfied that the left forearm had been forcibly twisted inwards, the arm probably being bent behind the back — the surgeon had seen such injuries on assault victims.

Perhaps most impressive of all was the left thigh bone, which had suffered a transverse, or greenstick, fracture — a splitting of the bone upwards and downwards, which is comparatively rare. According to the *Life of St. Oswald,* the King's body had been forced backwards over the saddle cantle and then dragged along the ground by the left foot; some time previously, Stowell had conducted a post mortem on a boy who had been dragged, feet upwards, along the ground by the driving belt of a lathe. He had sustained precisely the same type of fracture as that under examination.

Tibia fracture

The left tibia — the larger and stouter of the two leg bones — had also sustained a greenstick fracture of the type to be expected after a pressure such as the King was said to have undergone.

Finally, Stowell examined the right shoulderblade or scapula, the right humerus or elbow bone, and the right haunch bone, all of which bore fractures which were consistent with the body having fallen from the saddle and hitting the ground on the right side — the force being taken by the shoulder, elbow and protuberant part of the hip.

Stowell was satisfied. In his report he wrote that the bones were those of a male of the age of King Edward, and that they showed "a concatenation of fractures which precisely fit the story of the murder . . . the attack on the left upper limb, the drawing of the body to the right . . ." Stowell could not think of any other series of violences which would have produced exactly the same results. In conclusion he stated: "I cannot escape the conviction that, on historical, anatomical, and surgical grounds, beyond reasonable doubt we have here the bones of Saint Edward, King and Martyr."

A TRACE OF ARSENIC

The arsenic Dr. Taylor found in "bottle no. 21" almost ruined his reputation . . . and may have allowed an inept killer in the tradition of (insets, from top) Doctors Pritchard, Ruxton and Cream to escape.

COPY OF VERSES
ON THE
CHARGE OF WILFUL MURDER
inst Thomas Smethurst, for administering Poison to
Lady (whom the Prisoner had illegally married) at
No. 10, Alma Villas, Richmond.

A life interest of five thousand,
  And more besides by her father's wil.
To D c or Smethurst she got married,
  Yet his first wife was living still.
The marriage day was scarcely over,
  When Elizabeth Banks was taken ill,
With treacherous heart he waited on her,
  He beg'd of her to make her will.

He attended on her in her sickness,
  No one else woul f the Dr. trust,
He pretended to be all love and meeknes,
  The poison then was doing its worst.
He kissed her cheek—it was the kiss of s...
  With false tears he the girl betray...
The medicine himself he gave h...
  The murderer is alway...

Elizabeth Banks t...
  In health ap...
Done by the...
  Thou'rt...
The po...
  He...
Her...

ll good people and pay attention,
  these lines that I indite,
of poisoning I will mention,
  cruel deed has been brought to light.
ber the case of William Palmer,
  one does all exceed,
n unoffending woman :
l make the stoutest heart to bleed.

ed man is Doctor Smethurst,
  n in whom the sickly put their trust ;
amon stabber will meet you fairly,
  ruel poisoner he must be worse.
g and confiding woman,
  him her heart as we are told,
Smethurst, thy love was falsehood,
  ve was merely for her gold.

€ 1859
Se

A FICKLE PUBLIC agreed with the
anonymous verses above: that Dr.
Smethurst (right) was guilty of murder
and "the day must come when he must
die". But after successful prosecution
public opinion—especially other doctors
and scientists objecting to Dr. Taylor's
inconclusive findings of arsenic—
forced a last-minute stay of execution.
The "murderer" served a year for bigamy.

THE medical man who takes to murder
has, perhaps oddly, never been very
successful. Palmer, Pritchard, Lamson,
Cross, Cream, Crippen, Ruxton, and
Smethurst were all dealt with by the law,
and of them only Cross, Lamson and
Ruxton had any real professional qualifications, and none of them, except perhaps Crippen, showed real expertise.

One of the most curious cases was that
of Thomas Smethurst, a "doctor" who
obtained his degree through what would
today be called "a diploma mill", in this
case the University of Erlangen in Bavaria.
It is certain Smethurst practised and,
from somewhere, acquired a quite respectable medical knowledge.

He was born, according to some
sources, in Lincolnshire in 1805. It is
believed his father was a herbalist, and
that he had two brothers and a sister. In
1827 he married a lady 20 years his
senior, said to be a patient of his at the
time. Mary Smethurst brought to him a
very modest fortune, and this he put to
good use for six years by running a hydro-
pathic establishment at Moor Park in

147

Surrey, where Swift wrote *A Tale of a Tub*. This was a successful and profitable venture, for in 1852 Smethurst became a "gentleman of leisure".

The Smethursts seemed a pleasant and contented couple without any real roots, or children. In appearance he was a rather small and insignificant man, with thick reddish hair and a not very commanding presence which he managed to overcome with a slight pomposity, and the authority usual to medical men. In the autumn of 1858 the Smethursts were living in a boarding house in the better part of Bayswater, London, at 4 Rifle Terrace which was at the top of what is now Queensway, not far from Whiteley's Store.

In October a new lodger arrived at the house, Miss Isabella Bankes, a 43-year-old spinster of some means. She possessed £1800 in property and lived on the life interest of £5000 which, on her death, would revert to her family. There was an immediate attraction between Miss Bankes and the doctor. Smethurst managed to spend little time with his semi-invalid wife, but a great deal with Miss Bankes, and the affair became so marked to everyone except Mrs. Smethurst that the landlady, appalled at the boarding-house gossip, told Miss Bankes at the end of the first week in November that she would probably be more comfortable "elsewhere".

There was a quick exodus. Miss Bankes set up house in rooms at 37 Kildare Terrace, not far from Rifle Terrace, and there the "star cross'd lovers" — as a newspaper was to call them — were so enamoured of each other that they came together, Thomas Smethurst having calmly left his wife. The picture of Isabella Bankes that has survived does not suggest that she was a Victorian Helen of Troy, for she was "a gentle lady of quiet aspect, a bright eye and a kindly manner."

"United illegally"

But she was sufficiently attractive for Smethurst to bigamously "marry" her at Battersea Parish Church on December 9, 1858 — at his trial he was to excuse this action by claiming ". . . we united ourselves illegally, but it was for a permanency, and the marriage took place this way: At the request of Miss Bankes . . . she knew I was married — and in order that she should be protected from reproach hereafter, this marriage was preliminary to one at a future period, in the event of my wife dying — she is now 74 years of age".

"Dr. and Mrs." Smethurst now settled in rooms at 27 Old Palace Gardens, between The Green and the river Thames at Richmond. Here they lived peacefully or, anyway, without attracting notice — until March 28, 1859, when Isabella was suddenly taken ill with symptoms resembling those of dysentery.

The illness did not clear up quickly and on April 3 Isabella was still so unwell that her lover did something that has always puzzled believers in his guilt. He sent for medical help, seeking the co-operation of Dr. Julius and Dr. Bird, who were at that time the most prominent medical men in Richmond; Dr. Julius, as the senior physician, obtained all his information about the medical history from Smethurst and from the patient.

Smethurst was always present at every visit to the sick-room, though neither of the doctors found any fault with his medical knowledge. The patient was diagnosed as suffering from diarrhoea and was given medicines which, however, failed to help. It was felt that healthier quarters, above river level, might help, and the couple moved to 10 Alma Villas, on Richmond Hill. The move was made on April 15, when the doctor supported his weak spouse in a cab which took them and their possessions to the new quarters on the first floor of a very charming house.

Smethurst wrote to Louisa Bankes, sister of Isabella, at her home in Maida Vale. She came at once to Richmond on April 19, but did not stay very long. The doctors now diagnosed poison of some sort, but certainly Smethurst did not act like a poisoner. He treated the invalid with the greatest kindness and patience,

SERJEANT BALLANTYNE, prosecuting counsel.

and her genuine affection for him was obvious, yet he never permitted anyone to see her unless he was also in the room.

Smethurst called in a third, very prominent, doctor to see what could be done, and then on April 30 summoned a solicitor. The solicitor was shown the draft of a will drawn up "by a London barrister" — despite the fact it was wholly in Smethurst's handwriting. It left all Isabella's property to her "friend". A final will was drawn up by the solicitor, in haste, and was signed quite willingly by Miss Bankes.

Nevertheless this last action disturbed the two local physicians. They now became very suspicious, and decided to test the bodily evacuations of the patient; as a result of what they found they called the police, and Thomas Smethurst was promptly arrested. Over 20 bottles and containers holding, or having held, various medicines were removed from 10 Alma Villas. The unfortunate Miss Bankes appeared to have been only dimly aware of what was happening. Her doctors and her sister attended her, but in spite of every care she died on May 3.

The manifest suspicions of three well-known medical men, the arrest, and police evidence were not, just the same, sufficient to impress the Richmond magistrates. It was decided that Smethurst should be discharged on the basis of insufficient evidence; he went free, but only for a brief time.

The local coroner was less inclined to see the evidence and the suspicions in the same light. He considered the available facts and after various questions to witnesses issued a warrant for the re-arrest of Smethurst. It was not long before one of the greatest medical jurists of the time entered into the picture. This was Dr. Alfred Swaine Taylor, Professor of Chemistry at Guy's Hospital, who is remembered today as author of the classic *Taylor's Principles and Practice of Medical Jurisprudence* which, under succeeding editors, remains a cornerstone of forensic medicine.

As Government analyst, he gave evidence at the preliminary hearings to the effect that he found arsenic in vomit from the deceased. In one bottle of medicine — "No. 21" in the list of articles taken from Alma Villas — he also found arsenic. This naturally increased suspicion of Smethurst.

Dr. Taylor had arrived at his conclusions by using the analytical method known as the Reinsch Test, devised by a German chemist, Hugo Reinsch, in 1842 as a new method of detection of arsenic poisoning. The test was reasonably simple. Solutions suspected of containing arsenic were strongly acidified by the addition of hydrochloric acid. Pieces of copper foil were then introduced, and the liquid was heated to near boiling point. The presence of arsenic was shown by deposits on the copper. If present in any quantity, the poison showed as a lustrous black deposit, while a steel-grey coating indicated smaller quantities.

Remarkable contrasts

Dr. Taylor was satisfied after his investigations that arsenic was indeed present, but in the medicine bottle he examined he calculated that there must have been less than a quarter of a grain of arsenic mixed with the four ounces of matter in the bottle. Arsenic, he noted, presents remarkable contrasts, which tend to depend on the human body — adults have died from the ingestion of 0.12 grain, while others have tolerated, and overcome with medical help, as much as eight grains. However, Dr. Taylor's evidence at the preliminary hearing clinched the committal for trial.

Thomas Smethurst — still described as "Dr." in the newspapers — was taken to the Old Bailey's Central Criminal Court for his trial. Three years before, the Central Criminal Court Act of 1856 had been passed; Palmer, the Rugeley Poisoner, had been tried there through this Act by which an accused person could be tried for an offence outside the

IRATE FURY — and an unduly harsh sentence on the bigamy charge — was the reaction of Lord Chief Justice Baron Pollock to Dr. Smethurst's reprieve.

jurisdiction of the court, instead of at the local assizes, in order that he could receive a fair trial.

The hearing was held on July 7, 1859, before the Lord Chief Justice Baron Pollock with the great Mr. Serjeant Ballantine prosecuting. One of the great sensations of that bitter legal contest was the evidence of Dr. Taylor, for though he stated that he had received no less than 28 articles from Alma Villas through the police for examination, only bottle No. 21 was of any importance, plus the vomit. He had to make an admission which more or less turned the case upside down.

He stated that though he had found arsenic according to the Reinsch Test, he came up against a factor that was to fault his findings, and this was the presence of possible impurities in the reagents used. In other words, both hydrochloric acid and metallic copper invariably contained minute quantities of arsenic, with the hydrochloric acid often containing the larger quantity of the impurity.

The copper had shown the steel-grey of minute quantity, but Dr. Taylor's unhappy position in court was that he had to admit the arsenic may well have been in the reagents — the process of ensuring absolute purity is not a difficult one, but it is possible that either the doctor or, more probably, one of his assistants did not take the proper prior steps.

But medical opinion was on his side, in the shape of Professor Odling of Guy's Hospital, the Professor of Practical Chemistry, and others. The overall opinion was that there had been a continuous administration of some irritant poison, such as arsenic or antimony.

Against this the defence put forth its own medical experts, who claimed that the dead woman had died not by slow arsenic poisoning, but by idiopathic dysentery. Just to play safe, it was also suggested that ordinary bismuth, which Miss Bankes had been given from time to time, almost always contained arsenic.

It was revealed in court that the deceased had been nearly two months pregnant. It was also suggested that she might have died from "gastric complications" following her condition, while Dr. Taylor proposed that the accused might have given the woman potassium chlorate after the arsenic, to eliminate its traces.

The judge in his summing-up clearly indicated that he thought Smethurst guilty; this the jury obviously accepted, for they took only 20 minutes to return a verdict of guilty. The sentence of death was passed, but as so often happens, the public, which had been anti-Smethurst, promptly switched sides on hearing the verdict, and there was a great outcry against it. Experts in law, medicine, toxicology and other spheres began to join the passionate discussion.

Hard labour

A medical journal venomously suggested that "we must now look upon Professor Taylor as having ended his career, and hope he will immediately withdraw into the obscurity of private life, not forgetting to carry with him his favourite arsenical copper". This tasteless attack was quite without result. Dr. Taylor went on from success to success, and in 1865 he published the book on medical jurisprudence that immortalized his name.

The Home Office was disturbed by the raging controversy and directed a leading London surgeon, Sir Benjamin Collins Brodie, to look into the matter and study the trial record, to the surprise of the medical profession and the irate fury of Lord Chief Justice Baron Pollock.

Brodie offered as his opinion that there was "not absolute and complete evidence" of Thomas Smethurst's guilt. The Home Secretary did not intervene until two days before the execution date, when the condemned man was reprieved and freed, to be at once arrested for bigamy. He served a year's hard labour, an unduly harsh sentence when he should have received penal servitude.

After his release he went to live in a house off Vauxhall Bridge Road and, though still a comfortably situated man, aroused sensation by suing for the legacy left to him by Isabella Bankes and, to the distress of her family, winning his case. Nothing is known of him after that except an item in a local paper referred to "Dr. and Mrs. Smethurst", which suggests that, after all his troubles, he at last returned to his true wife.

THE PAJAMA GIRL

The body is charred, the features battered, but the dead woman is easily recognizable. Preserved in formaldehyde and studied for ten years, the corpse finally yields an identity (Linda Agostini, below) and a conviction (of her husband, bottom, with police). But doubts linger. The experts have botched the job . . .

MOST forensic scientists would confidently claim that given a body they should be able to identify it beyond reasonable doubt. In the last decade fragmented bones have been conclusively identified as belonging to a particular person.

But in the strange case of the Australian "pajama girl" no such positive identification was forthcoming: and the fault was at least partly due to the over-enthusiasm of forensic experts. In a word, they botched the job, and this despite the fact that they had had the body pickled in a special coffin and available for examination over a period of ten years.

The township of Albury lies on the borders of New South Wales and Victoria, between the cities of Melbourne and Sydney. On the fine, bright morning of September 1, 1934, a farmer was cleaning a culvert some six miles from Albury when, stuffed inside, he found the body of a young woman. She was clothed only in ragged pajamas; the head was covered

with a bag, the body was charred, and alongside it were patches of oil, which suggested deliberate burning.

The farmer contacted the police, and the corpse was taken to the mortuary at Albury, where a post-mortem was performed. It was immediately obvious that the girl had been subjected to considerable violence. There were extensive burns on the body's left side and a wound, roughly the area of an ordinary matchbox, had exposed the brain above the left eye. Another wound under the left eye had almost driven the eye-ball into the skull, the left temple was battered, and below the right eye was the entrance hole of a bullet. Death appeared to have taken place anything from one to four days before the discovery of the body, the three major wounds having been delivered with a "blunt instrument".

The only other immediate point of note was that the bag in which the head had been wrapped had also contained a towel which bore traces of what appeared to be laundry marks—in the normal process of things a vital clue, but in this case one which seems to have been ignored.

While police published details of the

dead woman in an attempt to identify her, the body was moved to Sydney University, where a second post-mortem was held. Here, pathologists confirmed that the wounds around the left eye and temple had been caused before death, the bullet having finally killed the terribly injured woman.

They concluded that the victim had been between 22 and 28, and noted that her hands and feet were large, her breasts small and firm, the body well shaped, and the ears unusual and highly individual in formation. The eyes, according to the Sydney experts, were blue-grey, and the race Anglo-Saxon. The second autopsy over, the body was placed in a special metal coffin which was then filled with formalin—an aqueous solution of formaldehyde which preserves organic tissues indefinitely.

Strangely shaped ears

By this time, reconstructed photographs of the girl's face had been printed in all the newspapers; a Mrs. M. Presley saw them and went to the police. The dead woman, said Mrs. Presley, was her grand-daughter, Mrs. Anna Philomena Coots, whose maiden name had been Morgan. She had lived in a Sydney flat with her husband, a writer. After seeing the body, Mrs. Presley "positively" identified her because of the strangely shaped ears and blue eyes.

From this point on all should have been straightforward enough, but in fact it was the beginning of a "search for identity" which was to last for ten years. For the first four of those years, a stream of witnesses viewed the grisly remains, lying suspended in their preserving fluid; Mrs. Callow, Anna Morgan's landlady, agreed with Mrs. Presley that this was her former lodger, and John Morgan, Mrs. Presley's first husband, also swore that the body was Anna's.

But one important witness disagreed with the others. Mrs. Jeanette Routledge, Anna's mother, looked long and hard at the battered corpse, and then told police officers: "I am certain that this is not my daughter." She seemed calm and rational at the time, and when police asked her to make a statement to this effect she did so.

Despite this, her testimony might have been disregarded, if a police sergeant named King had not seen the body in June 1938. He had known the dead woman, he said: even allowing for the wounds and the crinkling of the skin which was the result of steeping in preservative, he swore that this was Linda Agostini, a girl well known to King and his wife, but whom they had not seen since 1931.

Shortly after King had made this statement a coroner's court was finally con-

vened; five witnesses testified that the body was that of Anna Philomena Morgan, while Mrs. Routledge and Sergeant King disagreed. The coroner accepted the majority opinion, and the verdict was that Anna Morgan had been murdered by a person or persons unknown.

The inquest revived public interest and the "pajama girl" case hit the headlines once again. This time, the publicity caught the eye of Dr. Palmer Benbow, who, like a number of medical men before him, took a keen interest in criminology and had a reputation as an amateur investigator. His full methods were never revealed, but he gained access to the body and the other relics of the case—the tattered pajamas, the bag, and the piece of towelling. Unlike the police, Benbow examined the "laundry marks" on the towel minutely, and these somehow led him to a shack on a piece of common ground near Albury.

At the hut he found an old painted bedstead which, he alleged, matched up with flecks of paint found on the corpse, and some woollen material in the hut that corresponded with fibres found in the dead girl's hair. Proceeding with his investigations, the doctor traced an alcoholic who had known Anna Morgan; this person named a man who, he told Benbow, had beaten Anna up with a piece of the bedstead.

And here the doctor's investigations virtually came to an end. He later stated that he had been "obstructed" and the clear implication was that he had been obstructed by the police. Later he was

FLECKS OF PAINT (below) seem to point straight at an Australian VIP; the investigation is "obstructed", only to pick up six years later, ending with Antonio Agostini's "confession". Reluctantly, scientists and police agree the dead girl in the culvert must have been Linda.

to allege that the man—who was never publicly named by Palmer Benbow—said to have "beaten up" Anna Morgan had been an intimate of an Australian Commissioner of Police; had, in fact, been a member of the same social circle as both the Commissioner and the Commissioner's mother.

Whatever the cause, Dr. Benbow felt unable to continue with the inquiry. In an attempt to have his full findings published, Mrs. Routledge's lawyers applied to get legal control of Anna Morgan's estate—a token gesture as the estate was worthless—which was calculated to start a re-examination of all the facts. The attempt failed, and once again the "pajama girl" lapsed into obscurity.

No decent burial

For a further six years the pickled corpse lay in a corner of the medical laboratory at Sydney University; the files on the case were, of course, still open, and no one in authority seemed inclined to give the body a decent burial. Then, in March, 1944, the assertions made by Police Sergeant King seemed to receive corroboration. An Italian waiter named Tony Agostini appeared at police headquarters, and made a statement before the same Commissioner who was alleged to have "covered up" Palmer Benbow's investigations. Agostini confessed to the murder of his wife Linda.

Linda Platt, an Englishwoman, had married Agostini in 1930. She was an attractive woman, similar in height and build to the corpse in the formalin-filled coffin; she was even said to have had the same unusually shaped ears. The only positive difference between her and Anna Morgan was that Linda's breasts were "large and drooping".

Agostini told police that the marriage had not been successful, for Linda was a jealous neurotic who drank too much; in an attempt to patch things up, the couple had moved from Sydney to Melbourne. Linda had, the police knew, been alive in August 1934, when she was seen by a friend who knew her well but after that she had vanished, and Agostini had subsequently reported her as a missing person, claiming that she had run off with a lover.

During much of the Second World War Tony Agostini had been interned as an alien and it was after his release, while working as a waiter in Melbourne, that he had come forward with his confession. A rather short, balding and bespectacled man, Agostini appears to have given his long, rambling confession to the Commissioner quite freely.

Despite the move to Melbourne, he claimed, the couple just could not get along. One morning, after quarrelling the night before, they woke up in bed:

THE PICKLED CORPSE rests in obscurity for six years after Dr. Palmer Benbow uncovers a few explosive leads. Then a confession: but mystery remains...

Linda was pointing a gun at Tony. Agostini struggled with her, and the gun went off close to her right cheekbone and killed her. Panic stricken, he carried the body to the top of the stairs, but he was not a strong man and he dropped it; it bounced three times on the stairs, causing the three head wounds.

Next day, Agostini continued, he had driven out of Melbourne with the body, dumped it in the culvert where it was found, and then set fire to it in an attempt to prevent identification. To those who were familiar with the case there was an obvious discrepancy here: forensic experts at the second post-mortem had affirmed that the battering injuries to the head had been caused *prior* to death, and they certainly did not tally with the body having fallen down a flight of wooden stairs.

But the authorities decided to make an effort to solve the mystery once and for all, or at least arrive at some sort of truth. The pathetic, ten-year-old corpse again came under the hands of experts, this time embalmers and morticians, who were hired to "make the body more acceptable to lay viewers".

They had a formidable task, for the formalin, despite its many excellent qualities, had worked changes on the once-pretty features of the dead girl; the wounds had puckered slightly, the skin was wrinkled and fish-white, and the very outline of the features had become blurred. In spite of these difficulties the morticians, using wax, cosmetics, and

special hair cleanser, had the corpse prepared for viewing in record time, and on March 4, 1944, six friends of Linda Agostini, plus Police Sergeant King, were ushered into the mortuary to view the result. All of them "positively identified" the body as that of Linda Agostini.

On March 23 a second inquest was opened. This time the coroner was faced with a battery of lawyers—one for the police, one for Agostini, and two for Mrs. Routledge, Anna Morgan's mother. From the start there were violent arguments among the three legal teams; first an exchange, complicated and inconclusive, took place over whether or not the teeth of the corpse had been interfered with, and this was followed by a disagreement over the length of time which had elapsed since the witnesses had seen the living and the dead woman.

One woman witness introduced an important point when she claimed that the breasts of the corpse were not those of Linda—Linda had large breasts, and those of the corpse were small and firm. In answer to this the police contended that long immersion in the preservative liquid had caused the breasts to shrink, although experts counter-claimed that, though formalin would cause skin-shrinkage, it would not cause radical changes in the size and shape of the breasts.

A clumsy technique

Then came confusion about the colour of the eyes. Anna Philomena Morgan had had blue-grey eyes, while those of the corpse were brownish. But an expert stated that the dead woman's eyes were either blue or grey but neither brown nor hazel: the eyes had, like the rest of the body, suffered from the pickling process. To get a positive ruling on this, a pathological examination was put under way, but the technique was clumsy, and the eyeballs were destroyed during the experiment.

After further argument, the coroner somewhat wearily accepted the view that the corpse was that of Linda Agostini, a belief largely supported by the husband's confession and several moles found on the body which were said to be conclusive. Agostini was duly tried and convicted of manslaughter. He got six years' hard labour, and was released in 1950.

To some extent, the curious "pajama girl" case remains a mystery Over the ten-year period between the finding of the body and the last inquest a great deal of confusion had crept in; scientists had bungled, and the police had been obstructive, whether deliberately or not. Some experts still claim that the pickled corpse was that of Anna Philomena Morgan; but it was as Linda Agostini that it was finally buried in Preston Cemetery, Melbourne, in July 1944.

MURDER BY INSULIN

As a loving husband, he was naturally distraught after finding his wife Elizabeth dead in the bath. But why did Kenneth Barlow's dry clothes show no trace of his efforts to revive her? And what accounted for the strangely dilated pupils in the staring eyes of the drowned woman?

ON the evening of May 3, 1957, 38-year-old Kenneth Barlow and his wife Elizabeth decided to stay home and watch television. After tea, Elizabeth said she felt unwell and went to the bedroom to lie down. She told her husband to call her at 7.30 p.m. as there was a television programme that she particularly wanted to see.

Barlow called his wife at the requested time, but she decided to miss the programme and stay where she was. At about 9.20 Barlow heard her calling for him; she had been sick. Barlow changed the bedclothes and prepared to retire to bed himself. Elizabeth said she would have a bath. Barlow dozed off to sleep, and when he woke up at about 11.0 p.m. his wife was not in bed beside him.

He hurried into the bathroom, where he found his wife drowned in the bath. He tried to pull her out but could not manage it, so he pulled out the plug to let the bath-water drain away and then tried artificial respiration, but his efforts were of no avail.

Overcome by weakness

A neighbour called the doctor, who arrived just before midnight. He was met at the house in Thornbury Crescent, Bradford, by Barlow, and together they went up to the bathroom. Barlow's wife, aged about 30, lay on her right side in the empty bath. She had apparently vomited while in the bath and, overcome by weakness, had slipped down into the water and drowned. Her body bore no signs of violence, but the doctor noticed immediately that the pupils of her eyes were widely dilated. He called the police.

A detective-sergeant from Bradford C.I.D. was sent to the house. He had a quick conference with the doctor and then questioned Barlow, who said he was a male nurse at Bradford Royal Infirmary. Barlow was quite calm and related the story of how he found his wife. The police called in forensic experts. They were quick to note various suspicious signs. The dead woman's dilated pupils indicated the possibility of drugs having been administered.

Kenneth Barlow's pyjamas were quite dry, despite the efforts he said he had made to get his wife out of the bath. Moreover, there were no signs of splashing in the bathroom which would have been expected in the circumstances, but there was water in the crooks of the dead woman's elbows which threw doubt on the attempt to revive her by artificial respiration.

Two hypodermic syringes were found in the kitchen. Barlow explained their presence by saying that he was giving himself injections of penicillin for a carbuncle. He pointed out that he was a nurse and often had syringes in the house. He

IN THE KITCHEN of the Barlows' house police found two hypodermic syringes containing traces of penicillin. But there were no signs of injection on the body.

denied giving his wife any injections.

The forensic examiners took the syringes away with them, and Mrs. Barlow's body was removed for post-mortem examination. The doctors were at a loss to explain the sudden attack of weakness which apparently led to the woman's death. Her organs were sound and free of disease. She was two months pregnant, but that in itself offered no explanation of her death. No injection marks could be found anywhere on her body.

Traces of penicillin were found on the syringes taken from the house, which seemed to support Barlow's explanation of their use. But the doctors were still puzzled by the dilated pupils. Comprehensive tests were made of the body fluids and organs, but no traces of any poison or drug were found.

Baffled by these negative findings, the doctors suggested a further minute examination of the dead woman's body. They were looking for marks of an injection. This examination was made difficult by the proliferation of freckles over the dead woman's skin. But, with the aid of a hand lens, their persistence was rewarded. Two tell-tale needle marks were found on the

154

right buttock and then another two, more recently made, in the fold of skin under the left buttock.

The skin and tissue around the second set of marks was cut into, revealing unmistakable signs of inflammation—clear evidence of a needle having been pushed through the flesh. The appearance of the marks suggested that an injection had been made only a matter of hours before death. An injection had undoubtedly been given, but what substance had been administered? There was no ready answer, so a meeting of doctors, forensic experts and chemists was called to consider the facts of the case.

Blood sugar deficiency

Specifically they were asked to suggest what agent or drug might have caused the symptoms which preceded Mrs. Barlow's death. Her husband, a male nurse, had described them—vomiting, sweating and weakness. Added to these was the dilation of the pupils. The view of the experts was that these symptoms described hypoglycaemia—a deficiency of blood sugar and the opposite of diabetes.

Insulin treatment of diabetes had been practised for 30 years or more. It was well known that diabetic patients could die as a result of taking too much insulin. It was equally recognized that healthy persons given insulin by accident could also die from shock. The insulin deprived the blood of the sugar it needed and hypoglycaemia resulted.

Mrs. Barlow was not diabetic: that had been checked. It had also been found that blood taken from the heart contained an above average level of sugar—the opposite of what would be expected had she been given insulin.

Again the doctors had come up against an obstacle to their theories, but good police work confirmed that they were on the right track. Inquiries about Kenneth Barlow revealed that he was often given the duty of administering the insulin injections to patients at the hospital where he worked.

Perfect murder

A patient who had been treated by Barlow recalled a conversation he had with him. Talking about insulin, Barlow had said, "If anybody gets a real dose of it, he's on his way to the next world." Barlow apparently had also boasted to a fellow nurse that perfect murder could be committed using insulin. The police also discovered that his first wife had died in 1956, aged 33. No firm cause of death was found.

This was still circumstantial, however, unless insulin could be positively identified in the dead woman's body. The problem facing the experts was that there were no prescribed tests for detecting insulin. There was also the contrary evidence regarding the high sugar level found in the heart blood. The experts in this case were working at the frontiers of existing knowledge, and perhaps this made them conscious of the possibility of making forensic history. At any rate, they found in medical literature an explanation for the high blood sugar level in the heart.

The phenomenon of high blood sugar had been observed in several incidents where a person had died a violent death, and research on this biochemical change showed that in the moments before death the liver assisted the struggle to survive by delivering a heavy charge of sugar to the bloodstream. This reached as far as the heart before the circulation stopped. Consequently, the heart blood was disproportionately high in blood sugar.

In the case of Mrs. Barlow, therefore, the high blood sugar level did not contradict the possibility that she might have been given insulin. With this obstacle out of the way, the experts prepared to make extracts from the tissues excised from the dead woman's buttocks.

A number of mice were injected with various quantities of insulin and their reactions observed. In this control experiment the small creatures twitched and trembled and became very weak; they then went into a coma and died. Now, other mice were injected with some of the tissue extract from the dead woman. They showed exactly the same reaction —they went into a coma and died.

Some of the extracts were stronger than others; those made from the injection sites in the left buttock had a more rapid effect on the mice and confirmed the doctors' belief that this injection had been made only a few hours before Mrs. Barlow died, for the injection was so recent that much of the insulin had remained unabsorbed in the tissues. The estimate of the quantity in the body was 84 Units. But the actual quantity injected must have been a great deal higher than this.

The experiments were repeated with other laboratory animals. The results were the same. One doubt still had to be resolved in order to satisfy the doctors completely. It was current medical opinion—and that of Kenneth Barlow too —that, once injected into the bloodstream, insulin disappeared very quickly. If this were correct it would not have been possible to find any in the tissues of the dead woman.

Once again new research came to the aid of the forensic experts. It had been reported that acidic conditions preserved insulin. In Mrs. Barlow's case, the formation of lactic acid in the muscles after death prevented the breakdown of the insulin. Chemical changes in the muscles after death were known to produce lactic acid, but it had never been necessary to relate this to the injection of insulin. At least, not until the death of Mrs. Barlow.

On July 29, 1957, Barlow was arrested and charged with murdering his wife with insulin. He continued to deny giving his wife an injection of any kind for a while, but then admitted to giving her an injection of ergonovine to abort her pregnancy. He said that she had agreed to this. He had stolen the ergonovine from the hospital where he worked and gave the injection on the day that his wife died.

Abortion drugs

The forensic experts had made a routine check for abortion drugs when they analyzed the dead woman's body fluids. None was found. Barlow's confessed use of an injection appeared to be a move to escape the charge of premeditated murder. But it cut no ice with the police. Barlow's trial, which began in December 1957, created considerable interest on account of the scientific evidence involved. The work of the forensic experts had been thorough and their evidence was virtually unshakable.

A medical expert called by the defence suggested that there might be another, natural, cause of Mrs. Barlow's death. His thesis was that Mrs. Barlow might have had a fit of weakness which caused her to slide down into the bathwater. And, in a moment of fear when she thought she was drowning, her body reacted by discharging a massive dose of insulin into the bloodstream. The insulin induced coma and death. This shock reaction accounted for the insulin found in the body after death.

This theory contrasted sharply with the carefully presented scientific evidence of the prosecution. If it could be said to have offered a flickering hope of acquittal for the accused it was soon snuffed out. The theory was quickly and efficiently demolished by one of the prosecution's expert witnesses. He calculated that to account for the 84 Units of insulin found in Mrs. Barlow's body her pancreas would have to have secreted the unheard of quantity of 15,000 Units.

Kenneth Barlow maintained that the remarks made to a colleague about murder by insulin were only a joke. It was a bad joke. The judge, who commended the forensic scientists for their work, sentenced Barlow to life imprisonment.

INSULIN BY INJECTION

Insulin is a hormone secreted into the bloodstream by the pancreas. Its main action is to regulate the amount of sugar in the blood. When insufficient insulin is secreted, an excess of sugar builds up in the body—this is diabetes or hyperglycaemia. Until the discovery of insulin in 1921, diabetes resulted in death.

Treatment of diabetes with insulin can lead to an excessive lowering of the blood sugar—hypoglycaemia. Unless quickly corrected by giving sugar by mouth, hypoglycaemia can also lead to death.

Symptoms of hypoglycaemia

Weakness, giddiness, pallor, sweating, irritability, tremor, lack of judgment and self-control, dilated pupils and coma. These symptoms are likely to appear when the blood sugar level falls below 60 to 70 mg/100 ml.

Insulin for injection

Insulin is prepared commercially from ox and pig pancreas. Its strength is measured in International Units (one Unit will lower the percentage of blood sugar by 0·045%). Each Unit of insulin given to a diabetic patient enables him to use up to 2g more carbohydrate.

Unmodified insulin is soluble in the blood and tissue fluids. Its action is rapid and of short duration (4 to 5 hours). To prolong its action (to 15 to 20 hours), a protein form of insulin is commonly used.

Insulin is a clear, colourless liquid. It is supplied in sterile form in rubber-capped bottles ready for injection. The strength of the dose is always boldly marked on the bottles. 20, 40 and 80 Units per ml are the usual strengths.

THE BLAZE FAKERS

"Hot money" was given a whole new meaning by his gang. For, wherever there were flames, there was Leopold Harris. Inevitably, people began to talk. And could there, so to speak, be smoke without fire?

IF INSURANCE companies in the 1930s had possessed any degree of mutual co-operation, Leopold Harris—whose very name became synonymous with arson—could never have operated his successful business at all. The old-established firm of Harris & Company, Fire Assessors, of Finsbury Pavement, in the heart of the City of London, was eminently respectable when it was run by its founder, Harris's father, but when tall, bulky Leopold took over he was to find he had too little patience for the slow profits of legitimate commerce.

Harris & Co., under its shrewd and fast-moving new owner, had a way of maintaining contacts in the most unlikely places, and it began to get a reputation for "fire chasing". When a fire broke out, the firm's representative—usually Leo Harris—was quickly on the spot, having got authority from the policy owner, and hard at work assessing damage and preparing to negotiate with the insurance company concerned.

Fire claims have to be settled between the parties concerned by adjustment. Only too often the vital books, invoices, and records of a business go up in the fire itself, and assessment of actual loss becomes extremely difficult.

Leo Harris was perhaps a normal and decent-enough man, but his life style was expensive and money in quantities was needed. His daily contact with the insurance companies and Lloyd's underwriters, and the vast sums they handled, must have set his mind working: there seemed to be an easier, quicker way of making a living than by the daily grind of regular fire assessments on behalf of other people, who would get most of the money concerned.

In what must have been a moment of mental aberration, Harris made his first attempt to adjust the balance in his favour by faking a "burglary" at his home in Southend, Essex, and putting in a claim for £1500. Something about the claim—never yet explained—must have made the insurers suspicious, for they refused to pay. Harris brought suit, and lost. The judge said quite frankly that the claim "looked bogus to him".

Remarkable carelessness

It reveals the arm's-length attitude of insurance companies that they did not get together and, as it were, warn Harris "off the turf"—he was, later, to deal with individual companies, staying strictly in their own furrows, which is why he was able to succeed so long and survive so well. But his burglary claim had made him cautious, and he went to extreme lengths to make absolutely sure that no hint of his presence, other than as a simple assessor, was ever revealed in the arson cases he contrived.

To say he began on such-and-such a date is impossible. He may have tried mock runs, of which nothing is known; certainly his foolproof and *mentally* astute plans must have required a great deal of forward-planning. His ideas were excellent, and he could well have pulled off undocumented fires, only beginning his road to success and then failure when he brought in partners to assist him.

The case seems to begin with a man named Capsoni who, in 1926, was an

agent for Continental silk-makers. Capsoni heard that a customer and friend, Louis Jarvis of West London, had lost his business in a fire. On attempting to console Jarvis, Capsoni was astonished at his gaiety. It seemed, he learned on questioning, that the fire had brought Jarvis £21,500 insurance compensation of which, he explained with remarkable carelessness, only £3000 had gone to Leo Harris and his brother David for "services rendered".

Capsoni, hard-pressed by government duties imposed on imported silk, agreed

Adam L. Ball

William Herivel

Ernest Wolfe

Victor E. Cope

Bernard Bowman

Leopold L. Harris

Harry C. Priest

Harry Gould

Leonard Riley

Felix Bergolz

Louis Jarvis

to ally himself with Jarvis, in his real name of Jacobs. They formed a firm known as Fabriques de Soieries Ltd., of 196 Deansgate, Manchester, and bought a large quantity of bankrupt stock and "old soldiers" – salvaged goods from other fires, or damaged goods tastefully rewrapped – all of which made a fine display in the firm's showroom. The cost of setting up this superficially attractive and tasteful collection of goods was met in utter secrecy by Leo and David Harris. Capsoni, who possessed an artistic soul, put together what he called a "Confirmations Book", containing

FRONT-MAN Harris presented himself as a respectable, diligent fire-assessor. But the veritable organization which grew around his activities became too hot to handle. It was Harry Priest who put them on the front pages . . . and into the courts.

samples of the goods belonging to the firm, the quantities bought, and the low prices paid, which, if he had only known it, was to act as "a sword of retribution".

Policies for £60,000 were taken out; elegant lengths of silk were displayed in the Deansgate premises, exposed so that they would burn quickly. The fire arrangement was simple. Two photographic developing trays made of celluloid (a then popular and enormously inflammable material) were obtained. One was wedged inside the other, and a taper stuck in between. The taper, which had been timed, burned for 15 minutes before it touched and ignited the trays, a cheap and infallible device for arson which the "gang" was to use all the time. Between lighting the taper and the fire there was time for the arsonist, Capsoni, to get away and establish his alibi. By sheer "coincidence" Leo Harris was staying that night at the neighbouring Midland Hotel.

When the Fabriques de Soieries fire began one of Harris's many contacts advised him, and in his capacity of assessor he was on the spot almost before the firemen had unrolled their hoses. The fire was put out far too soon for Harris, but the firemen had worked hard, using enormous quantities of water, which did the required amount of damage. Harris put in a "reasonable" claim for £32,000, which was settled for £29,000. This was

divided, after costs had been allowed, by giving £1000 to Capsoni, £12,000 to Jarvis, £8000 to Harris and £1000 to David Harris. It was, Capsoni said, "money for old rope".

In the meantime the legitimate and slow business of Harris & Company went ahead assessing fires, something in which it had an enviable reputation, while the proprietor's mind concentrated on further aspects of fire-raising. An ingenious plan for future operations presented itself. Harry Gould was married to Harris's sister. His business, in which Leo Harris was a sleeping partner, was that of a buyer of salvage. Gould bought salvage from perfectly "respectable" fires – to which he was guided by Harris & Company.

When Harris brought Gould into the "arson" side of the firm, Gould was able to supply Leo Harris's nominees, who were setting up businesses for firing, with a few hundred pounds' worth of damaged but re-wrapped goods, and invoice them at huge prices. After the bogus fire claim was settled, Gould, who never missed a trick, was able to buy back his own now even more damaged goods for use in future fires. It was like printing his own money.

The next fire, in Leeds, was stocked with goods largely bought by Capsoni in Italy for the firm, Continental Showrooms, which was insured for £15,000, but certain insurance companies backed out for their own reasons; one being that the final insurance figure with another firm was £6300. The fire was a success but the assessor for the insurance company was a tough, sceptical Yorkshireman who did not like Harris's assessment at all. The settlement was finally agreed at £3350.

Paid without argument

Nor was Harris's next effort very successful. This involved Alfred Alton Ltd., a cloak and mantle business which had begun life as Cohen and Company, before being bought out by Harris. A branch was opened in Manchester, handsomely stocked with singed material and "old soldiers", and was duly fired with the reliable system of photographic trays and taper by Capsoni. Payment of the claim presented no difficulties as the assessor for the insurance company accepted Harris's assessment of the damage, and £9000 was paid without argument; in current values this was a considerable amount of money.

So far all had gone well, and the London end of Alfred Alton Ltd. was allowed to run down quietly into routine liquidation. Unfortunately the official liquidator was typical of his kind, an inquisitive and diligent man who wanted answers to a lot of facts – more, indeed, than Leo Harris could give with safety. The liquidator wanted books, invoices, records and details which would have resulted in showing the secrets of the Manchester branch and the bogus insurance claim.

It was vital that Harris should not be revealed as having any connection with the firm, other than that of assessor. With characteristic ingenuity he devised a neat and clever scheme.

Through a pliable nominee he made an offer to buy up Alfred Alton Ltd. at a rate that would give 15s. in the pound to the liquidator, something he could scarcely refuse. The offer was accepted and even though it galled Harris to pay out the money, he gained a period of time to carry on his activities.

Almost routine

Next came the Franco-Italian Silk Company, of 185 Oxford Street. By now the procedure had become almost routine, for the new firm was packed with "old soldiers" and damaged stock, and insured for £30,000. When, after various organizational delays, the place went up with the help of the inevitable photographic trays, the assessor, a Mr. Loughborough Ball, and Leo Harris seemed to get along like twin souls. A cheque for £21,966 18s. 4d. was eventually received.

In 1930 Leo Harris was the head of a veritable organization; he, Gould, and Capsoni were joined by the friendly Mr. Loughborough Ball. But their major recruit was Captain Eric Miles, Chief Officer of the London Salvage Corps, which acted for the insurance community. Miles had come into the organization by allowing Harris to guarantee a bank overdraft for him: the Corps, by nature of its duties, got news of every fire in London within seconds of a fire brigade being called. This information, it seemed, would be invaluable to Harris, and in connection with fires to which there was attached any hint of suspicion, since it would be more than possible for Miles's report, sent via the Corps to the insurance office concerned, to lean favourably in the direction of Harris, or his clients.

The Harris Fire Raising Organization, fully manned and highly efficient, was now set on a prosperous course, and might have gone endlessly about its business of profitable fires, had not the human element put an end to it all. One of the prime factors in keeping the scheme working was a supply of nominees, or dummies, who posed as the owners of respectable businesses and obtained insurance; Harris took over from there.

The man who found most of the dummies was a Harris employee named Harry Priest. Unfortunately Priest drank, and one day drunkenly approached a very respectable man named Cornock, suggesting he might like to be set up in a

STILL LAUGHING, Harris comes home to his wife after serving his time. He had a flair for spending, and had paid the best legal brains to represent him.

business, which would be capitalized by "a friend", and receive a share after the subsequent fire. Cornock was horrified, and went for advice to a friend, George Mathews, who had once been employed in the Intelligence Department of Lloyd's.

Audience of fire-bugs

This was the end. Mathews took Cornock to see a brilliant London solicitor, William Charles Crocker, who had been quietly solidifying his suspicions about Leo Harris. With this new information, and its content of facts and names, Crocker was able to move into top-gear, and laid plans enabling Mathews and Cornock to play the parts of greedy but fearful businessmen anxious to make money but apparently scared of anything to do with arson, although not beyond persuasion.

It was an outstanding performance that should have been played to a better audience than a collection of fire-bugs. Soon the plan yielded fruits, news of a *coming* fire. From that moment on Crocker could not be faulted, using his staff and laying plans which caused Harris to tie himself up in a tangle of his own making.

At the trial Gould and another man instantly pleaded guilty; Harris and a band of 13 men faced the judge in No. 1 Court

in a heat wave that did not add to comfort. Up to that time it was the longest trial in the history of the Old Bailey, running for 33 days and involving literally tons of documents, exhibits and relics, including Capsoni's famous "Confirmations Book" with its pieces of silk and the prices paid which, when laid against the insurance claim, was damning in itself.

The front pages of British newspapers were packed, day after day, with the constant sensations springing out of this notable *cause célèbre*. The hard work done by Crocker was the Crown's chief weapon, the more deadly because of the solicitor's remarkable talent for tying up seemingly unconnected facts, the careful probing which produced forensic support for the facts of arson, and a total achievement of personal detective work that could not have been bettered by a leading professional from New Scotland Yard.

Crocker had made sure that not a single error appeared in his testimony, and it had to be strong, for the fire-raisers had among their legal defenders some of the finest talent in the British courts, such names as Sir Henry Curtis Bennett, K.C., Mr. Norman Birkett, K.C., Mr. G. D. Roberts and Mr. T. Christmas Humphreys.

It was a remarkable fight but near the end Leopold Harris gave in and admitted his guilt; he went to prison for fourteen years, his brother for five, and Gould for six—the rest of the conspirators shared jail sentences totalling twenty-two years.